Getting Marriage Right

Other books by David P. Gushee

Christians and Politics beyond the Culture Wars: An Agenda for Engagement

Preparing for Christian Ministry: An Evangelical Approach

Toward a Just and Caring Society: Christian Responses to Poverty in America

Kingdom Ethics: Following Jesus in Contemporary Context

Getting Marriage Right

Realistic Counsel for Saving and Strengthening Relationships

David P. Gushee

BakerBooks
A Division of Baker Book House Co
Grand Rapids, Michigan 49516

Published by Baker Books
a division of Baker Book House Company
P.O. Box 6287, Grand Rapids, MI 49516-6287
www.bakerbooks.com

Printed in the United States of America

Library of Congress Cataloging-in-Publication Data
Gushee, David P., 1962–
Getting marriage right : realistic counsel for saving and strengthening relationships / David P. Gushee.
p. cm.
Includes bibliographical references.
ISBN 0-8010-1262-7 (pbk.)
1. Marriage—Religious aspects—Christianity. I. Title
BT706.G87 2004
248.8′44—dc22 2003023472

For my beloved Jeanie

Contents

Acknowledgments

This book is the product of the efforts of a large number of people. I am keenly aware of my indebtedness to so many who have made this project possible.

The list begins with the children of divorce whose honest discussion of their experiences motivated this book in the first place and forms such an important part of its content. I am also grateful to the sixty children of divorce who allowed us to interview them as well as the married and divorced men and women who participated in interviews over these last several years.

About half of these interviews were conducted by students in my Intensive Issue Seminar course on marriage and divorce in the spring of 1998, 2000, and 2002. I am grateful to these students for doing such an excellent job in conducting these interviews and transcribing the results. I also am indebted to a number of student workers and to the excellent staff in our college services department here at Union University for transcribing other interviews since 1996 when they began. Michele Bennett, Amy Maxwell, and Autumn Ridenour also played an invaluable role in analyzing the interviews and tabulating the statistics that are derived from them in this book.

Early versions of materials included in this book were presented as lectures at the Methodist Theological School of Ohio and at Messiah College as well as in my own classes and chapel talks at Union and sermons at my home church, Northbrook. I also have written chapters in several books and articles that are based on this material; the latter have appeared in a number of places, including *Faithworks, Prism,* and *Light* magazines. The intense responses to these published pieces (not always positive but always intense!) have convinced me both of the significance of this project and of its extraordinary sensitivity. I will not forget the profound conversations with many who have responded or sought me out.

I have received the help of several very thoughtful dialogue partners through the years of developing this manuscript. I am especially grateful to Greg Thornbury, Joshua Trent, Margaret Nell, Michele Bennett, Sondra Wheeler, Autumn Ridenour, Alan Asnen, Stephen Wilks, and my mother-in-law, Earlynn Grant, for reading and responding to the entire manuscript. I am also grateful to John Crouch, Fred Clark, Naomi Larsen, Alice Nelson, Janette Laughlin, Chad Cossiboom, Holly Coleman, and Don Browning for reading parts of the text and dialoguing with me about them. Don Browning was especially helpful in pointing me to resources that I had not yet discovered.

Since 2002 my wife, Jeanie, and I have led a marriage enrichment ministry at Northbrook in which this manuscript has been field tested and its principles explored. We are grateful to the couples who have participated in refining the book by being its first guinea pigs and are excited about many years of further leadership in this ministry at Northbrook.

I am deeply grateful to my parents, David and Jay Gushee, for modeling in their own way a gloriously successful Christian marriage, which not long ago passed its forty-year mark. I know without question that their influence can be felt on every page of this book. Words cannot express my thanks.

Nor are words sufficient to convey my gratitude to my own wife, Jeanie. I am so grateful that she read and commented on the entire manuscript, developed the marriage ministry with me, and has participated with me in countless sessions with couples over these nearly twenty years together. But it is her steadfast partnership with me in life for these twenty years, from college days to middle age, in eight homes across five states, in easy times and hard times, that I most cherish. “A wife of noble character who can find?” I did.

This book could only be dedicated to you, sweet Jeanie, the one and only love of my life.

Introduction

Like many college teachers, I am approached frequently by students struggling with personal problems. One week in the spring of 1997, my first year at Union University, I faced a particularly heavy week of unscheduled student counseling. One after another they came by. One after another they poured out their hearts to me. One after another their pain concerned the collapse of their families.

Late one afternoon, I remember almost staggering out of my office following a particularly intense conversation. I walked into my department chairman's office and said, "I feel like I need a broom to sweep up the pieces of all the broken lives around me."

Christian ethicists deal with moral issues facing the church and the world. That's what we do all day. Some people drive trucks, some sell clothes, some build malls; I talk about abortion, war, and euthanasia. So I had been dealing with marriage and family in the classroom for several years. Like most everyone else by now, I also had my own checkered past on this issue—child of a remarried father, brother of both a divorced sister and a never-married single mother, married father of three. I cared about marriage and divorce. It was one of many issues I had to address.

But this procession of students had an impact on me. These broken-hearted students were studying in a Baptist college that is serious about Christianity and located in the heart of the Bible Belt. If this level of misery is found here, what must it be like everywhere else? What kind of suffering is being visited upon an entire generation of young people?

Thus this book was born. Perhaps I am a glutton for punishment, but as a Christian scholar I find myself drawn to pain. My doctoral thesis was on the Holocaust. I have written about poverty, racism, war, and many other sources of human suffering. I think I'm inclined this way because my faith centers in a crucified God. Human sin and its resulting misery evoked God's compassionate response in Jesus Christ. We responded to God's response by torturing Jesus and nailing him to a tree, and in this maelstrom of blood and pain and sorrow, salvation was won. Ever since I first understood this story, somehow God has never seemed too far from blood and pain and sorrow, and he has called Christians not to stray too far either.

The pain of my students drove me back to the library. There I searched in vain for any Christian discussion of marriage, divorce, and family life that took adequate account of the devastating consequences of family collapse on children. I soon felt a sense of calling to write a Christian "ethic of divorce" that ended the invisibility of children. That is part of what now lies before you. But my sense of purpose broadened in the years between that initial sense of calling and writing this book. Studying divorce convinced me that it must not be discussed apart from marriage, as if divorce exists apart from the institution it collapses. In other words, it became vital to me to write a book about *marriage,* not just divorce.

My sense of purpose also broadened in terms of audience. Scholars have an unfortunate habit of writing mainly for other scholars. But as I talked with people about my project, they implored me to write a book that the nonspecialist could read. It is wrong to address an issue like this in a scholarly code language that excludes the people who most want to understand the issue.

The contemporary fragility of marriage is deeply perplexing to most thoughtful and sensitive people. I routinely encounter engaged couples, husbands and wives, ministers and lay leaders, parents and grandparents, children in troubled families and children of divorce *who want to understand what in the world has happened to marriage and how we can get it right*. They are deeply perplexed and want some answers. This book is "a guide for the perplexed," to borrow the phrase from Moses Maimonides. If you are perplexed about marriage, this book is for you.

In one of the most widely quoted works of the 1970s, Thomas Kuhn transformed discussion of science by introducing the concept of paradigms and paradigm shifts.

Kuhn argued that scientists operate on the basis of paradigms of what the world is like. These models function in all fields of science and are assumed to be true by scientists and nonscientists alike. They are the foundation for current research in any field.

Yet it turns out that paradigms do not last forever. They begin to weaken when they run into problems that they cannot adequately explain. Scientists are deeply invested in current paradigms and strive as long as they can to solve research problems within the framework of the existing paradigm. This may involve a series of amendments to the paradigm in order to account for troublesome problems.

After a while, however, the old paradigm becomes increasingly unworkable as it is buried under a thousand cumbersome qualifications. More and more effort is required to force the data to fit the paradigm, and even the amended paradigm is less and less able to explain what it is supposed to explain.

Finally, someone comes along and bulldozes the existing theory-plus-amendments in favor of an entirely new way of looking at the same evidence. This is what Kuhn meant by the term "scientific revolution." The outcome of such a revolution is a new paradigm—"a transformation of the world within which scientific research [is] done."[1] Kuhn argued that this is the usual way scientific progress occurs—through dramatic paradigm shifts.

Kuhn's discussion of paradigm shifts applies quite strikingly to the work you are now reading. This is a book about what Christians should believe and do about the deeply troubled institution of marriage. The argument Kuhn made about scientific theories applies to the development of moral thinking about marriage as well.

As I understand it, the Christian moral life is the quest to know and do God's moral will. If we believe, as I do, that God has chosen to reveal to human beings what we need to know about his character and will through the inspired Bible, then we can be confident that God's intentions for marriage (or any other significant aspect of human life) are both knowable and unchanging in their essentials. The Scriptures must be searched carefully and can be trusted to be truthful.

Yet this does not mean that Christian moral convictions never change. History clearly reveals that, like scientific theories, moral paradigms do develop and change over time. This happens as Christians in every generation who seek to be faithful to God's will examine the unchanging Bible amid ever-changing cultural contexts. Careful study of Scripture offers fresh insights that have been missed in previous generations or other settings. As well, study of the history of Christian biblical interpretation yields ancient insights that are remarkably applicable today. This process—the people of God reading the trustworthy Word of God amid the flux of changing cultures—results in the development of an ongoing Christian moral tradition that includes both continuity and variation across time and culture.

But there are moments when the church's moral reflection and practice on a particular issue fails. It can fail for many reasons, including a misunderstanding of Scripture, the impact of alien ideologies in the church, or because the pace and scope of cultural change overwhelms the church's ability to respond. I believe that the Western Christian church's approach to marriage today is in what Kuhn identified as the crisis stage; that is, it is failing. The church is getting along with jury-rigged and increasingly ineffective versions of a fading paradigm. Thus Christians are confused about marriage, prone to divorce and remarriage, and miserable both in marriage and in divorce. And it is undoubtedly our children who suffer the most.

I propose in this work that the church needs to undertake a thorough rethinking of marriage and, for that matter, divorce. I offer here an approach to marriage based on four foundational concepts: *the creation purposes of marriage, the covenant structure of marriage, the kingdom possibilities of marriage,* and *the community context of marriage*. I believe that a paradigm that rests on these four pillars can help replace the floundering paradigm still prevailing.

This is a book intended for those who are open to a Christian interpretation of marriage and divorce. But because marriage and divorce are universal human realities, this book also constitutes an invitation to any reader to consider its claims. The argument should be especially congenial to anyone who professes belief in God and in a God-given moral structure to human life. Readers who are not Christians should understand that though I am primarily addressing fellow Christians and my vocabulary reflects this, I do not intend to exclude any reader from the conversation.

In offering a Christian approach to marriage, I am not saying that Christians have it all figured out when it comes to building successful marriages. Therefore this book is not an invitation to the non-Christian to join the happy Christian love train, because that train seems to have jumped the tracks. It is instead an invitation to Christians to rethink marriage and divorce, and anyone who wants to listen in is invited to do so.

Let me say a word about the research for this book and how my book relates to other books about marriage and divorce.

Imagine yourself visiting a good local bookstore. Head over to the relationships or self-help section. There you will find dozens of books attempting to crack the elusive code of successful marriage or, such efforts having failed, books offering legal, emotional, or strategic guidance on how to go about divorce and live with its consequences. Such books have been an important element of my research, most visibly in chapter 5.

Now head over to the children's section and you will discover a number of books directed at the children affected by divorce. This section will range from those precious cardboard books for toddlers all the way to "coping with divorce" books for teens. There is no shortage of examples of what Barbara Dafoe Whitehead has acidly called "bibliotherapy" directed at the innocent victims of adult marital disasters. My own book is a passionate effort to help reshape adult thinking about marriage so that far fewer children have to be sent over to this sad section of the bookstore. The impact of this sort of book is felt most deeply in chapter 3.

If you make your way over to the current events section, you might find some recent books bearing witness to an intense struggle over marriage and divorce. Various social scientists and culture watchers are engaged in a debate over the changing shape of the American (or Western) family. The "marriage movement," which expresses concern about the institutionalization of mass divorce, will have its representatives here, but so also will you find the voices of those who claim that the family has never been better. Some of these books discuss whether reforms of our marriage and divorce laws ought to be attempted. Part 1 of this book wades into this literature; chapter 10 considers the issue of legal reform.

You might need a Christian bookstore for some specialized books available there on marriage and divorce. Hit the biblical studies section and you will find learned interpretations of biblical teaching about marriage and divorce. The church's scholars have been busy attempting to make sense of the biblical witness on this issue. This literature, well-intentioned but much of it profoundly unsatisfying, is important at several points in my own discussion. I will offer my own reading of scriptural teaching about marriage and divorce throughout this book.

Further browsing will lead you to the marriage section. Here you will find numerous books by the church's contemporary marriage experts, all of whom compete for market share with secular psychologists and others in the growing marriage preparation and enrichment business. I will interact respectfully yet critically with these books in chapter 5, offering my own take on the central skills and virtues of successful married life.

Perhaps in the same section of the Christian bookstore you will find evidence that all of this marriage enrichment effort is not proving uniformly successful. Books designed to help Christians deal with their own divorce experiences are found in increasing number. Books for ministers working with the divorced and their families also find a niche. I have written this book with ministers and church leaders firmly in mind. I would like nothing better than to see it used as a starting point for a marriage ministry in the local church. In particular, chapter 9 offers a very concrete treatment of how churches can strengthen marriages and prevent divorce.

In either store you may or may not find explicitly *moral* reflection on marriage, divorce, and remarriage. What should we be teaching, doing, and believing? How well are Christians doing in actually living in accordance with God's will?

That is the best overall description for my project. I intend a thorough rethinking of marriage. I believe that a moral vision based on creation, covenant, kingdom, and community provides the best paradigm for that rethinking. To make my argument, I interact with all the kinds of books just mentioned as well as others. Sound Christian moral reflection involves consideration not only of Scripture but also of history, theology, and sociology, not only of books but also of lives.

On that note, for several years my students and I have been interviewing the successfully married, the divorced, and especially college-age children of divorce. Sixty of the children's interviews form much of the material upon which chapter 3 is based. The appendix describes how we did these interviews and offers a statistical summary of the key results. I want to write about marriage as if children matter; one way to do this is to listen to children of divorce as they tell their stories.

First and above all, I write as a husband. My wife, Jeanie, and I have been married for nineteen years. Every word that appears in this book inevitably has been affected by our rich experience together. Married people don't understand marriage in the abstract; what they know about marriage is primarily what they know about their *own* marriage. The experiences of our life together have affected my perspective. I count our marriage a great success. We have enjoyed so many wonderful days together that they blur in my memory. But we have also experienced harrowing moments that have shaken us to the core. Without both the joyful and the difficult moments, we would not be the couple we are, and this would not be the book it is. A dewy-eyed newlywed could not have written this book. But neither could a brokenhearted cynic.

I write also as a pastor. All I do as a scholar is an expression of my prior and primary calling to ministry—and of my commitment to the local church as the focal point of God's redemptive engagement with the world. For two decades I have served in ministry with children and youth, college and seminary students, the engaged, the married, and the divorced. The last seven years have been as a copastor at Northbrook Church outside Jackson, Tennessee. This book is grounded in those experiences of ministry. It is not a book of lofty speculations or ideals. Its proposals are workable in real congregations and real lives, not just in theory.

Scripture reveals that marriage is very close to the heart of God. There can be no question that God reacts in outrage and sorrow to the mess we are making of marriage. I believe that in writing about this subject I am on holy ground. So I have prayed carefully over this project. My goal here is not to add yet another book to a library shelf but instead to offer a perspective that can help us obey God's command: "Guard yourself in your spirit, and do not break faith" (Mal. 2:16c). If this book can provide clarity amid perplexity, if it can help men and women keep faith with one another and with their children, it will have accomplished its purpose.

Part 1

Amid the Ruins

1

Fading Fast

The Decline of Marriage as an Institution

A *New York Times Magazine* story reads, "in September 1999, when Lise Krywy's husband walked out four weeks after their son's birth, she turned to her parents, who lived nearby, for support. Only five months later, Lise's father left her mother, Ruth DuBois. At first, mother and daughter talked about their dissolving marriages and particularly about Lise's hopes for a reconciliation with her husband. But eventually their pending divorces became the one thing they didn't discuss."[1] The one-page story goes on to offer four photographs of Lise and her mother. We see Lise holding her infant son near the four-bedroom South Brunswick, New Jersey, home in which she and her husband had planned to raise their children before he decided to move on. The second picture shows Ruth DuBois, looking shell shocked, sitting in her bathroom after putting her house on the market. We learn from the caption that her husband had left her because he "clicked" with his high school sweetheart at his fiftieth class reunion. Picture 3 shows Lise carrying her child near a block of what appear to be row houses—their newly downsized residence. The last photo, the most affecting, shows Ruth lying facedown on a pillow in her living room. The caption includes these words: "After 43 years of marriage, I was devastated."

It's just one clipping from my bulging "divorce in American culture" file. It's just one page, a few lines of text, four photographs. But the effect is nonetheless devastating, perhaps because of the pictures, which portray the commonplace pain of modern American life better than a hundred studies.

What's also significant about this little clipping is where it comes from—the *New York Times,* perhaps the leading voice of America's liberal establishment. The poignant treatment of divorce in this bastion of informed liberal opinion is significant and not coincidental.

In the period that began around 1965, a social revolution swept across American life (and more broadly, Western culture, though I will confine most of my discussion in this book to the North American setting, especially the United States). Marriage, that formerly sturdy social institution, which for generations had structured sexuality and family life, lost its way. During this time, Americans revolutionized the concept and practice of marriage. For most of this period, leading voices of American culture either embraced this revolution or let it pass without much comment. By the time the world learned of Lise and Ruth, however, this was no longer the case. It had become impossible not to notice that a revolution had occurred, and that revolution was now being met with expressions of bafflement, hurt, and in some cases outrage, from quarters as diverse as Focus on the Family and the *New York Times*.

This chapter seeks to offer a fair description of the social revolution that has swept over marriage in barely one forty-year generation. This is no easy task, for the issue we tackle is the subject of bitter cultural conflict that has produced competing bodies of research and comment. Yet as Christians we need to understand current realities as accurately as possible. We need to know where we are and how we got here. It is the necessary first step to thinking about how the church should approach marriage in our time.

Deinstitutionalizing Marriage

Those who voice any concern about the transformation of the American family are often caricatured as advocates of the notion that the 1950s family was a uniformly ideal experience for all involved. Others hasten to remind analysts of the family that there never was perfect conformity to the normative social vision of that time—or any time.[2]

Of course the so-called 1950s family was not ideal, and there never has been perfect conformity with a normative social vision or cultural ideal. Both these claims are true. But they are also irrelevant to the case I am making in this chapter.

In 1958, to pick a year, most American teenagers knew that there was a social institution called marriage; they knew what it involved (a man and a woman sharing a bed and a home, a lifetime commitment publicly made, an expectation of sexual fidelity, a context for bringing children into the world and raising them); and they knew that this institution called marriage would structure, even confine, their adult choice making, like it or not. By 1998, the American teenager did not know any of these things, because they were no longer true. What has happened is not a fall from perfection or a declining level of conformity with widely shared expectations related to marriage *but the near-collapse of marriage itself as a social institution.*

Various authors have used different vocabulary to describe this astonishing change. Maggie Gallagher calls it, too strongly perhaps, the "abolition of marriage." Barbara Dafoe Whitehead, and now Karla Hackstaff, write of a "divorce culture." Numerous authors speak of the postmodern or postnuclear marriage/family, while some refer to the "fade" or "decline" of marriage and the (traditional) family. Others, less worried about these quite visible changes, prefer to speak of a "transition" in marriage and family life. What is not disputed is that the marriage and family landscape is by now profoundly altered and deeply confused.

A parallel from the world of sports might be helpful. A sport works because everyone knows what the rules are, and it collapses into chaos when there is any uncertainty about those rules. It was possible to play football in 1928 or 1958 or 1998 and to play it in St. Louis, Washington, or Chicago because everyone knew what football was and how to play it. Rules in football and other sports do evolve from year to year. Yet this too is not random—the process is itself rule-governed.

Marriage in 1958 thus compares to a football league in that, while each couple had to negotiate specifics of living peaceably together just as various teams approach the game in different ways, the broader rule structure governing marriage was not in question. Marriage today enjoys no such situation. The very institution is in such a profound state of flux that it is nearly impossible for the "game" to be played. It seems that what survives are some rather musty old rulebooks, a nearly infinite variety of new rulebook proposals, and a number of rather unsteady teams trying to play the game. But there is no current rulebook that everyone acknowledges. As Susan Moller Okin put it in 1989, "Society seems no longer to have any consensual view of the norms and expectations of marriage. . . . There exists no clear current consensus in this society about what marriage is or should be."[3] Increasingly men and women don't know how to play this game called marriage. And for that matter, today many wonder whether the game *should* be played at all and search actively for alternatives. That is, indisputably, a social revolution.

Along with David Popenoe and others, I think the best single word for this social revolution is *deinstitutionalization*. It's a mouthful, but there is no better single term to describe what has occurred. Let's take it apart.

An institution is "a well-established and structured pattern of behavior or of relationships that is accepted as a fundamental part of a culture." Popenoe writes, "In sociological terms, a social institution is a relatively stable cluster of social structures (roles and norms) organized to meet some basic needs of a society."[4] Most people have been born into cultures in which an array of social institutions greet them; their legitimacy and stability are assumed; their values are communicated through socialization in school, home, church, and community.

An institution is a kind of grand social habit. Personal habits tend to structure our everyday lives and reduce the chaos that would result if we had to decide moment-by-moment what to do and how to act. Instead, most of us create routines that enable us to accomplish our daily goals with a minimum of confusion and fuss. Likewise, societies create habit structures related to many aspects of individual and group behavior that reduce the chaos that would result from unstructured decision making.

To deinstitutionalize something, then, is to socially disestablish it, to shatter its status as a fundamental and accepted part of a culture, and thus to disrupt the social habit structure related to that practice. My claim is that marriage is in various stages of the process of deinstitutionalization across the Western world.

Remember that the reason we create either personal or social habits is to enable us to accomplish goals. My morning routine, for example, exists in order to help me get ready for the day. It's hard to imagine accomplishing much else if I didn't find a way to get going in the morning. If I were to deinstitutionalize that particular habit, I would still have to find other ways to meet the same goal.

The institution of the family has existed in some form in every culture. Cultures here reflect a response to God's purposeful design in creation. Cultures have had no choice but to find a way to regulate the expression of sexuality, provide for the conception and rearing of children, organize economic cooperation, and offer provision for companionship, affection, and care.[5] In Western culture for many centuries, a publicly avowed, legally recognized, permanent-with-rare-exceptions, sexually exclusive, monogamous heterosexual marriage served as the only socially approved organizational center and foundation of the family. When a man and woman married on these terms, they initiated the formation of a family, which then was expected to fulfill the various functions for family just described.

But I am claiming that marriage is in the process of being deinstitutionalized. If this is so, and marriage has served as the foundation of family life, some new way is now required to accomplish the goals or perform the functions that marriage once accomplished for adults and children. This is the case unless we believe that families can perform these same functions quite adequately without being founded in marriage (at least, in any widely shared understanding of marriage); or, alternatively, if it can be shown that workable alternatives exist to which these previously family-based tasks can be transferred successfully.[6]

These are matters of empirical confirmation or rejection and on which the negative evidence is quite clear. The deinstitutionalized marriage fails and so does the family "system," if it can be so-called, that goes along with it. It fails the individuals affected by it—especially children—and the society that attempts to function without it. The particular social tasks once accomplished by families grounded in marriage are creation-based, wired into all human beings and social groups. They do not go away. The deinstitutionalization of marriage means that individuals and groups have to grope toward new ways of meeting these same needs and goals, at the price of considerable pain, confusion, and disarray in the process. That is the situation in which we find ourselves today.

How Marriage Collapsed

A social institution is like a cathedral. This is a favorite image of mine, for the institution of marriage in particular, and I will return to it regularly in this book. Cathedrals, like Notre Dame in Paris or the Cathedral of St. John the Divine in New York, are some of the most beautiful expressions of human creativity ever undertaken. My visits to these edifices are among the unforgettable experiences of my life.

A cathedral is built by a community, using human intelligence to transform raw materials into a beautiful edifice fit for human use. The same is true with marriage or any social institution. Maggie Gallagher puts it nicely: "Marriage is a sexual option carved out of nature by law, faith, custom, and society."[7]

Both cathedrals and social institutions take a long time to build and are not easily brought down. Marriage moved toward being deinstitutionalized under the impact of a series of exceptionally important cultural developments. Like a building damaged from all sides, marriage weakened dramatically under the cumulative impact of these cultural blows in ways that no one anticipated. In the end, it seemed that marriage had become a lost art. A vague memory of how to "do marriage" still survived, but few had access to its secrets. Couples spoke wistfully of the enduring marriages of their grandparents but did not know how to replicate them. Marriage had reached a stunning state of fragility.

Let us consider the most significant factors that contributed to the virtual collapse of marriage as a social institution over the last forty years.

The Sexual Revolution

"Bill and Sally, sitting in a tree, K-I-S-S-I-N-G. First comes love, then comes marriage, then comes a baby in the baby carriage."

This seemingly ageless playground rhyme confirms our institutionalization thesis better than a shelf of scholarly reports. Children once chanted to each other the fundamentals of the prerevolution marriage ethic: Bill and Sally like each other. They date. They kiss. They fall in love. They marry. They have sex. They have babies. They push those babies around in baby carriages.

It is hard to know where this set of social expectations began to change first. The best candidate is likely the sexual revolution. We catch glimpses of it in the mid- to late-1950s. Contrary to what many think, movies and music of the era already show hints that the expectation of sexual restraint until marriage was beginning to weaken. American culture began toying with the notion that sexual mores needed liberalization. Indeed, hints of what was to come can be seen in popular culture as early as the 1910s and 1920s.

That liberalization came upon us with a vengeance by the mid-1960s. For a variety of reasons and from a variety of sources came the cry for sexual freedom. Two new sexual standards emerged and were widely embraced. A moderate approach urged that sexual intercourse should be confined to "loving relationships." A liberal stance claimed that sex should freely be enjoyed whenever desired, as long as there was "mutual consent." These two approaches still jostle for mainstream dominance today, with the sex-within-marriage-alone crowd still present but, let's face it, quite marginal overall and often viewed as an archaic medieval leftover.

Forty years later, of course, the cutting edge of the sexual revolution lies elsewhere. Advocates for the full social acceptance of homosexuality, whose voices began to be heard in the 1970s, now occupy a place very near the cultural mainstream. Meanwhile, out on the fringes, advocates can be found for the acceptance of adult-child sexual contact. And, of course, in the intervening years pornography has grown into a $40 billion industry whose tentacles reach into most American homes via the Internet. Child pornography is its most appalling manifestation.

The sexual revolution mattered for a lot of reasons. For our purposes, its greatest impact was in breaking marriage's cultural monopoly. As an institution, marriage confined and structured sexual activity. It did so imperfectly, to be quite clear. But it did so effectively enough to help coerce/entice most men and women to the altar at some time in their lives. Once married, the strongly held cultural norm against adultery kept most men and women faithful despite the existence of an immoral double standard allowing men more sexual license than women. The loving relationship and mutual consent approaches undermined sexual restraint both before marriage and in marriage. More profoundly, these views have dethroned marriage as the normative context for sex. If sex need not be confined to marriage, marriage becomes less significant or necessary.

The Contraception and Abortion Revolutions

The development and widespread distribution of the birth control pill and other effective birth control devices in the 1960s was intertwined, as both cause and effect, with the sexual revolution.[8] It is unlikely that wide swaths of society would have embraced liberalized sexual practices if birth control innovations had not made the prevention of pregnancy much more certain than ever before in human history. But now couples could choose sex without risking pregnancy, or so it was widely believed. This marked the culmination of many decades of efforts on the part of those who believed that birth control could break the tyranny of nature over human sexuality.

It is interesting to recall the initial opposition to such birth control innovations that surfaced both in the broader culture and in the church. It took a Supreme Court decision (*Griswold v. Connecticut*, 1965) to gain married couples the freedom to obtain birth control. Opposition to the easy availability of birth control for the unmarried was much more intense but ultimately proved futile, as a 1972 Supreme Court decision required states to extend access to contraceptives to these individuals and couples as well.

Most Protestant church groups and their leading thinkers, even the most conservative, rapidly embraced the use of birth control by married couples for spacing their children and fostering full enjoyment of marital sex. The Catholic Church remained a holdout and to this day refuses to grant its blessing to any "artificial" form of birth control. The church's stance was and remains hotly contested and has been widely disregarded by the people in the pews since the 1960s. Perhaps the most public dispute within Catholicism of that era was when Pope Paul VI in 1968 refused his own study commission's majority recommendation that he bless the use of artificial birth control by married Catholics.[9]

The Catholic Church's opposition to birth control can be critiqued, but it is based on an ancient and fundamentally important insight. That insight is that human sexuality at its highest occurs in a context of loving and permanent mutual commitment in which there is openness to the gift of new life; that is, in marriage as traditionally understood. The use of birth control by a married couple in order to space children adequately is the best-case scenario for the use of birth control. However, the use of birth control to undermine the links between sex, marriage, and procreation and to underwrite a cultural practice of casual or marriage-free sex is quite another thing altogether. Catholic leaders feared that it would not be possible to bless the former without opening the way to the latter. Here they were right. It is in this sense that the birth control revolution joined the sexual revolution in weakening marriage.

It is not a coincidence that the sexual revolution and the birth control revolution were accompanied in short order by the legal acceptance of abortion on demand with the Supreme Court's *Roe v. Wade* decision in 1973. The ensuing abortion revolution, in which for a time one out of every three American pregnancies ended in elective abortion (before "settling down" to one out of four or five today), carries profound social consequences that extend well beyond the "mere" killing of more than one million developing children a year.

For our purposes, the significance of mass abortion includes at least two other phenomena relevant to our thesis. One is that locating the full authority for making the abortion decision in the hands of the pregnant woman contributed to marginalizing both men and marriage. Abortion within marriage—without a husband's consent or even over his objections—marks a socially significant weakening of the marriage bond regardless of the justifications that can be offered for it on grounds of female self-determination and autonomy.

Second, the abortion license, as it has rightly been called, constitutes a fateful diminution of the rights and interests of children over against those of adults. Abortion sacrifices a developing child's life for the sake of an adult's life, health, or happiness. In this way, *Roe v. Wade* (and parallels in other nations) communicated in the most fundamental way imaginable that the interests of children must give way to the interests of adults. This had enormous implications, not merely for the issue of abortion, but across the entire range of adult-child relations and decision making. As David Popenoe puts it, current transitions in the family mark a shift "from child-centeredness to adult-centeredness."[10] This shift is fundamental both to our analysis of marriage and family decline and to any Christian rethinking of marriage and family life (for more on this theme, see chapter 3).

The Illegitimacy Revolution

Remember that the birth control revolution was supposed to prevent unwanted pregnancies and free men and women for fearless sex. But a funny thing happened on the way to utopia: lots of unplanned conceptions—not to mention sexually transmitted diseases. Of course, there was nothing funny about it.

In 1960, 5 percent of all pregnancies occurred to unmarried mothers; as of 1999, the percentage stood at 33 percent. Think about it—one out of every three children born in America is born to an unwed mother, a rate that has held fairly constant since 1994 but compares quite strikingly to the numbers, not just from 1960, but from 1970 (10.7 percent), 1980 (18.4 percent), and even 1990 (28 percent).[11]

This development makes for an eye-opening example of the iron law of unintended consequences. The birth control revolution was supposed to prevent any upsurge in unwanted pregnancies. A whole lot more people were having sex outside of marriage, but this was supposed to be sustainable because birth control would prevent conceptions.

It turned out that the God-given procreative power of the human body is not easily blocked. Missed birth control pills do not prove very effective at controlling births. Condoms break. Every birth control method fails sometimes, and people fail to use birth control correctly other times. Forty years after the pill was supposed to have solved all these problems, it has been estimated that over half of all American pregnancies are unintended. Of course many, perhaps most, unintended pregnancies end in abortion—22 percent of all pregnancies in the most recent statistics, roughly one for every three live births. But many of the rest contribute to the 33 percent out-of-wedlock birthrate.

Sometime in the 1970s it became viewed as insensitive or oppressive to describe this phenomenon as *illegitimacy*. This word was viewed as unfairly stigmatizing to both mother and child. Sometime in the 1980s, it also became viewed as prehistoric to describe this out-of-wedlock birth phenomenon, whatever it might be called, as a *problem*. Finally, by the mid-1990s, the findings of social scientists about the diminished life-chances of the out-of-wedlock child population and their mothers made it respectable, in some circles at least, to begin raising such questions again.

But by then the damage to the structure of marriage as an institution had been done. If one of marriage's key purposes had been to structure the birth and rearing of children and to provide a structure of family relations as architecture for a child's world, then the illegitimacy revolution marked the crumbling of one of the fundamental pillars of marriage as a social institution.

This is what was going on with the surprising flap over the *Murphy Brown* television show in the late 1980s. Some readers may remember that Vice President Dan Quayle criticized this show, starring Candace Bergen, for its depiction of the main character's decision to conceive and raise a child without benefit of marriage. Quayle's reputation never quite recovered from the scathing attacks he received as cultural assassin of the reputations of single mothers.

Yet the former vice president was making two basic claims, both of which have turned out to be true. First, for most single mothers and their children, life is far more difficult than it is for those whose context is marriage, beginning with economic circumstances but extending to many other aspects of life including basic survival.[12] Second, the glamorization of (especially voluntary) single motherhood contributes to the weakening of cultural commitment to marriage. Barbara Dafoe Whitehead made both arguments quite devastatingly in her epochal article "Dan Quayle Was Right," which appeared in the *Atlantic Monthly* in 1993. It was an article that contributed considerably to changing the terms of the public discussion. However, by this time the deinstitutionalization of marriage was all the further along.

The Cohabitation Revolution

Related to all of the above was the simultaneous cohabitation revolution. It is well-known that couples live together without benefit of marriage at a rate unprecedented in American history. Over four million American couples currently live together, and some reports indicate that nearly two-thirds of Americans now choose to live together before getting married if they ever get married at all.[13]

One of the social purposes served by marriage as an institution is in providing structure for family ties and the formation of households. Again, it would be a gross mistake to claim that family life in the Western world, or in America, has ever been confined to the nuclear family of father, mother, and their own biological children. Well into the twentieth century it was not uncommon for extended family members to reside in various households of their married relatives. Household employees sometimes lived in residence with well-to-do families. And the far greater rate of early death in days of more primitive medical care meant that families took on unexpected shapes on a regular basis—and marriages rarely lasted more than twenty years.

But again, all of these were viewed as variations of a basic and well-understood norm. Sexual relations were to occur among adults within the confines of marriage. Those who had sexual relations and slept in the same bed within the same household were to do so only after having crossed the threshold of marriage—after mutually exchanging promises before a gathered community and thus participating in that rite of passage, which signified the permissibility of sex and living together.

The deinstitutionalization of marriage has been marked by the virtual collapse of this particular boundary marker. It is a natural accompaniment of the other changes already noted. Regular sex outside of marriage tends to lead to the establishment of more or less regular patterns of cohabitation—who wants to get up at four in the morning and stagger home? Unplanned pregnancies resulting in births (as much as 25 percent of all out-of-wedlock births) tend to bind cohabiting couples somewhat more closely together, even without marriage, and can result in semipermanent but still unstable cohabitation arrangements.[14]

Moreover, in a classic example of the "feedback effect," the instability of marriage itself has contributed to cohabitation. Afraid of the heart-rending failure of marriage, couples hesitate before ascending the altar. They try living together to see if the arrangement might work. Their very experiment has the ironic effect of blurring the line between married and unmarried, between permanence and impermanence, and thus weakens the institution of marriage for everyone, themselves included.

In a sadly ironic twist, cohabitation also fails to prepare couples very well for marriage. According to Linda Waite, a leading researcher on this issue, "Cohabitation isn't marriage and cohabitating people don't act the same way as married people do. They don't have the same characteristics; they don't get the same benefits; and they don't get to pay the same costs."[15] Studies show that many couples expecting to marry never do—the average length of a cohabitation relationship is a little over a year. Those live-in relationships that do result in marriage are much more likely than other marriages to end in divorce. Cohabitating partners suffer higher levels of conflict, domestic violence, abuse, and infidelity than married partners do.

Over a third of all cohabitating couples share their homes with children under the age of fifteen, according to 1998 Census Bureau statistics. Sadly, these domestic arrangements are rarely placid. Relationships between live-ins and the children of their significant others have been shown to be less stable and satisfying and far more likely to be characterized by sexual and physical abuse, including assault and murder, than in families where the adults are married to each other. In a study by Leslie Margolin of the University of Iowa, boyfriends were twenty-seven times more likely than natural parents to abuse a child.[16] Waite argues that "the parenting role of a cohabiting partner toward the child(ren) of the other person is vaguely defined. The non-parent partner . . . has no explicit legal, financial, supervisory, or custodial rights."[17]

Whatever the dynamics driving this pattern of abuse, the results are clear, as Heather MacDonald so memorably puts it, "The risks to children living outside a two-parent home go beyond social failure, as witnessed by New York City's never-ending cortege of tiny coffins containing children beaten, suffocated, and scalded by their mothers' boyfriends."[18]

Remember that these individual traumas, horrible as they are, are not the end of the story. The bigger picture is that the mass pattern of cohabitation functions as yet another sledgehammer blow to yet another portion of the cathedral that was marriage.

The Reproduction Revolution

In 1978 the first test-tube baby was born. Hailed as a medical miracle, the birth of Louise Brown through in vitro fertilization inaugurated a change in the social landscape, the full implications of which were not anticipated at the time—and have not yet been fully realized.

The reproduction revolution marked the seeming triumph of medicine and technology over the all-too-fallible natural processes of conception and gestation. In a society in which 10 to 15 percent of couples seeking to conceive a child prove infertile—unable to conceive after a year of unprotected sex—technologically assisted reproduction (AR) offers the promise of overcoming nature's obstacles and producing the baby so deeply desired.

After twenty-five years, dozens of varieties of AR techniques have been developed. While the failure rate remains quite high, this industry offers enough successes to continue to attract tens of thousands of anxious and hopeful couples a year.

However, there is a downside to these technological breakthroughs that goes beyond the moral question of whether AR itself ought to be undertaken. For our purposes, the key problem is this: AR makes child conceiving and childbearing, at least theoretically, available to any person or combination of persons willing to pay for it.[19]

Thus, two men can use AR to procure a baby. So can two women. So can an unmarried couple. So can a single woman or a single man. So can two men and one woman. And so on. While AR is still primarily employed to enable married heterosexual couples to have children, AR companies themselves do not limit their services to such couples. Nor have state or federal governments attempted to do so. The result is a further weakening of the connection between (heterosexual) marriage, childbearing, and parenting, not to mention the link between sex and procreation. The historic locating of childbearing and child rearing within the institutional context of heterosexual marriage takes another significant hit.

The Gay Rights Revolution

Prior to the mid-1970s, medical professionals understood homosexuality to be a psychological disorder requiring research and treatment. Under significant pressure from the increasingly organized homosexual community, the American Psychiatric Association voted in 1973 to remove homosexuality from its list of disorders. This step was significant in mainstreaming homosexuality both in medicine and eventually in popular culture. It was of enormous social significance and anticipated a broad shift in cultural understandings of homosexuality, indeed, of sexuality.

Of course, despite the earnest efforts of many activists, homosexuality has not won the full acceptance that long has been the dream of the gay rights community. Evangelicals and Roman Catholics have been perhaps the most significant force preventing the triumph of this aspect of the gay rights agenda.

Sadly, and inexcusably, Christians frequently have responded to homosexual persons with hatred and contempt. In doing so, we have embarrassed rather than distinguished ourselves. That homosexual people should be treated with respect and Christian love should go without saying. There is no place for antihomosexual crusades of any type.

Yet resistance to the full social acceptance of homosexuality is, at its best, rooted in a recognition that here we find another blow to the historic social institution of marriage. The challenge posed by homosexuality to marriage takes two very different forms. Promiscuous or multipartner homosexuality can be viewed primarily as one more example of the challenge to marriage posed by the sexual revolution in general. To accept promiscuous gay sex is to say, "Not only is sex outside of marriage socially permissible, and not only is promiscuous sex outside of marriage permissible, but promiscuous sex without regard to gender distinctions is also permissible."

The late 1980s introduced an entirely new and far more significant dimension to the challenge homosexuality poses to marriage. Here I speak of the move on the part of many in the gay community to press for full civil equality, even "marriage," for committed homosexual partnerships.

The demand for gay marriage sometimes is presented as a socially conservative move, even as a defense of marriage. The argument directed toward those who oppose gay marriage goes something like this: "We press for marriage because we, like you, value the stability of lasting romantic commitments. In a society that devalues such commitments at every turn, we are your allies, not your enemies. Grant us the right to marry, and let us join you in defense of marriage as an institution." Andrew Sullivan put it this way: "Far from weakening heterosexual marriage, gay marriage would . . . help strengthen it as the culture of marriage finally embraces all citizens."[20] While this argument has not yet prevailed in our culture, it is making great inroads.

The net result of the press for gay marriage is less social certainty about whether marriage necessarily must be viewed as exclusively a bond uniting one male and one female, and thus gay marriage is another bewildering challenge to the historic understanding of the institution of marriage.

The Divorce Revolution

I have saved until last what is undoubtedly the most significant single social development affecting the health of marriage as an institution and the one that will receive the most attention in this book: divorce. From 1964 to 1975, the divorce rate doubled in the United States. It has stabilized since then, but still we have by far the highest divorce rate of any major industrialized nation.[21] Americans long had a higher divorce rate and easier access to divorce than did most other Western nations, so divorce had always been a part of American life. Andrew Cherlin has shown that the divorce rate in the United States had actually risen steadily since 1860, with incremental surges after World Wars I and II.[22] But those numbers were dwarfed by the explosive growth in the divorce rate after 1960 and especially after 1965.

No individual or group sat down and planned to double the divorce rate in ten years. No one imagined a scenario in which by 2001 nearly half of all marriages contracted that year were projected to end in divorce if current trends continued; nor did anyone plan a society in which over one million children a year would experience the divorce of one or more of their parents, many for the second or third time, or more.

Prior to the 1960s, divorce (and its more cautious colleague, separation) had always existed as a kind of small exit hallway out of the marriage cathedral. In nearly every political context within Europe, Canada, and the United States in the last three hundred years, there has been some way to get out of marriage, maybe not to gain an outright divorce, but at least to be spared the most hideous forms of ongoing conjugal suffering by gaining the freedom to flee. These exit hallways have varied in width and accessibility. But political and even religious authorities have reluctantly recognized the need for an emergency exit from marriage and have usually found a way to provide it.

But during the same period in which the other revolutions were occurring, the divorce emergency exit grew beyond recognition. Imagine a bulldozer gouging massive chasms in the south, east, and west sides of our cathedral, with signs afterwards posted: "Exit Here, Please."

Both in law and in cultural attitudes, divorce moved from rare exception to routine practice. Indeed, it can be argued that divorce emerged as an alternative cathedral; that is, a new social institution paralleling marriage in a kind of parasitic way, thriving as marriage weakened, somehow absorbing much of the cultural energy that once was given to marriage itself. As Barbara Dafoe Whitehead puts it: "At such high and sustained levels, divorce is not simply a legal mechanism for dissolving marriages but a social and cultural force that opportunistically reproduces itself everywhere."[23]

With the rise of divorce came the related rise of remarriage, blended families, and a practice that came to be called serial monogamy. Most divorced people later cohabit or eventually remarry; two-thirds of divorces involve children, who are brought along (in one way or another) into cohabitation and remarriage—thus the phenomenon of blended quasi-families and blended families. Statistically, remarriages and especially cohabitation relationships are even less enduring than first marriages, which are shaky enough to begin with, and so postinstitutional marriage involves the practice of multiple cohabitation and remarriage—serial monogamy. Contemporary marriage involves the mixing and matching, mending and blending of human families into loosely tethered fragments. It's a far cry from that sturdy old social institution we once knew as marriage. A frothy little story from a Christmas issue of the *New York Times* helps paint the picture:

> Ameena Meer . . . will celebrate the holidays this year with a cast of (practically) thousands. There is her immediate ex-husband, James. And her first ex-husband, Andrew. There is her 9-year-old daughter, Sasha, by her first husband, and her two children by her second husband, Zarina, 6, and Jahanara, who is almost 3. At a Christmas Eve dinner Ms. Meer is planning in Washington, Andrew will bring Stephanie, his girlfriend, and one of Ms. Meer's ex-boyfriends is also coming. . . . "Sometimes I need a flow chart to keep everybody straight," she said.[24]

A hundred years ago, relatively few men took the path of Lise Krywy's husband and abandoned their wives and newborn babies. Some days they may have wanted to; many days they may have wanted to. But they didn't. It was unthinkable. And few men abandoned their life partners of forty-three years, as did Ruth DuBois' husband. This too was unthinkable. Equally unthinkable was a family Christmas party along the lines of the one thrown by Ameena Meer.

Marriage has faded as a social institution in American life. If marriage is a cathedral, we stand among its partial ruins. One way we know that this is true is because of the kinds of things that are happening to people like Lise, Ruth, and Ameena.

The statistics, as we have seen, also tell the tale. The combination of nonmarital childbearing, cohabitation, and divorce, among the other factors we have discussed, has rocked the institution of marriage to its foundations. A nearly 50 percent divorce rate, 33 percent illegitimacy rate, and 50 to 60 percent cohabitation experience has made the married two-parent family with their own resident children an increasingly rare phenomenon in American life.

The anthropologist Margaret Mead once wisely wrote, "There is no society in the world where people have stayed married without enormous community pressure to do so."[25] In other words, the social institution of marriage, attaining strength through social sanction, has helped govern human passions and restricted their expression in ways intended ultimately to serve the best interests of most marriage partners, their children, and the society as a whole.

In the United States, and in similar ways in the rest of the developed world, Mead's "community pressure" has been abandoned. Under a series of dramatic cultural revolutions—sexual, birth control and abortion, cohabitation, gay rights, illegitimacy, reproduction, and divorce—marriage has moved toward deinstitutionalization. Now the understanding of marriage, entry into marriage, and exit from marriage are all purely voluntary decisions of autonomous individuals if they choose to partake of the institution at all.

But all this raises the suspicion that deeper forces are at work. Our metaphor may need to shift a bit. So far we have pictured the cathedral of marriage being hammered by a variety of seven outside forces. From the West comes the illegitimacy revolution, from the East the cohabitation revolution, and so on.

It may be that these revolutions are more effect than cause. In other words, it may be that the marriage cathedral has collapsed, not primarily from dramatic external blows inflicted within a single generation, but instead from the slow rotting of its foundations and weakening of its support beams over many generations. It may be that there are termites in the marriage cathedral, weakening marriage (and the various cultural values and practices that sustain it) so profoundly from the inside that it took little more than a few pushes from without to make the cathedral collapse.

In the next chapter, we will consider the historical and social origins of the collapse of marriage.

2

Structural Damage

Why Marriage Collapsed

Tell me the kind of family you have and I will tell you the kind of society you have.

—Frederic Le Play (1806–1882)

The fading of marriage is not the result of some kind of shadowy conspiracy hatched in an office building in Zurich or New York.

Don't laugh. Through the years many have been tempted by such theories. The social changes we are considering are so vast and so great in their significance that many have stumbled toward conspiracy thinking to try to make sense of them. Perhaps this gives evidence of the difficulty of arriving at an adequate account.

Instead, tracing the factors leading to the decline of marriage as a social institution requires the most careful historical analysis. As the quote from Le Play suggests, understanding marriage (or family) in contemporary society involves nothing less than understanding contemporary society—and those societies that came before it.

I will not attempt an original historical analysis here but will instead sift through the best accounts offered by others in recent decades. I will also not attempt to consider all the religious, legal, national, and cultural traditions and all the particular historical eras that could be named and isolated for discussion. Such an effort would take us too far afield.

Our goal is to understand how we arrived at the deinstitutionalization of marriage. Too many contemporary Christian treatments of marriage lack any kind of historical and social context. They seem to assume that the high expectation, high failure rate, high confusion marital climate of our time has ever been thus. But this is not the case. Understanding how we got here is critical to easing our perplexity and moving toward a more adequate Christian approach.

Beginning my account with the first century, my approach will be to argue that there have been three distinguishable cultural periods in Western history—the premodern, modern, and postmodern—with three correspondingly distinguishable approaches to marriage. In looking at these transitions, I will focus on Western Europe and the United States, with special attention to critical developments in Christian thought, law, economics, and the role of women in society—all of which contributed to shaping the practice of marriage in each era.

The Premodern Marriage

The premodern Western marriage grew out of the soil of Christian convictions in interaction with pre-Christian cultural practices that varied in different regions of Europe. Yet the heart of the story must be located in the Catholic Church, the institution that became the intellectual, spiritual, and political center of Christianized Western Europe after a rocky beginning as a powerless, frequently persecuted religious minority on the outskirts of the pagan Roman Empire.

The convictions that the Church developed about marriage were rooted in its understanding of the meaning of biblical texts as filtered through historic interpretations of such texts by church leaders, in the context of broader traditions of thought that characterized the formation of Christian belief and practice in other arenas as well. In short, the baseline starting point for historic Western thought and laws about marriage and divorce is found in the Bible, as interpreted by the Catholic Church, and all later developments represent a revision or abandonment of Catholic thought in one way or another.

We will say much more about what the Bible *should be interpreted as saying* about marriage later in this book. Here our project is historical—identifying what the Church over time made of those texts in developing its treatment of marriage.

Early Christian convictions about marriage, for example, were rooted foundationally in belief in the God revealed in the Bible and in the Bible itself as inspired revelation of the divine will—such convictions have the same roots today. There is a God; this God is the Creator of the heavens and the earth and the author of human life; this God wants to be known and obeyed by the humans he has created; despite human rebellion against God, God chooses to act as Redeemer of humankind by making covenants first with Israel and then the church; as part of redemption, God reveals himself to us in various ways, including through the written Word; the people of God, gathered together in the church, are those who love and serve God and bend their wills to the divine will; one day the entire creation will acknowledge the sovereignty of God and the lordship of Christ. Here is the foundational story that transfixed the Christian mind and provided the context for every particular moral belief.

The premodern church thus sought out God's will for marriage by reading and interpreting Scripture and attempting to put its teachings into practice. The development of the Catholic tradition shifted the locus of interpretation to official church leaders whose charge it was to offer authoritative interpretation of Christian faith under (it was believed) the ongoing inspiration of the Spirit.

As the Catholic tradition developed, a pattern of interpreting Scripture emerged that had several very significant and influential components. Many of these convictions remain essentially unchanged within Catholicism to this day, even though the Church's social power has declined enormously since these beliefs first crystallized. Many of these convictions are shared by other Christians today as well. But they no longer serve as the basis of public law or dominate a nation's cultural ethos, as they once did throughout the Christian West.

What follows are the key biblical texts and motifs that were drawn upon in Catholic teaching about marriage and the main lines of interpretation that developed.

On the basis primarily of Genesis 1–2, the Church understood marriage as a divinely established institution for structuring sexual and family relations. Indeed, marriage was viewed as the one and only normative context for the expression of genital sexuality and the birth and rearing of children, who were to be trained "in the service and love of God."[1] The Church would always press those under its jurisdiction to confine their sexual activities (if any) and family formation to marriage as thus understood, even though it would never achieve perfect compliance with its vision.

Jesus' and Paul's teachings about marriage (Matt. 5:31–32; 19:1–12; Mark 10:2–12; Luke 16:18; 1 Cor. 7; Eph. 5:22–33) pointed back to Genesis but also implicitly critiqued patterns of sexual and family life often apparent elsewhere in the Hebrew Bible. These authoritative New Testament teachings thus served as the foundation for the Catholic Church's rejection of polygamy, prostitution, homosexuality, adultery, fornication, divorce, remarriage, and any other alternatives (other than celibacy) to sexually exclusive monogamy in a lifetime heterosexual marriage relationship.

The Church also developed a theology of marriage, emphasizing the God-given aims, goals, or goods of the blessed estate. The writings of Augustine (354–430) were especially important here. These marital goods were described by Augustine as including procreation (and child rearing), chastity (marriage serving as a way to harness the dangerous sexual passions, thus as a remedy for lust), and for Christians, "the bond of permanent union."[2] The emphasis on procreation was rooted in Genesis 1:27–28; the remedy for lust was based on Paul's teaching in 1 Corinthians 7:1–9, 36–38; and the permanent (sacramental) union was founded on Ephesians 5:22–33.

Ongoing ambivalence about sex plagued Christian thought, leading many church leaders to prefer celibacy (sometimes even *within* marriage) and leading some to condemn sex, women, or both.[3] And yet an (increasingly grudging) acceptance of sexual expression within marriage solidified within the tradition. The companionship dimension of marriage also sometimes made it into the standard list of marriage's aims (often based on a reading of Genesis 2:18–25) but usually in a subsidiary role. Augustine actually begins his treatment of marriage here: "The first natural union of human society is the husband and wife."[4] Yet this theme is not developed thoroughly by Augustine, and it can be argued that it remained a secondary theme in official Catholic teaching until the twentieth century.[5]

The Pauline comparison of the relationship of husband and wife to that of Christ and his church (cf. Matt. 9:15; John 2:1–11; 2 Cor. 11:2; Eph. 5:22–33; Rev. 19:7–8; 21:2) became foundational in the twelfth century and thereafter for the evolution of a *sacramental* notion of marriage in the Catholic tradition. As Catholic thought about marriage grew more systematic and refined, marriage was brought into the "Holy of Holies," as it were. It was viewed as being as much a means of grace as baptism, communion, or any of the other sacraments. According to John Witte, "The temporal union of body, soul, and mind within the marital estate symbolized the eternal union between Christ and His Church, and brought sanctifying grace to the couple, the church, and the community."[6] This exalted perspective on marriage stood in considerable tension, however, with the ongoing preference of Church leaders for celibacy as the higher and more spiritual path.

Still, this sacramental analogy between the Christ/church and husband/wife relationships became the subject of very rich reflections on both.[7] It became instrumental in raising the status and expectations of marriage and eventually in leading to an acknowledgment of the rich spiritual and relational possibilities within marriage. We are here still far away from a modern or postmodern emphasis on love and romance; there was no thought of hanging either marriage or the possibility of divorce on the emotional quality of the marital bond. Still, the sacramental vision planted seeds for the development of a more positive vision of the spiritual and moral significance of marriage, a vision that has been articulated richly in the Catholic personalist theology of marriage in recent decades.

This vision also played a key role in the Catholic Church's decision finally to ban divorce altogether. For, as Thomas Aquinas argued, just as the relationship between Christ and the church can never be dissolved, so it must be with the bond between a husband and wife.[8] The church came to believe that marriage is *literally indissoluble* in this life and thus can be ended only by the death of one spouse. While interpretations of the difficult biblical texts varied and were the subject of considerable debate among church scholars for a thousand years or more, indissolubility was settled upon as the authoritative and enforced Catholic stance during the thirteenth century.[9]

Marriage could thus be exited only if church officials could determine that it had never been validly contracted—this was the *annulment* tradition. Marriage partners could *separate* "from bed and board" only on the basis of narrow, specific grounds (essentially: adultery, heresy, desertion, and cruelty) and under church adjudication, but full-fledged *divorce* as we understand it—the dissolving of marriage with the possibility of remarriage—was not permitted at all.[10] Church laws established elaborate codifications of these rules related to who had permission to marry, separate, and have their marriages annulled, and any such cases were heard in church courts.

At the same time as these theological developments, the Church was solidifying its political and legal grip in Europe. The Catholic Church had long held, in part based on its understanding of Jesus' delegation of authority to Peter (Matt. 16:18), that through the pope as Peter's successor, it bore the authority to govern the lives of believers. Christians were required to submit to the authority of the Church in contracting and conducting their marriages, as in other areas of life.[11] But from 1200 on, in part due to a vacuum of political power in Europe, the Church was able to extend its reach fully into Western law. Now canon law (Church law) became civil law. The official Christianization of the Roman Empire under Constantine's successors in the fourth century had given the Catholic Church its first taste of cultural power. Now the Church began to experience the fulfillment of its fondest hopes for directing the course of Western societies.

There remained some local resistance and variation, but on the whole the result of Catholic cultural domination was the institutionalizing of its vision of marriage across the Western world. Marriage was God-given, sacramental, contracted by consent of the parties, heterosexual, procreative, monogamous, sexually exclusive, remedial (for lust), and indissoluble. Canon law provisions for annulment and separation were decreed by the Church and enforced by the state. The only social alternative to marriage was the superior state of celibate singleness through religious vocations.

The medieval Catholic vision of marriage was strongly reinforced by broader economic and social circumstances as well. Catholic Europe was dominated by agriculture; most people eked out a living on farms or in small trades. Most were born and raised, lived and died within a confined geographical location. Social roles were rigid, and thus social mobility was quite limited as well. Those seeking an alternative to social norms had little recourse anywhere in Catholic civilization.

Women, in particular, lived their lives under quite constrained circumstances. A woman was viewed as under the sovereignty of her parents until that sovereignty was transferred to her husband. She could not own property, could not seek employment outside the home, could not resist her husband's will in any significant way, could not seek or obtain a divorce, faced ferocious social and legal sanctions if found engaged in illicit sexual activity, and could not serve as a political or religious leader (except in the monastic vocations). Her lot in life seemed as unalterable as the sunrise and sunset.

To fix this long-lost world into view, I ask you to imagine an ancestor of mine, Robert Gachet, a farmer living and working in southern France in 1400. He is married to the former Madeleine Bouvier. They have six children. If we were to ask Farmer Gachet whether he might like to divorce his wife, he would respond that the question makes no sense at all.

It makes no sense *religiously*. Robert is a Roman Catholic in medieval Europe. His marriage was celebrated in a church that believes that the bond between married couples is indissoluble. It is spiritually impossible for him to divorce his wife.

Our question to Farmer Gachet also makes no sense *legally*. The Church has the power in southern France to establish its view as the law of the state. Thus Farmer Gachet is not legally permitted to divorce his wife. He can separate from her under narrowly construed grounds (arbitrated by Church courts), but he cannot divorce her.

The question also makes no sense *economically*. Mr. Gachet needs his wife and the oldest of their children to help him run their farm and care for the younger children. If he divorces his wife, he is suddenly short at least one very significant pair of hands. These hands likely spell the difference between survival and starvation.

The question of whether Farmer Gachet should divorce his wife also makes no sense *relationally* or *culturally*. Any attempt on his part to divorce his wife (or even to separate from her) would gain him the rejection of every significant person in his social world—his neighbors, extended family, and the entire community. He would face a wall of social rejection and opposition.

Finally, Farmer Gachet would likely respond to our question with one of his own—why should he even consider divorcing his wife? If we respond that he might consider divorcing Madeleine because he appears unhappy in the marriage, or not "in love," he will scratch his head in complete astonishment. He will say that whether he is happy with his wife is utterly irrelevant. A spouse is for economic partnership, having and raising children, providing a sexual outlet, and imitating the relationship between Christ and the church. An effective partnership in shared labor and living is enough; no one dare expect more, though when more comes, it is a welcome gift.

In its essence, this was the status and understanding of marriage in Christian Europe when Martin Luther tacked his ninety-five theses to the church door at Wittenberg in 1517.

Toward Modern Marriage

Perhaps the most far-reaching effect of the Reformation that Luther unintentionally launched was the collapse of the monolithic cultural and political supremacy of the Catholic Church. At least in Western Europe, there had been no alternative to what might be called the Catholic Way. All (legitimate) debate took place within the Church; illegitimate opinions were legally suppressed by the Church. This extraordinary cultural monopoly was soon gone with the Wittenberg wind.

The two primary Reformers (Martin Luther and John Calvin) did not break entirely with the Catholic tradition on marriage. Nor were they uniform in their own views. However, it is possible to identify several key moves they made that took both Christian teaching and Western law in some new directions.

Emphasizing Scripture as they did, these two Reformers taught that marriage was God-given, heterosexual, procreative, monogamous, permanent, and a remedy for lust. However, they rejected on biblical grounds the concept that marriage was sacramental. They strongly rejected the tradition of celibacy as any kind of "higher way" for Christian sexuality; many, including Luther, lived out this conviction by leaving religious orders to marry. The Reformers also recast the theology of marriage, situating it within the context of their broader theological vision. For Luther, marriage was one of three foundational "social estates" within the earthly (rather than heavenly) kingdom. For Calvin, marriage was treated as a covenantal association of both the civil and church order.[12]

The Reformers emphasized the human purposes of marriage. Created by God, marriage was still a humble human endeavor, neither eternal nor a means of divine grace, yet no less valuable for being accepted for what it is. The Reformers tended to lift the value of partnership ever so slightly in considering marriage, though again we are a long way from contemporary "wine and roses" expectations. Both Reformers emphasized the social importance of marriage as well as its benefits for individuals. They strongly emphasized that marriage was a remedy for sexual sin. In the latter part of his life, Calvin developed a rich covenantal theology of marriage. Marriage was a covenant akin to the divine-human covenant relationships described in Scripture. Among other implications, as a covenant it must be entered by free consent on the part of both spouses, with the participation of parents, peers, ministers, and civil rulers, in pursuit of particular covenant obligations. And as a covenant it was unbreakable apart from the grave breach of specific biblical provisions (for more on covenant, see chapter 6).[13]

While both Luther and Calvin were strongly opposed to divorce, they rejected the Catholic understanding of indissolubility because they believed it to be without biblical basis. Thus they made the historic move of broadening the grounds for separation and of opening up the possibility of divorce and remarriage—though on very limited grounds, which they believed to be in keeping with biblical teaching. Luther's thought on the issue developed over time, but eventually he settled on adultery, desertion, and refusal of sexual intercourse as legitimate grounds for divorce (and impotence as grounds for annulment). For Calvin, only adultery and "malicious desertion" (which he treated as a type of adultery) were acceptable grounds for divorce.[14] For both Reformers, a legitimate divorce opened the way to a legitimate remarriage for the innocent party.

There was no question for Luther or for Calvin of doing away with Christendom, however, or of accepting a pluralistic society in which many competing notions about ultimate questions could be tolerated. Both men still believed in church leadership or even dominance over culture, though their visions of exactly how that would work varied. Marriage was seen as a matter of the divine will; any responsible Christian ruler would treat it as such. Thus control over the legal aspects of marriage and divorce could be shifted to civil magistrates with the confidence that the reigning Christian vision would there be enforced. While retaining for the church aspects of Christian practice and church discipline in the area of marriage, Lutherans handed legal control over marriage and divorce entirely to the state. Calvinists, beginning in Geneva, tended to develop a joint approach involving both church and state. Calvinist Puritans in New England, however, brought marriage entirely under civil control.[15] This shift of legal control over marriage and divorce would prove especially fateful in later centuries, when the churches lost their grip on the hearts and minds of the populations they once dominated.

The long and bloody battle for religious and political control of Europe that followed the Reformation eventually led to a checkerboard of conflicting treatments of marriage and divorce in different jurisdictions both in Europe and eventually in colonial territories. Lutheran parts of Germany had one kind of law; Calvinist Geneva and Scotland had another; Zurich and Basel had yet others. Catholic sections of Europe continued on the course charted above, while Anglican Great Britain developed its own quite distinctive and quite restrictive Anglo-Catholic approach. Religious and legal treatment of marriage and divorce literally varied from city to city.

This collapse of *Catholic* cultural and political domination in the sixteenth century foreshadowed the gradual collapse of *Christian* cultural and political domination in the seventeenth and eighteenth centuries. What emerged over time was the loss of the church's (*any* church's) ability to control the West's worldview and, along with it, the laws and cultures of Western Europe and its colonies. Provoked in many ways, ironically, by the Reformation itself, a secularizing wind blew across the Western world. The Renaissance, the scientific revolution, and ultimately the philosophical shifts that take the name "the Enlightenment" eventually led to the triumph of secularism in Western culture. The center of authority shifted from Scripture and Church to reason and science. Truth was discovered by reason and observation, not mediated by the Church or dictated by its priests. Autonomy and freedom were treasured rather than submission to external authority. Humanity was coming of age, or so it was thought, and it was leaving its old tutors and schoolmarms behind. These worldview shifts began with the elite and took many centuries to penetrate into the highways and byways of both the Old World and the New. And yet penetrate they did.

A significant aspect of the historical trajectory related to marriage was the Romantic Movement, which emerged as a kind of alternative tradition to the Enlightenment's dry philosophical and scientific rationalism and empiricism. Romanticism shared with the Enlightenment its humanism, its rebellion against traditional authorities (especially the church), its celebration of the individual, and its "restless quest for human freedom, fulfillment, and bold exploration of the new."[16]

However, the Romantics broke with the musty philosophers and fussy scientists of their age by emphasizing human emotions in all their depth, individual self-expression, passion and imagination, the interior states of human consciousness, and the ineffable possibilities of human relationships. In other words, the Romantics were "romantic" about life and especially about love, sex, and relationships. They sought to plumb the depths of human experience and were unsatisfied with anything less.

At its broadest level, this cluster of values eventually crystallized into what Lawrence Stone calls "affective individualism," and it is a critical part of our story. It began in elite culture but trickled down to the masses in the eighteenth and nineteenth centuries through novels, plays, romances, and many other expressions of mass culture. The Western imagination—large portions of it, anyway—was captivated by the vision implicitly and explicitly communicated and still is today.

It was a vision that when addressed to family life made historic Christian treatments of love, sex, and marriage look crabbed and confining. If marriage was to be preserved as a social institution, it would require a total rethinking. Individuals would have to be fully free to pursue their own mates. There could be no more arranged or coerced marriages. And marriage would have to be based on privately considered matters of love, affection, and compatibility, not just (or not at all) shared piety, money, family preferences, or even the ability to milk cows and bake bread. Sex would become more than what was sometimes a merely obligatory remedy for lust, though it took some time for frankness about sexuality to become a cultural norm. Romantic love would now govern the choice of marriage partners, and the sense of whether marriage was or was not a "success." Spouses would now be "collaborators in a joint emotional enterprise," which took precedence over any other aspect of family life, even children.[17]

Cultural analyst Anthony Giddens points out that while erotic or passionate love is a feature of every culture, romantic love, as we understand it, is a unique, recent cultural development. It swept the Western world beginning in the late eighteenth and early nineteenth centuries and has not yet eased its grip. It is possible to identify a number of historical factors contributing to this concept of romantic love. Historic Christian piety, especially in its mystical strand, fostered a passionate conception of the interpersonal relationship between God and individuals that in a more secularized time could be transferred to human relationships. A forerunner to romantic love also could be found in the "courtly love" tradition that emerged in France in the twelfth century, though in this case the love object was always beyond reach, to be pined after rather than captured. Economic transitions (discussed below) placed the home within the woman's domain, and womanly dreams of domestic bliss and emotional warmth began to spread very widely. Giddens claims that romantic love "was essentially feminized love."[18] However we trace the origins of romantic love, it eventually came to define the cultural understanding of marriage.

Economic changes contributed to this broad social transformation. The decline of medieval feudalism and eventual rise of industrial capitalism had a profound impact on the intellectual and social world of Western humanity. In feudalism, just about everything in the social order was given; in capitalism, men (and eventually women) were much more free to make their own way in the world and rise above their origins. Capitalism created an ethos of individual self-advancement through cunning preparation and hard work. Economic relationships were governed less by trust and family or community connection and more by contracts between strangers enforced by law.

The shift from an agricultural to an industrial economy rearranged the work and household patterns of vast millions of people. The family farm was in many ways a self-contained social unit, in which all family members lived and worked in the same space and all shared the common purpose of ensuring the family's economic survival. Factories pulled men (and often boys and later women and girls) off the farm and into the city for endless hours of work. This diminished the presence of the husband and father in the home and contributed to a reorganization of the dynamics of family life. The "work" and "family" spheres were split, and marriage subtly shifted from a relationship based on shared work to a relationship based more on shared affection and mutual enjoyment. This opened up greater potential for emotional fulfillment in marriage; but it inevitably raised emotional expectations of marriage as well. Indeed, as Eli Zaretsky argued, these shifts led to the rise of "subjectivity" and the quest for personal identity that so characterizes all Western cultures.[19]

Eventually, millions of families migrated to the cities. Urbanization created an entirely new social environment in which to conduct marriage and family life. The net result was a decline in the sense of stability, continuity, and community and an increase in individualism and social dislocation. The world was changing dramatically, and marriage changed with it.

Beginning in the mid-nineteenth century, the feminist movement pressed for a transformation of the role of women in society. Women demanded improved, and eventually, equal rights with men, especially basic property and political rights as well as enforced protection from domestic violence. They pushed for changes in social customs that demeaned them and limited their economic, social, and political freedom. Some agitated for marriage and divorce law reforms in order to give women more freedoms in marriage and more opportunities to escape oppressive marriages. Eventually, by the mid-twentieth century, women had broken through many of the economic and social barriers they had so long bumped up against in law, though fewer gains had been achieved in culture and attitudes. Women now had much broader access to economic life (though still only 30 percent were in the labor force by 1960) and had begun to move in the direction of the level of freedom and self-determination that men had long enjoyed.[20]

It is important to note that the sharp reduction in family size in the Western world, which began in the mid-nineteenth century, also had a profound impact on every aspect of marriage and family life, as well as on the culture as a whole. Giddens points out that for the first time sexuality began to be separated from nature and to come under the control of individuals and couples. Life no longer was an endless round of pregnancies, births, and regular fetal and maternal deaths. The way was prepared for sex to become, in Giddens' words, "a potential property of the individual," who could decide what sexual involvements to engage in, with whom, and with what meaning(s). Eventually, as we saw in the last chapter, the great improvement in contraception created a full-blown "plastic sexuality" that could be, and often is, separated from marriage and childbearing.[21]

Throughout this period and into the early twentieth century, Western countries were still rather slow to change their marriage laws, even as these dramatic cultural changes occurred. What now appears to have been a relatively brief period of equilibrium was reached in the late nineteenth and early twentieth centuries that combined something of the historic Christian vision with the exciting but dangerously unstable romantic vision. It is often identified with the Victorian era. Marriage was now freely contracted by the individual on the basis of affection and perhaps romance, but once contracted it was permanent. Both the surviving Christian ethos, as well as a concern about the well-being of children, led to the maintaining of high barriers against divorce. Thus, divorce remained a rare exception, discouraged by both culture and law. These social pressures prevented most unhappily married people from divorcing, despite disappointed romantic hopes—until these pressures collapsed later in the twentieth century.

In understanding events in the United States, dynamics distinctive to our nation are important to consider. The constitutional disestablishment of religion in America meant that, though the churches had great cultural influence, they did not have the power to force their particular visions of marriage into law.[22] Courts and legislators responded to the broader public will, whether the churches liked that will or not. Indeed, from the beginning of colonial settlement, most colonies treated marriage as a civil matter, and divorce was more accessible than almost anywhere in the Old World.

Barbara Dafoe Whitehead has argued that pivotal American cultural attitudes—freedom, personal reinvention, individualism, rebellion—from the very beginning helped shape a greater openness to divorce in the United States than anywhere else in the Western world (with the exception of the radical revolutionary regime in France).[23] As well, the United States (except for some sections of the Old South) never reproduced the static, aristocratic, and hierarchical social order that existed in Europe. We did not have to make the move from feudalism to capitalism, or from monarchy to democracy, because we were born democratic capitalists. Of course, this is a generalization, but it is not without merit. It created an environment far less favorable to binding commitments, and to social pressure to maintain such commitments, than anywhere else in the world.

Even with all this, due to the continuing influence and social power of the churches and the Christian ethos of the nation, divorce was still quite limited. The marriage cathedral may have quivered a bit, but by the late nineteenth century it was still standing pretty firm.

Still, consider the dramatic shift in the view of divorce by visiting with Almond Gushee (my grandfather) of Milton, Massachusetts, in 1935. Many generations earlier, two French brothers named Gachet fled to America in 1699 as persecuted Huguenots. They settled in New England and changed their name to Gushee. Their descendant Almond and his wife, Genevieve, have four children. When they can get there, he and his family attend a Congregational church. It's the heart of the depression. To provide for his family, Almond delivers milk, runs a general store, and gets whatever other employment he can.

If we ask Almond Gushee whether he might like to divorce his wife, the question is no longer ridiculous. At a religious level, his church teaches that divorce is permissible on grounds of adultery and that remarriage is also permissible. But because he has no evidence of adultery, his church would not bless his divorce. However, the state might permit it if he could establish certain other limited grounds, and at that point it wouldn't matter what his church thought. He could always go to another one or just stop going.

At an economic level, however, the question remains nonsensical. Almond needs his wife to care for their children and their home. Moreover, she is a homemaker with no employable skills. She would be bereft if he were to abandon her. If he walked out, she and the children would be at risk of starvation.

No one in his immediate circle of family and friends would support him in this irresponsible decision. And though Almond is not a particularly religious man, he operates by a strong moral code. He would not consider breaking his marriage vows. Marriage is for life. Genevieve is a good and loyal wife and mother. Even though it is not an intimate relationship, he has few expectations in that regard.

For all these reasons, though divorce might be legally permitted, it would not be an option that Almond Gushee would ever consider. Despite the awareness that divorce is increasingly available and more and more frequent, he knows that it is ruled out—for him and for any *respectable* person. He would be disturbed by our questions and would send us away to go bother someone else.

The Postmodern Marriage

From the example of Almond Gushee, it is easy to see the differences as well as the continuities in social context and internal consciousness between the premodern and modern marriage, which of course track closely with broader shifts in culture overall.

In both periods there was no question that marriage was *the* institution in which sexual expression and family formation were located. In both, divorce was very rare. Religious, legal, economic, moral, and community pressures combined to hold men and women to their marital covenants, and it was understood that marriage was a matter of social and public concern, not just a private issue between consenting individuals.

But, alas, the "center did not hold." After World War II, and especially beginning in the mid-1960s, Western culture, and thus Western marriage, made another transition. The new era still lacks a satisfactory name—for now, *postmodernity* will have to do.

We have already discussed the visible signs of postmodernity when it comes to the progressive deinstitutionalization of marriage: the divorce revolution, the sexual revolution, and the birth control revolution came first, beginning in the mid-1960s. The gay rights, abortion, and illegitimacy revolutions gained steam in the 1970s, followed in the 1980s by the reproduction revolution and today by the cohabitation revolution.

But what social pressures contributed to this extraordinary set of developments? Theories abound. Social changes of this magnitude could not have had a single cause. In any case, here is my account, focused on events in the United States.

Postwar America entered into a long period of sustained economic growth that brought prosperity to larger sections of the population than had ever known it. The struggle to survive that had characterized human existence for millennia and that resurfaced with a vengeance during the depression gave way to the ever-increasing comforts of affluent suburban life. Advertisers both catered to the growing desire for more creature comforts and, of course, created it. The "baby boom" generation, those born between 1946 and 1962, entered a society in which for the great majority there was no question of economic survival, just what level of affluence each person might be able to enjoy.

This almost unprecedented extension of affluence shifted the entire context in which life was lived. Economic need focuses the mind. If the question is whether we will eat this week, there is little energy for other concerns. But if survival is assured, the mind and spirit have the space to wander to other issues. There is room to find new mountains to climb, new projects to undertake.

There is much debate over why this wandering did not begin in the 1950s, as affluence began to rise, instead of in the 1960s. Andrew Cherlin's review of the sociological data suggests that the cohort of marriage-age men and women in the 1950s (born in the 1920s and 1930s), having experienced the trauma and suffering of the depression and World War II, were both toughened by these experiences and predisposed to seek stability at their work and in their home life. Simultaneously, and perhaps in tandem, a shift in social values emerged during the 1950s that also marked a return to more conservative standards related to family and marriage.[24]

However, in America (and the rest of the industrialized world) in the 1960s and 1970s, the new horizon (besides the task of accumulating more consumer goods) became *the self*. This was not unprecedented—the same focus was part and parcel of the Romantic Movement, and in the early twentieth century Freud's invention of psychoanalysis, with its emphasis on self-discovery, identity, freedom, and the inner life, also played a critical role in inventing the modern self.[25] For a time, both of these were primarily elite trends, reserved for those with time and space to contemplate the endless depths and distortions of the self. But by the latter third of the twentieth century, most Westerners had opportunity to make the quest for self-actualization the focus of their lives. The late modern self—that striving, searching, self-actualizing beast—was widely disseminated as the normative self during this period. Anthony Giddens notes, "By now, the self . . . is for everyone a reflexive project."[26] What he means is that, in large part due to the constant reinforcement of the idea in all forms of mass culture, the need to interpret, improve, and actualize one's self has become a nearly universal cultural project.

As Christopher Lasch and Barbara Dafoe Whitehead point out with devastating clarity, the "helping professions" and culture-forming elite in American culture (psychologists, sociologists, educators, etiquette experts, and media) fostered and rode this wave by articulating an ethic of "one's sacred obligation to oneself" over against the older ethic of obligation to others.[27] It was not just that Americans had the luxury and psychic space to pursue self-actualization; they were now told by their "therapeutic culture" that they had a *moral obligation* not to let anything stand in the way of "finding oneself" and "becoming what you were meant to be."[28]

I can still remember all the books that my dear mother collected during those years. A steady stream of self-esteem and self-actualization books graced her bedside table, including *I'm OK, You're OK, Passages, Jonathan Livingston Seagull,* and so on. This vision of life was also communicated in the television shows we watched and the advice columns Mom faithfully read each morning. (Fortunately, she lived a different ethic than she read.) The fact is that one did not have to go out to find the self-actualization ethic—it came looking for you. All you had to do was have any exposure whatsoever to the organs of mass culture, and it would seep into your soul without any effort whatsoever. This is what Giddens means by "reflexivity," and it is an extraordinarily powerful force.

The second wave of the feminist movement won its grandest victories during this same period. Remember that the purpose of the feminist movement, at its origins, had been to win for women the most basic rights of participation in political and economic life. These goals were met in the 1960s, and no analysis of the postmodern marriage and family fails to observe the dramatic and still unfolding implications of these achievements for restructuring marriage and family life.[29]

But, under the guise of finishing the job begun in the nineteenth century, second-wave feminism embraced the self-actualization ethos of the era.

Thus, not only did this movement settle the question of whether women would have the legal opportunity to participate in the economy and provide leadership in business, cultural, and political life; it also became critical in advancing the sexual revolution, the abortion revolution, the illegitimacy revolution, and the divorce revolution—along with the men whose behavior made them just as responsible for these social changes. Women were now more economically self-sufficient than ever before (though still lagging behind men in economic opportunities, in part because of their disproportionate responsibilities in family life). They also were more apt to be imbued with the ethic of self-fulfillment than ever before. They were thus far less likely to settle for the disappointment of their expectations in marriage; and for the first time, some had gained the economic means to consider leaving abusive or destructive marriages.[30]

The roots of this revolution of marital expectations, according to Roderick Phillips, can be traced back as far as the nineteenth century.[31] I suspect that rising expectations of marriage relate very closely to rising hopes for marriage as the romantic love ethos gained ground, beginning in the late eighteenth century. Rising expectations of marriage, especially on the part of women, in combination with weakening constraints against divorce, fueled the explosive growth in the divorce rate across the Western world. As more and more came to be expected of marriage, fewer and fewer marriages were able to meet those expectations—at least to the satisfaction of one of the partners—and all it took for divorce to be initiated was for one spouse to decide that their unmet expectations merited it.

The law both responded to and fostered the weakening of constraints against divorce, as well as the broader self-actualization ethic. As I will discuss in detail in chapter 10, in the 1960s and 1970s lawmakers began to lose confidence that they had any business structuring laws in such a way as to encourage permanence in marriage. So they retreated into neutrality, rewriting divorce codes to replace or supplement fault-based divorce with no-fault divorce. The purpose of the law was to provide a minimal legal structure to encompass marriage and an apparatus to sort out divorce as painlessly and quickly as possible.

Andrew Cherlin argued in 1981 that legal changes in this era are best considered responses to changing cultural norms rather than a cause of more divorce—but it is clear by now that easy access to divorce plays a fundamental role in reproducing cultural attitudes and in multiplying divorce.[32] Because "today nearly everyone has been touched by divorce," the sheer omnipresence of divorce "may have some kind of intangible power," as Hackstaff puts it, to affect social attitudes and actions.[33] Such tentative claims by sociologists have long been articulated by moral thinkers—as far back as Aristotle—who have recognized that individual character and behavior are affected by a society's moral climate.

As for organized religion, it never knew what hit it. As I will argue in chapter 9, the church responded to these successive social revolutions in varying ways. A large and fateful section of the church capitulated to them, "updating" their ("embarrassingly quaint and old fashioned") moral teachings to fit with the spirit of the age—sometimes even embracing the self-actualization/self-esteem ethic and teaching it rather than the Bible, the Creeds, or the Confessions. I experienced that as a young Catholic going through catechism classes in the early 1970s.

Conservative churches, such as the Baptist congregation I joined in 1978, attempted to hold onto biblical moral teachings as they understood them but found increasing percentages of their membership out of compliance. This created agonizing dilemmas for ministers and other church leaders. What does it mean to hold onto biblical morality when chaos is erupting in half to two-thirds of our families? How do we balance grace and accountability? Many gave up trying. And yet it is now clear that a remnant of churches survived the entry into postmodernity with their repertoire of moral convictions intact and with a member population still willing to attempt to live accordingly. These were a minority, however.

Let us have one final conversation with a Gushee relative. It is 2002, and we are speaking with Samantha Gushee, not a real relative but a pretty good imaginary thirty-seven-year-old composite of my family—and most families—well into the postmodern marriage era.

If we ask Samantha whether she might like to divorce her husband, she will reply that she has already walked down that road. In her first marriage, her husband left her and their two young children because he said he was bored with her. It turned out that he had been sleeping with his secretary. They divorced after six years, in 1995.

As a young single mother, Samantha was lonely, tired, overworked, and economically stressed. After several years of this difficult life, she met a man at work named Jake, a divorced father of three. She had some questions about him, but she sure appreciated the attention and affection and was hungry for another chance at happiness. She decided to try things out by living with him, beginning in the fall of 1998.

However, within six months she knew she had made a terrible mistake. It turned out that Jake had a problem with alcohol, and he was an angry drunk. He also had accumulated considerable debt, which he had managed not to tell her about before they moved in together. His kids were a mess and were shuffled between his ex-wife and his new household. And he seemed to show just a bit too much interest in Samantha's daughter. So Samantha pulled the plug on the relationship. She took her kids and left, staying with her parents for a while.

Samantha has remarried. Bill is an older man, in his fifties. The kids from his two marriages are grown and gone. Samantha met him at church, where she is involved again for the first time in years. They married in 2001. So far, despite some adjustments, things seem to be going okay. Bill is kind to the children and to her. The relationship has its problems, but Samantha shows a tentative confidence that this time she might have found her "soul mate," that this time it might last.

So Samantha answers that she would not be interested just now in divorcing her husband. It is not that divorce is difficult to obtain legally; while her divorce was a hassle, and expensive, she is free to initiate divorce in her state at any time. At a religious level, Samantha has always believed that divorce is wrong, but she also believes that God doesn't want anyone to have to suffer for a long time in a bad marriage. Her church doesn't talk about divorce, and so she is not sure where the people there stand on it. If they got unpleasant about it, she could always go somewhere else or stop going.

In terms of money, Samantha knows that divorce would be tough. She and her children benefit from Bill's income. However, she has survived as a single mother before and, if she had to, could do it again. She has a good job, her children are now school-age so childcare is less of a problem, and she feels that her position at her company is secure.

Family and friends would not stand in Samantha's way if she decided to divorce Bill. After all, most of them are on their second or third marriages anyway. "Everyone knows that marriage is tough these days." They would stand with Samantha no matter what she did. Everyone has to do what they think is best.

For now Samantha Gushee is happy to stay in her marriage to Bill. She is tied to him by rather tentative bonds of affection and mutual satisfaction, but these bonds are strengthening rather than weakening. She is aware that divorce is always an option, both for herself and for her husband. No external pressure will keep her from choosing divorce if this relationship proves unsatisfying. Everything hinges on whether she and Bill continue to find happiness and love with each other.

Samantha has arrived at what Giddens calls the "pure relationship," "a situation where a social relation is entered into for its own sake, for what can be derived by each person from a sustained association with another; and which is continued only insofar as it is thought by both parties to deliver enough satisfactions for each individual to stay within it."[34] Now stripped of all external supports, no longer functioning as a social institution in any recognizable way, marriage is for Samantha (and millions of others) just one more voluntary relationship to enter and exit on the basis of current perceptions of its benefits and satisfactions.

I suggested at the end of the last chapter that the marriage cathedral has collapsed, not due to external blows since the 1960s, but instead from the slow rotting of its foundations over a long period of time. The story told in this chapter should help to support this claim. There are indeed termites in the marriage cathedral—deep structural forces in culture that have brought down marriage from the inside.

This is an important claim because it helps us understand that there is no enemy group or some kind of conspiracy to topple marriage. We need not look for scapegoats, which too often is the Christian response to unwelcome social changes.

We see through this analysis that any issue-by-issue strategy related to the family is doomed to fail. Some Christians have taken on the abortion issue; others have focused on divorce, the gay rights movement, illegitimacy, you name it. While Christians must continue to make their moral witness clear and live according to biblical standards, it is important not to confuse symptoms with causes.

The deinstitutionalization of marriage is a cultural phenomenon rooted in some forces that cannot be reversed, some that should not be reversed, and others that can and should be reversed. It is not possible to return to premodern economic and population conditions, for example, nor would many of us want to do so. It is not right, in my view, to press for a rollback of women's moral status before the law and in culture. It is also not right for Christians to attempt to reestablish Christianity in law and thus try to coerce men and women to return to an earlier way of living that in some ways was more in keeping with Christian principles and in some ways was not.

We can do several things, however. We can clarify a Christian understanding of marriage and divorce and live accordingly. We can strengthen faith communities so that they no longer capitulate to destructive cultural trends. And we can bear witness to the culture. Through our lives and through our words, we can call our neighbors to a better way.

One way to do that is to tell the truth about the consequences of the collapse of marriage. Those consequences are disproportionately borne by a group whose stories have not yet been heard in this book and whose stories have not been heard nearly enough in the broader culture. That group is our children.

3

Squandered Legacy

The Consequences of Divorce for Children

Here is a letter from a father to his college student daughter, and her response. All names are pseudonyms, and the letter is used by permission.

Dear Sally,

Thank you for the birthday card. I do not wish to appear cynical, but this is the first birthday card you have sent; so I suspect you want something. (Furthermore I feel your mother's hand in this.)

To be honest, Sally, if you want something, why don't you ask for it straight out. I know this is not the way you were brought up, . . . but you now have the opportunity and hopefully the maturity to be straightforward.

In your last letter (again motivated by your mother), you stated you were attending college. I wish you the best most sincerely.

In the same letter, you stated you didn't hate me, . . . but you hated what I did. Specifically, what did I do that you hated? I doubt your mother would want you to say; most assuredly she would not want me to answer.

Hopefully we will continue corresponding, with the criteria that we be honest. I abhor hypocrisy. (I had ten years of it.)
Love,
Jim Peters

[No salutation; Sally told me that she didn't know what to call her estranged father.]

Hey!
Where do I begin? I suppose that "You're welcome" is appropriate. Actually, you don't have to thank me for the card; I should have been sending them all along.

I want nothing but a relationship with you. I have finally come to my senses. I've realized that I've missed out on a big part of my life. My only intention in writing is patching up our differences and trying to make my wrong right. I'm sorry if I caught you off guard.

As for hating you, I could never do that; you are my father. As for hating what you did, well, did you forget me? Or did you just give up? Did you care what I was doing or . . . the person that I developed into? My last letter was sent only to inform you of what is going on in my life. I thought that maybe you wondered. . . .

I hope that you believe my sincerity in that I truly want to know about you. Again, Mom has no hand in this.
Sally

We have seen that Western society has reached the stage of the deinstitutionalized postmodern family. Marriage has not disappeared, but the marriage and family practices of our culture are different from any prior era. We are living out of the anterooms of a ruined cathedral.

Yet not everyone agrees that the situation should be described so bleakly. A great debate about marriage rages in our society. By now, everyone agrees that the family has changed and that marriage is less likely to last a lifetime than ever before. But whether this development should be evaluated negatively finds no consensus.

It is possible to identify three main patterns of thinking on this question. The *declinist* stance views these changes as disastrous. Marriage and the family are in freefall, and the results are destructive for individuals, families, and society. The response is a combination of sharp critique with some prescription for a return to health. Advocates for this stance include, not just many religious leaders, but a number of psychologists, philosophers, political leaders, and other culture watchers.

On the other end of the spectrum are those who argue that the changes we are experiencing have been needed for a long time. Let's call this the *liberationist* stance because of the view that the transformation of the family represents a liberation of love from the shackles of outmoded institutional forms. This liberation frees individuals to create their own family structures as they see fit. Some argue that shifts in marriage offer a decisive advance for women (or for men or even for children). The prescription offered is that Americans should stop pining for an earlier era's marriage and family, do what we can to ease the transition into this new era, and even celebrate the beginning of freer and more satisfying marriage and family relationships.

A more cautious position—the *reformist* stance—rests somewhere in between. Reformists argue that while marriage is in transition, there are also positive dimensions to the new kind of family life that we are creating. Almost by necessity, men and women are learning how to improve their skills in relating to each other. Thus marriages that do survive are likely to improve in quality. Some in this camp argue that the tectonic shift toward a more equal sharing of power between men and women represents a sharp improvement in the morality of society and of the family. Advocates of this view often chide traditionalists with the claims that social change is irreversible and that the good old days weren't so good after all, especially for women. Thus the prescription is that we need to find ways to manage the inevitable passage into a reformed kind of family structure as effectively as possible.

Which approach is closest to being right? It is impossible to make a fair judgment about this without hearing from the children whose daily lives are shaped, for better or worse, by the decisions made by the adults in their lives. The children's experience of postmodern marriage is the last piece of the puzzle we need for understanding where we are and for preparing the ground for a Christian rethinking of marriage.

It has never been easy to be a child. We spend our first years dependent upon the character and goodwill of the adults who happen to be placed in our lives. Children in all societies are physically, legally, financially, emotionally, and socially dependent on adults. They live or die, thrive or wither, due to the decisions of their parents. They have no political power and little voice even in the decisions that affect them most directly—including whether their mother and father get or stay married.

Sentimentality about little children is a recent phenomenon. It is easy to see—whether in scriptural accounts or in literature or in history—that children have often been treated as nuisances, playthings, exploitable rag dolls, or simply as miniature adults. The existence of a dependent period of life called "childhood" is by now taken for granted, but it took a long time to reach this point. Children are not the same as adults but are indeed vulnerable, dependent, and easily frightened and harmed and thus must be treated with special care. Children don't need adult sentimentality, which is a cheap commodity in any case; but they require the loving and just treatment appropriate to their vulnerability.

Of course, this insight is not new. It is taught throughout Scripture that children—especially orphans—fall under the protection of the God whose heart is with the last, the least, and the lost (see Exod. 22:22–24; Deut. 10:18; 14:29; Job 31:17–21; Pss. 10:14; 82:3; Isa. 1:17). The God of justice inclines his ear to the cries of the victimized and the vulnerable—to the widows, orphans, aliens, and sojourners—and demands that his covenant people do the same. It is impossible to be God's faithful people if we do not stand in solidarity with the marginalized, voiceless, and oppressed. We are called to employ whatever influence, voice, and power we have to protect the vulnerable from exploitation, victimization, neglect, and ruin.

After many hours of conversations with college students whose parents have divorced, I find myself deeply struck by this essential biblical mandate: "Defend the cause of the weak and fatherless; maintain the rights of the poor and oppressed" (Ps. 82:3). In other words: stand with those who have no one to stand with them; give voice to the cries of those who are not heard. Through their tears and anger, my students have begged me to hear and eventually tell their stories. They have been comforted by the prospect that someone might benefit from their misery. Many have never been permitted to communicate their pain even within their own homes. Silenced at home (in their *many* homes), silenced by the courts, often silenced in church, these young men and women are the epitome of powerlessness. It became clear to me that if I did nothing else for the rest of my entire professional life, I must do at least this one thing: provide a platform for these children to be heard. Not just so that they can shout their sorrow into the wind, but so other children might be spared having to suffer as these children have.

In the rest of this chapter, I will quote from some of the interviews that I (and supervised student researchers) have undertaken over the past six years with sixty children of divorce. At the end, I will reflect on what these stories mean for understanding marriage and family life. *What would Christian thinking about divorce look like if children mattered?*

Most of my interviews were with eighteen- to twenty-three-year-old undergraduates; a handful were with adults in my geographic area. All interviewees were avowed Christians, though they come from a variety of denominations and varied greatly in their church involvement and level of commitment. They hailed from different geographic and economic backgrounds, though most were middle-class kids from somewhere in the southern United States. The stories reflect the trends indicated in most of the psychological/sociological studies of children of divorce, some of which are cited here. For more detailed information about the interviews, see the brief appendix at the end of the book.

The Children Speak

The stories of children of divorce do not fit into a single neat pattern. Much depends on variables such as the age of the child when the divorce occurred, what life was like prior to the divorce, why the divorce happened, how the parents handled the divorce process, what shape family life took after the divorce, and whether or not a significant social support network existed for the children. Even so, certain recognizable patterns emerge.

The way to begin is by saying this: from the children's perspective, their parents' divorce is almost always the most significant event in their lives. While, as Judith Wallerstein has shown, at least some of the time adults are able to absorb divorce and even benefit from the experience, this is less often the case for children.[1] Divorce leaves its mark, not just for a brief period of time, but for a lifetime. This does not mean that its effects cannot be surmounted; it does mean that there are real effects *to* surmount. As one of these children of divorce has said:

> Every day I think of my parents' divorce at least once. I consider the ramifications of their decisions and actions. I wish that I could remember the good memories from my childhood. I wonder what my life would be like today if my past were different. . . . I think about what a childhood without adult responsibility would have been like. . . . Every day I relive the pain in some way. Every day.

Life before Divorce

It is assumed that every divorce is preceded by intense conflict. This is not in fact the case. Some divorces seem to come out of the blue, especially from the child's perspective. In a result that correlates with the work of Paul Amato and Alan Booth, over 60 percent of students interviewed were surprised by the announcement of divorce and experienced their parents' marriage as low-conflict.[2] For these children, divorce comes as a total shock, disrupting a childhood they understood as positive and relatively free of marital troubles. In the retrospective shadow cast by divorce, these childhood memories are particularly bittersweet:

> I remember my younger sister and I would sit on the roof and my dad would hit plastic golf balls up to the roof, and he would say, "Scoot back. Don't get too close to the edge." And we would catch those. My favorite meal was ribs, rice, and green beans, and we had this little grill, . . . and my dad would cook the best ribs on that.

A surprising number of students report many positive impressions and memories from childhood. Life was once good, but then there was a turn in the road, a change of atmosphere. Dad changed, Mom changed, or their marriage took a turn for the worse.

> When I saw them together, I could tell they were in love. It was no big deal to see Dad with a hand on her leg or to see them hug and kiss. . . . They seemed happy during my childhood days. During my teen years, I began to notice a kind of tension between them that I did not understand, . . . but I knew there was something that was not right with their relationship. . . . Their relationship [had been] founded on Christ, . . . but somewhere something went off course with my dad.

There are other cases, though, in which the entire experience of family life is remembered with pain and sorrow:

> My father abused us, mostly verbally. We heard just about every name in the book. I guess mental cruelty could be a part of it. He accused my mother of being a whore, which she never ever was. . . . He said she was the worst wife and mother in the world. . . . They believed in fighting in front of the children because they did not want us to grow up thinking that there were no fights in marriages. . . . The physical abuse was not terribly bad. . . . We were never beaten to the point of death.

The degree of conflict in a child's home affects their perception of the moral legitimacy of divorce—and has implications for an overall Christian moral approach to divorce. Those who had suffered through high-conflict or abusive marriages understood and almost always supported the decision to divorce. In their effort to make moral sense of a decision that changed their lives, children of divorce from high-conflict families have an ironic advantage over those for whom divorce came as a surprise. In the latter case, the great pain associated with divorce does not seem to correspond with any justifiable cause for it. This may help account for the finding by Amato and Booth that divorces in low-conflict situations are more detrimental for children than divorces following high-conflict marriages.[3]

Liberationist and sometimes reformist voices in the marriage debate argue that most of the long-term emotional and behavioral problems of children of divorce should be attributed to the circumstances that preceded the divorce, rather than to the divorce itself. This claim has some validity, especially in cases of high conflict and abuse prior to divorce. Still, research also shows that the divorce experience itself and the patterns that tend to emerge in its wake carry their own negative consequences regardless of the prior state of the marriage. No child of divorce to whom I have spoken would disagree. There is no one for whom divorce marked a clean transition from struggle and suffering to wholeness and well-being, even in that minority of cases in which divorce brought a halt to a high-conflict marriage.

Reasons for Divorce

Why are so many people getting divorced? My interviews reveal a distressing litany of problems. They include the following main causes, as mentioned by children of divorce.

- Adultery/infidelity (57 percent). "Mom had an affair ten years prior to the divorce that had just come out two or three months before they split up. . . . There were two or three other occasions that she had not had an affair but had come close."
- Communication breakdowns (28 percent). "They said [only] the things that needed to be said. I don't remember them having any good times together. . . . Dad was basically uncommunicative."
- Work-related stresses and absences from home (25 percent). "My dad, he always traveled . . . every week, all week, coming home only on the weekends. . . . My mom was frustrated with my dad."
- Financial problems/conflicts over money (23 percent). "I can remember the water being turned off and not having a telephone like everyone else. . . . Dad was really bad with money, and it frustrated Mom. . . . When there was trouble in the marriage, it was mainly over money."
- Violence (15 percent). "She was afraid of him, when she thought he was going to break her neck. My sister and I were going to call the police, and he said he would kill us if we did."

- Substance abuse/addictions (12 percent). "Dad drank a lot, and because of that, he was verbally abusive. He yelled a lot."

These six causes dominated the accounts of my students. However, a wide range of other troubles also received mention. These included:

- Midlife crises. "There was a point where things snapped and changed for Dad."
- Criminal involvements. "Eventually Dad was sent to a . . . federal prison where he served one year. . . . [They] had him on financial misdeeds."
- Depression/mental health problems. "He was really depressed, . . . and basically he wasn't real open to anybody. . . . My mom was afraid he was gonna commit suicide for a while."
- Lack of (or dissatisfaction with) sexual relationship. "There was a lot of talk about sex between my parents, and my dad would mention things about how mom wouldn't have sex with him. It was just a big deal in their relationship."[4]

Some divorces happen for no reason that the children can articulate, often because the parents cannot say why their marriage ended. This is profoundly disorienting for children. Sometimes neither parent will reveal to the child why the divorce happened; it becomes a secret that they keep from the child. However well-intended, this decision has led these students to feel cheated of essential information concerning the most important event of their lives.

The amicable "mutual divorce" is rare, at least as experienced by children (and articulated by the angry and unhappy adults in their lives). Most divorces stem from actions that eventually break the marriage relationship. Usually one of the two spouses initiates the end of the relationship, while the other resists.[5] Once begun, the divorce process almost always worsens existing conflicts and whatever sense of injustice that already exists in the relationship, tempting both parties to give in to a poisonous bitterness and hatred that can last a lifetime.[6]

The Experience of Divorce

Sometimes divorce comes upon a household with great suddenness. Other times the tension level has reached such a crescendo that everyone knows separation or divorce is imminent. In either case, children of divorce almost never forget the moment in which they get the news that their family is being torn apart.[7] Far more important to children than the actual day that the divorce becomes official, the heartbreaking announcement of separation or pending divorce is seared in their memories:

> When [my mom, sister, and I] pulled into the driveway, Dad had all of his things packed into his car. As we opened the door to go in, he was on his way out. He was very surprised that we were there. It was a strange confrontation. He was just slipping out. . . . I don't know how he was planning to tell us. . . . Dad sat us down and said that he was leaving and that he had an apartment. . . . It was fake because he was saying how much he was going to miss us and that he loved us. I was on an emotional roller coaster and not able to sort out everything.

> I remember the events of that day [this child was six at the time]. It was in the morning time, and our dad brought all three of us and sat us down, sat me and my middle brother, one on each leg, and my oldest brother was sitting in the chair next to him. And he was explaining to us that he and my mom were having problems and . . . were gonna separate . . . for a while and that he would . . . still love us and would still keep in contact with us, but that he was gonna move out for awhile.

> In October they called us into the living room and they told us that they were getting divorced. And . . . my initial reaction was anger. I was really mad, and I got up [this child was eight at the time]. . . . I ran around the house a few times, and I threw myself into my dad's lap, and I slapped him in his face. I'll always remember that. And then we all kind of cried, and they said they were sorry.

> Dad had all of his stuff in his car. I just remember that Mom was very adamant about him not leaving. . . . I remember them arguing the whole night, and then the next day arguing again. He got in the car to leave. It was extremely intense—their words, tone of voice, actions. I remember being in the garage. The whole time I was just standing there [this child was eleven at the time]. . . . Anyway, Mom told him he couldn't leave, and he would have to run over her to leave. I remember Mom laying down in front of the car and telling him he couldn't leave. At this point, I was just horrified. . . . Then he left and never came back.

Despite the significance of "announcement day," divorce is not so much an event as a process. Divorce is preceded by one or more separations. Children's lives are disrupted by the conflict and chaos of their parents' lives as well as a significant series of changes in their own lives: new living arrangements, new schools, new religious involvements, changing relationships with extended families, new lovers for Mom and Dad. It is striking how important the loss of a stable household is to children.

In my study, 45 percent of children had to move as a result of their parents' divorce—for many, this marked the beginning of what became a jumbled blur of moves. These moves pulled children away from the friends who could serve as a critical source of support, especially for preteens and teenagers:

> I didn't really blame God as much for the divorce as for the move. The move's what was hardest on me the way I saw it—because I was in a situation where I could've handled it before, the divorce and all, but then I was put in a totally different situation.

As all of this is going on, Dad has usually moved out, requiring a crisis-driven renegotiation of that critical relationship in children's lives. Mom is likely present but distracted, angry, busy, and sad. Children are sometimes required to get involved in the legal process of divorce—giving testimony, indicating their custody preferences, and so on. No-fault divorce has the benefit of limiting the direct exposure of children to the legal process of divorce. Most students reported that they had little contact with the legalities of the divorce and spent no time in court. Ironically, children of divorce sometimes resent the relative ease with which their parents obtained the divorce that shattered their world. Yet they also frequently suffer through endless legal struggles over custody and child support. The end result is the paradoxical perception that at a legal level divorce is both too hard and not hard enough.[8]

> As hard as it was, I think it was too easy. They both went to lawyers, and they said okay fill out these papers. . . . It was almost like buying a car. You have decided to do something, and the lawyer says yeah give me this much money, and I'll milk the other for all he or she has. There is no justice there. . . .

> I think that the legal system is crap! Right now, you could walk into a lawyer's office and get divorced in no time at all. You don't even have to have a reason. . . . I hate it. I hate how easy it is now.

Relating to Parents after Divorce

The most common pattern for children after divorce is to live with their mothers in a new home while struggling to have some workable relationship with their fathers. In my study, 79 percent of students lived with their mothers after divorce, with the fathers being given regular visitation rights. Just under 14 percent of the children split time evenly between father and mother, while only 3.7 percent lived primarily with their fathers. The remaining 3.3 percent lived with grandparents and in a small number of cases foster parents.

Those who claim that our nation faces a fatherhood crisis can find ample confirmation of this claim in my study.[9] Over two-thirds of students interviewed reported that the quality of their relationship with their fathers declined after divorce. By the time they were interviewed, very few of my children of divorce enjoyed a satisfying relationship with their fathers. It is true that a very small number of my students never had a relationship with their father at all: these were the children of men who never married their mothers or who disappeared after a divorce during the child's infancy. Some lost contact with their fathers after interstate moves. We witness the sad spectacle of young people like Sally, quoted above, who has not seen her father in ten years yet apologizes to *him* for *her* supposed failure to maintain the relationship—and her father, whose sense of himself as Sally's father has become so attenuated that he signs his distrustful and rather stiff letter, "Jim Peters." Sally's alienation from her father and her desperate desire for any kind of relationship represents a common experience among children of divorce.

Deep frustrations and hurts are apparent even among that majority of students whose fathers lived within a reasonable distance and had opportunity to maintain some kind of presence in their lives. As David Blankenhorn notes, the entire concept of the visiting father is a difficult one. It is almost impossible to establish satisfying parenting patterns when visiting every other weekend—it is an unnatural way to parent a child.[10] In my study, a clear pattern emerged: the official court-ordered visitation pattern deteriorated, sometimes quickly. Students put it this way:

> Dad was kind of hit and miss. . . . He was just not very responsible; he would call and say, "Hey, I'm going to be at this event," [but] he wouldn't show up. I'd get a call from him later saying, "Hey, something came up, I wasn't able to be there."

> When I was eight, we would see my dad once a year, and that was at Christmas. Half the time we wouldn't see him. He lived twelve miles away. What he would do was he would bring our presents. If we weren't there, he would leave them on the living room floor and leave. That was all we saw of him and pretty much heard of him. . . . He could have seen us any time he wanted.

> He lived five miles from us, and he had to drive by our house to get to his house [in a rural community]. . . . A lot of times I would be out in the yard

playing, and he would drive by, and he wouldn't look or wave or honk or anything, like we didn't even exist.

This next student's account symbolizes the slow demise of the father-child relationship that occurs so often after divorce. Notice the stages, marked numerically.

> (1) Even before the divorce actually happened, . . . they had already started the every other weekend thing. . . . Sometimes he would [also] pick us up after school, so we saw him a lot in the months after. (2) And then the divorce took place, and it was . . . just strictly every other weekend. . . . We did faithfully go to his house every other weekend for three years. . . . (3) Then he got married to this much younger woman. And she didn't like us very much at all. So during that time it was more like once every two months. . . . (4) [After another divorce and remarriage], my dad just pretty much dropped off the face of the earth, and we didn't hear from him for around six months. . . . (5) By the time I was a sophomore in high school, we saw him maybe once or twice a year, if that. . . . (6) Now I have not seen my dad in two years. . . . And I talked to him on the phone once, last summer, for a few seconds. . . . (7) Last year I even quit calling him my dad.

Visitation arrangements with an absent, long-distance father are often a dreadful part of children's lives. The court-ordered summertime visit to a father inspired these comments from one of my students:

> The court decided that we had to spend a month with him in the summer. . . . He moved to Mississippi and married Joanne. So we had to go all the way down there to see him. He didn't care about seeing us, though. The only reason he wanted us to come down was to piss Mom off. He didn't care a thing about us. He forgot what grades we were in. The visits were hell.

The longing for a father is palpable in many of my interviews—it is the single most consistent theme. One student summed up his thoughts as follows:

> To my dad I would probably ask "why," but mainly, "Where have you been?" Just because . . . through so much of my life the man doesn't know me. . . . I still long for a father, for a physical, earthly father that I've never really felt like I had. . . . I want to be able to take hold of something and say, this is my dad.

Other children of divorce, after years of abandonment, lose any interest in relating to their fathers at all, even if the fathers decide to try to (re)connect, as some do. The children claim not to care. And yet the sadness is striking:

> I had the first conversation with my father that I've ever had, this year. It was weird, really weird. . . . He really wants me to come see him. I don't think I want to, though. I mean, I'm not really angry towards him. I just think it's indifference. I'm nineteen years old, and I've gone through most of the developmental stuff where you learn from your father. . . .
>
> Sometimes he tries to be a father and stuff. He actually came to a few of my ballgames last year, and he sent a Christmas present this year, but I just got it a few weeks ago [in April] and it was a broken picture frame.

Economic Consequences of Divorce

My findings confirm those of many researchers that the standard of living for single mothers and their children tends to drop, sometimes dramatically.[11] Two-thirds of my students offered evidence that their economic circumstances declined after divorce, at least for a time.

There are various reasons for this decline. Even an unsatisfying or unhappy marriage is a kind of economic partnership, in which husband and wife pool paid and unpaid labor to manage the various needs of their household. They may occasionally argue over the division of labor in the family economy, but at least both are present and offer some kind of contribution.

Separation and divorce are costly enterprises. The couple moves from one household to two. Labor is no longer pooled, and so duplication of costs and services is required. Many times there are substantial legal bills, especially in a contested divorce. Most profoundly, the invisible but critical spirit of cooperation that undergirds the family economy is shattered.

After divorce, the state intervenes to enforce a highly strained kind of economic sharing between a man and woman who often hate each other. Custody of the children is usually awarded to the mother. The extra expense associated with caring for these children is addressed by ordering monthly child support payments from the father. However, most child support awards account for a small portion of the actual costs of raising a child. And only half of noncustodial parents pay all that they are supposed to pay (men who never married their children's mothers pay far less frequently than divorced men).[12] These "deadbeat dads" are some of society's favorite whipping boys. The irresponsibility of many such men marks one of the gravest moral issues in our society. But, as Blankenhorn points out, there are reasons besides individual moral failure that account for the massive noncompliance with child support obligations. And any way you look at it, child support from afar is a lousy way to organize the economic support of children—because what children need is not the $3,000-a-year child support payments of the compliant noncustodial father but the $30,000 per year child investment of the residential father.[13]

One aspect of the economic sharing that characterizes many marriages is an implicit husband-wife tradeoff: the husband will invest in his career to gain the skills to support his family well, and in turn the wife will limit her workforce investment in order to provide domestic support. It is an arrangement that works well for millions, but its costs and risks are revealed at divorce, when many women are left in a catastrophic economic situation. Their trust that marriage would last led them to sacrifice the one thing they now need the most—a wage-earning skill lucrative enough to support a family. At the same time, many fathers—for whom neither marriage nor divorce has cost them their professional skills—are often doing quite well.[14] The economic injustice of divorce for many women is not lost on my students:

> Mom had to go to court with the IRS and was audited and hounded because they considered her responsible for Dad's finances and debts he had not paid. . . . Eventually she got to the point where she had no money. . . . She has pleaded with my dad to pay, and he says he will. . . . He travels internationally and lives very well. . . .

> We stayed with my mom. And so she took on two jobs. I remember . . . she took on three jobs at one point.

Meanwhile, child support requirements almost always end when a child reaches eighteen. Yet the reality is that the need for a father's financial support rarely ends on a child's eighteenth birthday. There is the small matter of college. Many of my students struggle to make their way through college because they lack the financial support available to their peers. Some fathers are uninterested in helping, while other students are afraid even to initiate the contact that would be required to ask for help. One student told me that each semester the battle over college funding erupts between her parents, inevitably drawing her in as well:

> I constantly have to deal with the anger and mistrust they have with one another because that impacts whether or not I am going to have college money. . . . Parents should have to write in a clause [in divorce agreements] about how the college education is going to be paid for.

The evidence from many sources is indisputable—divorce hurts the educational attainment and employment prospects of children. We are at risk of creating an even more sharply stratified society than we already have—one tier consisting of those with two financially supportive parents, the other without such support. The economic well-being of postdivorce mothers and their children is one of the major social justice issues of our time. As one very typical student testifies:

> There was an economic impact on our lives. . . . He did not pay child support and alimony. . . . My mother suffered tremendously so my sister and I would not feel the impact. I remember her sitting down with us and showing us her paycheck and saying this is all we have. These are the things we need, and let's all make out a budget and see how we are going to make this work.

Many children of divorce tend to admire their mothers for such heroic efforts to maintain the family, to "keep body and soul together."

> I think it was devastating for Mom too, but she felt a responsibility toward us and could not show it. I think she felt that if she broke down, the entire family might. I don't know how she dealt with it. . . . She put all of herself into work and making a good home. She said that it was hard, . . . and by the time the divorce took place, she had already cried all she could.

Yet we can see that even when single moms manage to make ends meet, the effort of working two or more jobs, raising a family alone, and dealing with the grief of divorce takes a huge toll. The tremendous effort involved in surviving, coupled with loneliness, grief, and anger, sometimes distorts the mother's personality and relationship with her children. Children end up in many cases raising themselves and even, at times, caring for their mothers and sometimes fathers in a strange role reversal (called "parentification") that can be deeply unsettling.[15] As one young man said of his teenage years after a divorce:

> My mom emotionally looked to me for counsel. . . . I just sat there listening because I didn't really know what was going on. She tried to explain things to me. . . . I got to hear a lot of stories, . . . and I just remember my mom being upset at times and wanting to hold me and me not wanting to be held.

Two other students described it this way:

> I was taking care of my dad. My mom was trying to fulfill her desires. And I was just kind of sitting there in the middle hoping somebody would pay

> attention to me. . . . I feel cheated. I absolutely do, because I had no childhood. I went from being a third grader to being a mother, basically.

> It just got to the point where I was going to have to grow up or she [her mother] was going to have to grow up, and I knew that it wasn't going to be her and it was going to have to be me.

Divorce costs children a normal relationship—or sometimes any relationship at all—with *both* of their parents. Thirty percent of students interviewed reported a decline in their relationship with their mothers (less than half the rate of father loss, but still significant). Some men and women end up either so emotionally broken or so consumed by new relationships or so alienated from their children that the children end up emotionally orphaned, drifting away in search of other meaningful relationships with adults:

> Mom and I got kind of emotionally separated. . . . Then when I moved in with [adult friends from church], I think that has been harder on her because she sees how well I relate to them, and she knows how happy I am with them and how well they can provide for me. . . . I saw her recently for the first time since she divorced, after eighteen months. . . . I've seen her about once a year, . . . and it is awkward. . . . There is not a whole lot to talk about.

Postdivorce Family Forms

Life after divorce is affected by whether or not a child's parents date, cohabit, or remarry, which most parents do. The experience of witnessing Mom or Dad's new romantic life is difficult. My interviews show how cohabitation and serial marriage have penetrated the heartland, including the avowedly Christian homes from which many of these children come. In my group of sixty children of divorce, they reported a total of 117 remarriages on the part of their parents, for an average of just under two parental remarriages per child (after the original divorce of their parents). As well, they reported fifty-seven extra divorces or just about one per child.

The most devastating single pattern is multiple divorce and remarriage. Listen in on the following exchange:

Q: How many times has your father been married?
A: Let's see—there was Jill #1, then my mom, then Jill #2, then he married again in there, then Belinda. So I think we are on #5.
Q: How many times has your mother been married?

A: I think this is #10. I kind of lost count, and one of them she married twice so I don't know how you count that. But ten's a good guess.
Q: Did anything positive come out of this experience for you?
A: I can pick up and move and blend in different social situations. My ability to pack boxes. I'm a master at that one. I guess that would be all. I can't think of anything else.

While this is my most extreme case, it is not unique. For all too many children, childhood consists of a dizzying array of unstable and ever-reconfiguring families, with the various moves, homes, and fluctuating step- and half-siblings and other in-and-out householders that this means. When we speak of children of divorce, we must understand that for many this means the heart-numbing experience of multiple divorces and constantly shifting blended families. Asking some children of divorce to draw a family tree produces cynical laughter.[16] Some cannot even recount all of the places they've lived and the people with whom they've lived. One student said, "I had beds; I didn't have homes." In some cases, whole years or more have been forgotten, or the memories are hazy, perhaps linked to traumatic school years. Imagine yourself having this childhood:

> I grew up not knowing my father. My mom was married once before my dad, so I have two brothers from that marriage, and then she married my dad and they had me. Then they divorced when I was very young, and so I grew up for awhile in a single-mother home. My mom remarried when I was probably in third grade, but then she divorced again, and there was a single-mom family again for awhile. Then she remarried again when we were in, I think, fifth grade. She lived with this guy for awhile, but then she remarried. So I grew up most of my life with my mom and my stepdad, which was her fourth marriage. . . . Then they divorced when I was in high school, so she is remarried again, but I don't really consider her new husband my stepdad or anything. He's just her new husband. Does that make sense?

As parents cohabit and remarry, their children from former marriages experience profound ambivalence and pain. As new household arrangements develop, they often feel neglected, with a sense that they are unwanted leftovers of Mom or Dad's earlier life.[17] There's Mom, stepdad or boyfriend, stepdad's children, Mom's and stepdad's *new* children, and the child of divorce, "on the outside looking in," witnesses to a family in which they are not a full member. In many cases they carry a different last name, a potent symbol of their outsiderness that is visible in any school directory in the nation today—as one of my students pointed out. Succeeding at navigating blended family relationships is one of the most difficult human relations challenges that has ever existed. It can be navigated, as the liberationist voices on this issue never tire of saying. But it is extraordinarily difficult. Many interviews strike these themes:

> We found out my dad was getting married just one week before from someone my mom knew. So the whole week leading up we kept saying, "Man, why hasn't he called?" . . . Finally, the day before, he called. I remember listening to this message on my answering machine, just yelling at the phone because I was so mad. . . . So my sister and I went. And I cried through the whole thing. . . . I was not happy about it.

> I was so mad because I still had the image in my head that my family was me, my brother, my mom, and my dad. . . . Even though I was young [eight years old], I think I kind of knew that if she got married, I didn't really have a family anymore. [After the remarriage, my stepfather and my mother] had two kids, and I hated them both. I couldn't stand him. I never called him Dad.

> When we first moved in [with mom's boyfriend], he and I had a falling out in our relationship. Basically it accumulated to him asking me if I hated him, and I said, "I've always hated you," and there proceeded six months of silence between us, absolute silence.

The grief is so deep. I was not prepared to discover the depth of the chaos that now constitutes family life in America. Despite some stepfamily success stories, the broader pattern is clear: the consequences of divorce and subsequent family disorganization for children are severe. Several of my students remind me of trauma survivors. One articulate student put it this way:

> I don't know if there is fury and wrath in nature that would be as devastating as divorce. [The divorce is comparable to] an earthquake, . . . probably just the worst earthquake you can ever imagine—that would make rivers flow backwards and just totally change the face of the earth to where you don't even recognize it anymore.

Violence

Divorce is, tragically, sometimes preceded by family violence. One student described her life before divorce this way:

> My father never hit me or my brother. My mom took it all. One time he broke her nose. . . . He would hit her and then cry with her afterwards. He would do the same thing with us after whipping or yelling at us. . . . He came home one day, and they got into a fight [related to him impregnating another woman]. They were yelling, and he hit her; then she said she was going to call the cops. Then he went outside and started yelling, "Call the cops, call the f—ing cops."

This event precipitated the divorce, which in the case of this student finally brought an end to the violence of her childhood. However, divorce sometimes heightens rather than ends violence. The divorce process itself kicks up a storm of passions and emotions that many adults have difficulty handling. In my study, while 15 percent of students reported incidents of domestic violence that occurred before their parents' divorce, 20 percent reported violence during the divorce process or in a subsequent cohabitation or remarriage situation. Judith Wallerstein's results are similar but even more extreme—one-fourth of the marriages in her study involved acts of violence to a spouse prior to the divorce, while over half included violence during the process of divorce.[18]

Those who fail to divorce successfully—that is, those who fail to end the former relationship and move along peacefully into the next stage of life—are prone to violence against themselves or others.[19] Newspapers are full of tragic tales of the violent end of a relationship between ex-spouses and their children. An entire cottage industry exists in our society related to the violent episodes that rock the lives of the divorcing: restraining orders, domestic violence calls to the police, legal hearings, and so on. And domestic violence is far more likely in cohabiting relationships and remarriages than in first marriages.

Perhaps the most shocking moment in my interviews so far was the following comment from one of my older interviewees who, along with her brother, was asked by her mother and her mother's new lover to kill their father. She describes her recovery of this memory in the following way:

> Years later when I had kind of pushed things aside, . . . I kept thinking to myself, "I must have dreamed this." I started having flashbacks. I had had my first child, and I didn't even tell my husband because I couldn't believe that this really happened. I was talking to my brother one day [on the phone]. I said, "Do you remember—I hope I really imagined this—but do you remember that they talked about killing [Dad]?" And he said, "Don't you remember? He had said that we should do it, and that was the only way to solve the problems." I just broke down because I can't imagine someone telling a child that. . . . "Oh," he said, "you might get sent to a reform school, but we'll come visit you." He's an evil man.

Emotional Impact

David Larson of the National Institute for Healthcare Research is among those who have shown that divorce has a lasting negative impact on children in various aspects of their lives: in parent-child relationships, self-esteem, peer and dating relationships, academic and vocational success, behavioral/emotional adjustment (such as delinquency, substance abuse, early sexual activity, depression, suicide), physical health, and economic well-being.[20] Of course, the form, extent, and timing of this impact vary considerably, and conflict within marriages also causes great stress. But such qualifications do not diminish the reality: children of divorce suffer profoundly.

My interviews tend to confirm Larson's conclusions. While my students respond to their experiences with different emotional mechanisms, none is unaffected. Some, especially the young men, have flattened out their grief into a kind of hard, cynical anger. For others, especially women, the grief is at, or very near, the surface. I remember Jenny, who began to cry even before we started talking and ended her interview with the same tears and these wrenching words: "I think I would have been a daddy's girl." I will never forget her sorrow.

Many report a continuing sadness, and this shows on their faces. Many, especially girls, have struggled with fear and depression. One young woman told me, "I didn't do anything my senior year; I didn't play any sports, I wasn't involved in anything. I was out of it." Some have developed stress-related health problems, such as stomach disorders. They often continue to struggle with financial worries. And their emotional base of support from "the folks back home" also tends to be far less stable than the average student enjoys—though the active involvement of a strong extended family network proved to be hugely important for several students in my study.

My children of divorce desire trusting and intimate relationships but frequently are quite tentative in getting to know members of the opposite sex and are wary of marriage. They have no model for how to make an opposite-sex relationship succeed, and so they grasp in various directions for help: friends, professors, other adults, the Bible itself. Some fear the prospect of marriage, while others are eager to get married and to "do better than my own parents"—a nearly universal refrain.[21]

> I saw how good marriage can be but how quickly it can change. No matter how much one person wants it to work, you can't make the other person stay there. . . . It scares me to think that things can be that great and then get that bad, and it is out of your control. . . . I completely trusted who my dad was. He was a man of Christian character and honesty, but all

> that changed. Now I have trouble with trusting people. Who's to say that somebody else won't do the same thing?
>
> You want your parents to be the ones that you get direction from: "This is what you should do; this is the model you want to have." But I didn't have that. I had the opposite, what you should not do, what marriage does not look like. . . . I have great examples of what not to do. . . . I have been studying marriage since I was eight years old because I am very fascinated with male-female relationships and how it's supposed to work. . . .
>
> It definitely makes [relationships] harder because I don't want to get hurt. I've already dealt with enough of that for a lifetime. I don't want to invest time in relationships that are not going to go anywhere. . . . I don't see the point in spending a whole lot of time with somebody just to get hurt.
>
> I wear my dad's [abandoned] wedding ring as a reminder of my commitment . . . that I would not have a marriage like my parents. It says . . . that the cycle stops here. . . . It's not going to happen to me. It's not an option.

Many students have a clear sense of what is required to make a "true Christian home" happen. As I talk with them, I am given reason for hope. But it is clear that they enter adulthood without all of the emotional or relational tools that most of us take for granted. They offer fearsome evidence that the divorce crisis has become an intergenerational phenomenon and may only worsen.

Divorce, Church, and Faith

While most of my children of divorce come from Christian homes, they almost universally report that the supposed Christian faith of their parents played no role in inhibiting the move toward divorce and the behaviors that led to it. Their parents were ministers, deacons, every-time-the-doors-were-open Christians who committed adultery (sometimes with other church members), got in trouble with the law, beat their spouses, and otherwise destroyed their families. It seems that nearly all of my students, and not just the children of divorce, are aware of some sordid divorce-related scandal in their home church. There is little evidence in these stories that our churchgoers are thinking coherently about how their behaviors fit with their supposed faith or are living out that faith with any kind of integrity. A local judge told me, "I have never seen Christian faith stop a single divorce." All of this, of course, is disillusioning to these Christian college students seeking to discover the reality and meaning of their faith.

Likewise, most churches in which these crises occurred offered few if any resources that could make a difference. While there were some constructive exceptions, my interviews show that the churches generally stood impotently by as their members' families disintegrated. In only two cases did churches attempt to intervene to hold members accountable to their marriage vows as an aspect of Christian commitment. Sometimes the divorced were pressured to remove themselves from church leadership positions or from church membership, but this is an inadequate response to divorce. Frequently divorced adults and their children stopped attending church altogether. Even when they kept going, many children of divorce seethed with frustration at their churches' responses:

> To my knowledge, to this day, more than four years later, not one person has addressed the issue with my dad, who remains a member of my church. No one has tried to help. No one has questioned his right to retain membership in light of his actions. What happened to church discipline? Does anyone care that my life has been torn apart and I still do not know what is going on?

> I feel that they were very unchristian in the way they treated her [this student's mother, during the divorce]. It's possible that if they had been more loving and less judgmental, things might have been different for my family. I resent . . . the church for pushing her away.

The children of divorce often sought out Christian friends for personal support, and thankfully this support was sometimes available. But other times these children faced rejection as the parents of their friends quietly severed their children's ties. Could it be that children of divorce became too potent a symbol of adults' fears? "If my kids play with you they may bring some of your trouble back home with them." The overall picture of the role of the church in either preventing divorce or helping to pick up the pieces is distressing.

However, Christian faith did play a significant role in sustaining many of my students through divorce. While the church often failed them, and their suffering led to many profound faith struggles, most children of divorce found comfort and strength in their relationship with God. Most concluded that though the divorce was deeply painful, God had used their experiences to help shape the kind of people they were becoming.

Beth told me of the time that her father was moving out. Dad and Mom were sitting at the kitchen table exhaustedly sorting out details of his departure after one last frantic fight. Beth found one of her father's shirts, put it on, and climbed up onto her roof. It was raining. As the rain mixed with her tears, she considered jumping to put an end to her pain. Yet as she considered this, she felt a strong sense of God's presence. She reported to me that she sensed the love of God, and she felt he gave her a message that he had a purpose for her life. She did not jump. Now she wants to be a minister to youth, especially children of divorce. This is a bit of good news in the midst of the bad. Just a bit.

Rethinking Marriage and Divorce as if Children Mattered

As the divorce rate skyrocketed from the mid-1960s through the late 1980s, many of the most influential Christian moral thinkers weakened their opposition to divorce—or remained silent. Meanwhile, church leaders struggled to find a way to proclaim biblical moral standards in a context in which those standards were being violated by many congregants. The issue tended to drop from the radarscope.

But now, thirty-five years into the age of mass divorce, the times call for a new approach. Even contemporary film reflects the growing tide of revulsion at the misery that divorce is visiting upon so many of us—especially our children. The film *Hope Floats* is one of the most striking of several dozen movies that have divorce and its costs at their core. Those who saw the movie will long remember the devastating scene in which little Bernice (about seven years old) tries to go with her father after he tells his wife that he wants a divorce so he can be with his new lover. As he forcibly removes Bernice from his car and gets ready to drive away, she cries out her anguish in a way that chills the soul. Watching that scene, or listening to much of today's music, the thoughtful observer recognizes that we are witnessing the tears, not just of a young actress, but of a generation. Consider these words from the song "Father of Mine" by the popular grunge-rock group Everclear:

> Father of mine
> Tell me where have you been
> You know I just closed my eyes
> My whole world disappeared
> Father of mine
> Take me back to the day
> When I was still your golden boy
> Back before you went away . . .[22]

The need of the hour is not to help those who want to break their marriage covenants to feel good about their quest for self-actualization. During the last generation, some may have thought that was what was needed. There are individual marriages in which a disastrous oppression is the rule and divorce becomes a kind of liberation. But overall the press for liberation is not the direction we need to go. Today we must instead push back with energy and creativity against the divorce culture in which we all are engulfed.

When, for example, a wealthy Christian businessman/deacon chair leaves his homemaker wife and children for a younger woman, refuses to pay child support or any money toward college tuition, lives a comfortable life while his ex-covenant partner and abandoned children scrape by to survive, and loses contact with his children altogether after two years, we need to be able to call such behaviors what they are—*sin*. It doesn't matter if he's happier or if he thought the marriage was "dead." What he did was wrong. We need to remember how to say that. The man has won his liberation at the expense of breaking sacred promises to those who had built their world on his fidelity.

Over one million children each year experience the kind of trauma I have outlined above, many not for the first time. Their lives are marred by the actions that others visit upon them. Postmodern marriage occasionally wins benefits for individual adults. Whatever benefits adults may sometimes gain come at the cost of enormous misery for the children who must be dragged along for the ride. There was a need for the reform and improvement of the quality of marriage. Women, in particular, have the opportunity to experience more just and satisfying marriages than ever before. But at what cost?

Our divorce culture has set up a tragic conflict of interest between adults and children, and in a contest involving such uneven distribution of power, it is obvious who will win. To the charge that children's perspectives about divorce are only partial, we can say that the same is true of adults. The difference is that it is adults, not children, who have the power to make *their* partial perspective prevail. Our culture remains sentimental about children even while we sacrifice their basic needs—and the basic requirements of justice—on the altar of our self-interest. In all of the ways young people know how to communicate—Internet sites and instant messages, song lyrics, films, and books—they are screaming out their pain. Divorce is a *justice* issue—not *only* for its children but *especially* for them. And if it is a justice issue, biblical people have no choice but to respond on behalf of injustice's victims.

If children matter, we will need to integrate their interests and needs into our theology of marriage and our interpretation of key biblical texts about divorce. On the one hand, this will lead us to strengthen our commitment to the permanence of marriage that God intended from the beginning. The entire biblical concept of the "one flesh" nature of the marriage relationship looks even more important in light of children, who are a permanent "one flesh" embodiment of their parents' (previous) love. Even the Catholic doctrine of marital indissolubility has a peculiar resonance today—for the testimony of children of divorce is that they and their estranged parents are locked into a permanent relationship, of whatever quality, or have a desire for such a relationship where it is missing. One student told me:

> There's not any closure—I will always be dealing with this, one way or another. I deal with it now in the dating relationship I am in—the day I get married, I will deal with it. The day I ask my wife to marry me, I will deal with it. . . .

"There is no such thing as divorce" when children are present, as songwriter Bob Bennett has written in a haunting collection of songs about his own divorce.[23] It is almost impossible to dissolve the bond between children and their parents. The cost of doing so, when it occurs, is grievous, worse than death.

Yet, in what may appear to be a paradox, the witness of children of divorce should also lead us to a rethinking of our interpretation of the legitimate grounds for divorce. Here is where the lawyerly reading of Jesus' teachings offered by many biblical scholars tends to lead us astray. The argument in this subculture has tended to be about which narrow circumstances might permit divorce. Is it adultery only or mere sexual misconduct or perhaps desertion, and can that mean "spiritual" desertion?

Yet children of divorce have tales to tell us about the various ways the marital covenant of their parents was destroyed. They help us to see that rather than a narrow list of grounds for divorce, we need to speak of covenant keeping and covenant breaking more broadly. The issues of abuse and violence are particular challenges to the old paradigm. One cannot find a biblical text in which burning a child or a wife on the arm with a cigarette (or throwing them down the stairs or banging their heads against the wall or enlisting them in a murder plot) is listed as grounds for divorce. Such actions, however, constitute a fundamental assault on the meaning of the marriage covenant. Repeated instances will lead a woman (or man) to take their children and flee. If children matter, we will find a way to move from older legalisms to a broader principle of just marital covenant making and covenant breaking—and then focus our attention on how to nurture the former rather than the latter.

The marriage cathedral lies in ruins. Its falling beams have knocked altogether too many men, women, and children to the ground. Anyone wondering how to evaluate the status of marriage in our time should consider this summary of what we now know:

- The collapse of a marriage inflicts emotional pain on the partners themselves, most acutely the partner abandoned by a spouse.
- The collapse of a marriage inflicts considerable and lasting pain on the children who experience it.
- The collapse of a marriage causes pain and sorrow for the extended families and friends of the divorcing couple and children.
- The collapse of a marriage causes considerable economic fallout in most cases, often especially damaging to single mothers and their children.
- The collapse of a marriage kicks up passions that lead to tremendous emotional distress and sometimes lead to violence.
- The collapse of a marriage can be the first step in a pattern of relational instability that places children at increasing risk of physical and emotional abuse and neglect.
- The collapse of a marriage requires the intervention of the legal system, sometimes for long periods of time—restricting the freedom of family members, increasing the power of the state, and costing every taxpayer money.
- The collapse of a marriage has proven negative health consequences.

More broadly, even when people divorce successfully, as they see it, the *total pattern* of constant divorce and remarriage leads to subtle but real social consequences:

- Social capital diminishes as couples and families have less energy for contributing to the common good, instead spending that capital either fighting to preserve their marriage or to "win" their divorce.
- Multiple generations of divorce, remarriage, and cohabitation increase the overall level of misery in society and continue to deinstitutionalize marriage.
- Intergenerational ties weaken as children of divorce grow up without satisfactory relationships with one or both parents; this raises critical questions about how or whether these now grown children will care for their aging parents.
- Every particular marriage is rendered less certain, less stable, through a "feedback effect" in which the omnipresence of divorce makes divorce more of an option for everyone.

- Economic resources in society are diverted as fewer couples pool their resources to invest in the next generation but instead waste money on paying divorce lawyers, maintaining separate residences, and supporting kids in a variety of quasi-family arrangements—and as society pays the costs of judicial and police intervention.

In light of all of these considerations, I conclude that what some are calling a "restructuring" or "transition" or "liberation" of marriage and family is in fact a disastrous collapse that must be met by determined resistance. While I am sympathetic to aspects of the reformist position, I find it hard to resist the main lines of the declinist stance in light of the evidence.

By now we have a pretty good idea why marriage collapsed and what the structural damage looks like. But we also have within Scripture and the Christian tradition resources for its reclamation. In the remaining chapters of this book, I offer a biblical vision for rebuilding the marriage cathedral. Its pillars are creation, covenant, kingdom, and community. Consider this vision with me as we proceed.

Part 2

Rebuilding the Marriage Cathedral

4

The Creation Purposes of Marriage

> This love is more despotic than any despotism: for others indeed may be strong, but this passion is not only strong, but unfading. For there is a certain love deeply seated in our nature which knits together these bodies of ours. Thus even from the very beginning woman sprang from man, and afterwards from man and woman sprang both man and woman. . . . There is nothing which so welds our life together as the love of man and wife. For this many will lay aside even their arms, for this they will give up life itself.
>
> —John Chrysostom

It is easy to despair about the future of marriage as a social institution in Western societies. There seems to be little hope of reclaiming any broadly shared vision of marriage or even for the survival of marriage as the premier social institution for structuring adult love and family relations.

James Q. Wilson, reflecting on this dismal scene in his recent book *The Marriage Problem,* hopes for "retail" solutions to be offered by families, churches, and neighborhoods rather than the government.[1] He hopes that marriage can be reclaimed in society by the cumulative impact of creative local solutions. I think it quite possible that the society as a whole is a lost cause. But if it is to be changed, it will only occur through the modeling and witness offered by faith communities that are still able to make of marriage a coherent, compelling, and successful institution.

That is my purpose in the remainder of this book. Having sketched the near collapse of marriage as a broader social institution, I want now to offer a distinctive Christian vision of marriage. This vision is Christian in that its four pillars—creation, covenant, kingdom, and community—are grounded in the Scriptures and developed in the theological traditions of the Christian faith. It is also Christian in that it is written primarily for those who believe in Jesus Christ and for application in communities of Christian people.

But this vision is *not* Christian in the sense that I am arguing for a unique thing in itself called "Christian marriage." Instead, there is *marriage,* an institution given by God to humanity in creation, with a certain constitution to it, which human beings are both intuitively aware of and routinely spoil. I will argue later that the marriage of Christian people has unique possibilities for the advance of the kingdom of God, and that the New Testament does strike some distinctive notes related to marriage, sexuality, and family life. Every aspect of life in Christ, including marriage, has its own distinctiveness by virtue of the fact that Christ lives in us and we live for him.

But in its essential purposes and structure, the successful marriage of a Hindu is little different from that of a Christian believer, because it is, as it has sometimes been called, an "order of creation." The account of marriage that I offer should be especially recognizable to those operating in the Jewish or Christian traditions, because it is grounded in Scripture. But it should resonate with those of other faith traditions or no faith tradition, because of its correspondence with human nature as designed by the Creator God. Knowledge of God's intentions for marriage is at least partially accessible to any human mind through reason, observation, and intuition. The biblical witness about marriage thus articulates fully what apart from scriptural revelation is dimly sensed.

In this chapter, I will develop the theme that marriage is an institution designed by God and given in creation to all humanity. The God-given creation purposes of marriage are both personal and social; they apply to all who participate in the institution, and rightly undertaken they accomplish good both for God's agenda for creation itself and for the particular human beings who "do" marriage. Marriage in this sense functions as a kind of mute witness to God the Creator, who is responsible for the very institution of marriage and the powerful yearnings that draw men and women toward the altar, whether they know it or not (cf. Rom. 2:14–15).

A Narrative

My concept of marriage was revolutionized through a pastoral experience.

A man was locked in a miserable marriage. Financial complications and young children kept this man and his wife legally married. Both husband and wife had been unfaithful. The wife had physically attacked her husband and uniformly spoke of him and to him with contempt. The husband had run his business into the ground and left the family nearly bankrupt. They eventually separated and saw each other only in court when battling over various disputes.

Before that separation, however, a woman in our church became involved with this man. She struggled to keep the relationship within moral bounds, but at every stage her resistance was insufficient. The relationship seemed to have a momentum of its own that defied every obstacle placed in its way, including the desperate pleadings of her friends and church leaders. Their friendship soon turned into a romance; then the romance took on a sexual dimension. They began dreaming and talking of marriage but over long months of waiting often despaired at ever having the opportunity to marry.

Eventually, the possibility of finding a new chance at love motivated the man to resolve the remaining legal issues and get divorced. Just as soon as the divorce was final, the new couple wanted to get married. They came to me and asked if I would perform their ceremony.

The reason I tell this tale is because of what it taught me about the nature of marriage. In considering their request, I looked through my standard premarital counseling material and realized that it was geared toward the committed young Christian couple. It assumed that the couple was Christian and was undertaking marriage on that basis.

I prefer to see a couple enter marriage this way—the joining together of deeply committed and well-prepared Christians is one of a minister's great joys. But the revelation that hit me was this—*marriage is marriage, whether the couple is explicitly Christian in their approach to it or not.* This new couple sitting before me—the man coming off an atrocious marriage, neither now attending church, just then involved in an illicit relationship—were still about to embark on *marriage*. As a minister, my task was to explain the nature of marriage to them as God designed it, to urge them to reflect on the wrong decisions they had made, to make restitution for these decisions, and then to invite them to invite God into their new life together. I was able to tell them that God was the author of marriage, whether they were willing to acknowledge it or not, and that their chance of success at this new bond would increase exponentially if they would acknowledge it and attempt to live according to God's will and in the power of his Spirit.

At the wedding, I was struck by the primal human beauty of the experience. A man who had been lonely and humiliated for many years and a woman who wore many scars of her own had found comfort and companionship in each other. The relationship had begun immorally despite furious objections from Christian friends and the couple's own individual sense of right and wrong. Yet a force that proved more powerful than these moral objections had drawn the couple to each other and, finally, to the altar. It would be too simple to call that force "sin," but it did in fact tempt the couple to transgress moral boundaries. It is better to call the force itself the *impulse toward intimacy*. It is an impulse given to men and women by God in creation. Any account of marriage—and, by the way, of divorce—must take into account that very powerful, very primal, and under conditions of sin, very dangerous force.

Marriage and Creation

The biblical accounts of creation in Genesis 1:26–28 and 2:18–25 are pivotal for a Christian theology of marriage. Many rich theological treatments of these passages have been offered. Here I will try to summarize basic truths about each account that are relevant to a theology of marriage, realizing that the richness of these texts makes them inexhaustible.

In Genesis 1, God is depicted as creating the heavens and the earth in an unfolding process that takes six days. Light and darkness, sky and seas and land are created and placed where God wills. By God's command the land produces vegetation; God creates all the creatures that dwell in the sea and the animals that dwell on land.

On the sixth day, a new element is introduced—God speaks in second-person voice. "Let us make man in our image, in our likeness, and let them rule over the fish of the sea and the birds of the air"—over all creatures and all the earth (Gen. 1:26). As the church father Gregory of Nyssa noticed, we catch a glimpse here of a *deliberative* process prior to God's creation of humankind, a deliberation not spoken of in relation to any other aspect of the creation.[2]

We also catch a glimpse of a relational God prior to his relating to any creatures of the earth. Who exactly the "us" is that God is deliberating with has been the subject of considerable debate. The Jewish tradition tends to argue that God was speaking to his heavenly court; Christian theologians traditionally have seen here a striking reference to God's interior interaction as Father, Son, and Spirit (John 1:1–13; Col. 1:16).

In either case, but especially if we accept the Christian interpretation, implications follow concerning what it means to have been made in the image of God. "So God created man in his own image, in the image of God he created him; male and female he created them" (Gen. 1:27). Whatever else the much-debated concept of *imago dei* (image of God) means, it does at least mean that we human beings correspond to God's nature, reflect God's attributes, and relate to God in a manner that no other creature does. The prevailing opinion in contemporary biblical scholarship is that the image relates to the human exercise of dominion or rule over the earth. We "image" God to the rest of creation in that God delegates the authority to us to represent him, to "image" him to the other creatures of the earth.[3] We "stand in" for God in exercising power but are implicitly called to do so in a manner that is responsible and resembles God.

It is a fair inference to push beyond this to argue theologically with the historic Catholic and Orthodox churches and more recently with the best of Protestant theology, that *being made in the image of God means being made as relational beings,* for the God who makes us in his image is an intrinsically relational being. God is not alone in the heavens and neither are we alone on the earth. Not only do we relate to our Creator but, in the Genesis 1 account, the very creation of human beings is relational: we are made as male and female. God has created, simultaneously, a form of life (humankind) that is a single entity and exists in community, especially in that first community of male and female but extending to all other forms of community. Just as God is simultaneously *three* and *one,* humanity is simultaneously *one* and *two* or even *one* and *three* (male, female, and male-female "one flesh" bond; or male, female, and children of the marital union).

Some theologians overstate the significance of this male-female sexual polarity in its relationship to the image of God, as if to say that only as male-female couples are human beings made in the image of God or even fully human. This is where the great theologian Karl Barth went astray, despite brilliant insights on these issues.[4] Full humanity and the potential for full experience of life in the image of God are not reserved for the married couple but belong to all people. And yet that full experience of life in God's image is intrinsically relational. We were created for community. One of community's forms—the first and most fundamental, to be sure—is that bond between male and female for which most of us reach most of our lives.

"God blessed them and said to them, 'Be fruitful and increase in number; fill the earth and subdue it'" (Gen. 1:28a). God speaks to his creatures for the first time with a mandate to reproduce after their own kind. The first command is to exercise dominion over the earth.

Fulfillment of this command requires the propagation of the species. Propagation requires humanity functioning precisely as male and female, having sex and bearing children.

This account of the creation in the first chapter of Genesis concludes with the exultant declaration that God "saw all that he had made, and it was very good" (Gen. 1:31). All of it—earth and sky and heavens, land and sea and air, vegetation, sea creatures and land creatures, man and woman made in God's image and commanded to join together in sexual intercourse and bear children.

The so-called second creation story focuses on the creation of the first man, his placement in the Garden of Eden, and the eventual creation of woman. It differs in considerable detail from the account offered in Genesis 1. For our purposes there is no need to get bogged down in the details or origins of those differences; our goal is to consider the significance of the story as we find it in Genesis 2.

God creates the earth and then out of the "dust" of the earth forms the first man. He breathes life into him and sets the man in the Garden of Eden. There the man enjoys the pleasures of unspoiled nature as he tends the garden and communes with his God.

"The LORD God said, 'It is not good for the man to be alone. I will make a helper suitable for him'" (Gen. 2:18). The livestock, beasts, and birds are brought to him for companionship. Significantly, he names them, but they are not adequate as companions, as helpers. So God performs surgery, putting Adam into a deep sleep and creating from his own bodily substance a woman. Upon awaking, the man exults, "This is now bone of my bones and flesh of my flesh." He gives her a name as well: *ishshah*, wo-man, a true companion at last, taken from the very flesh and bone of man (2:23).

Then the narrator interjects: "For this reason a man will leave his father and mother and be united to his wife, and they will become one flesh." Then continuing the story: "The man and his wife were both naked, and they felt no shame" (Gen. 2:24–25).

Before the story of Eve's creation is even complete, the man and woman have rather surprisingly become man and "wife." The male-female relationship is embedded in the institutional framework of marriage before we are even out of the garden. Before there was sin; before there was either Israel or the church; before there were laws or governments; before there were children; before there was any other institution, there was marriage.

If we believe the biblical record, marriage is a *structure of creation*. This has certain pivotal implications for thinking rightly about it. It means that marriage comes from God. It is not a merely human creation. This means we are not free to abandon it, disdain it, or reinvent it at our whim. We are obligated to attempt to discover what God intended by and for marriage when he created it. As theologian Brad Green has argued, a healthy doctrine of creation requires us to acknowledge the "givenness" of certain created realities.[5] "There is indeed a reality outside of the human person, and the human being finds himself in a world that is not of his own making."[6] Marriage has always been understood in Christian thought to be one of those discovered "givens" of human life. It is a God-given institution that structures male-female relations and the conception and nurture of children and was intended to do so from the beginning.

Because marriage precedes sin, its purposes must be understood as being wired into the very constitution of the human person and the created order. God did not create marriage *because* Adam sinned but *before* Adam sinned. Human beings are programmed to need what marriage offers. Historian Steven Ozment writes that the family is "proving itself to be humankind's bedrock as well as its fault line."[7] Social critic James Q. Wilson speaks of the stubborn "persistence of marriage among people for whom it could so easily be dismissed."[8] We can damage it, we can fail at it, but we just can't seem to get away from it. We keep returning to marriage.

Because it is a structure of creation, marriage applies to all people. It is not an institution unique to believers. It is not merely an expression of a particular culture. In its essential constitution, whatever marriage is, it is for all. This does not mean that every adult is required to marry; the New Testament teaches that celibate singleness is an option (cf. 1 Cor. 7). However, it does mean that marriage (monogamous marriage, as taught in Genesis 1–2 and reaffirmed by Jesus and Paul) is the context that God has established for the human "mating process," wherever and whenever humans mate.

Because God created all that he created for some reason, it is appropriate to seek out the divine goods that were intended in marriage. Marriage exists for some reason or reasons, and these reasons will not change until the created order sees its last day. While various cultures rework marriage in their own ways, underneath changing cultural forms will be unchanging divine purposes.

In a culture where nearly half of all marriages end in divorce, nine-tenths of marriages are viewed by some analysts as unsuccessful, and a significant percentage of people have rejected marriage altogether, something fundamental has gone wrong. Social practices are failing to accomplish the divine purposes for marriage. Part of getting things right is figuring out how our cultural practices align, or fail to align, with the creation design for marriage.

God's Purposes for Marriage

On the basis of the Genesis passages reviewed above, it is possible to sketch a basic overview of God's purposes in marriage.

Companionship

Contrary to the myth of self-sufficiency, the human being was made for companionship. Our dependence on relationships with other people is one of the most obvious facts about us. We are drawn to other people and they to us. We are social creatures, inescapably.

Our lives begin in utter dependence on others. We do not create ourselves but instead come into existence through the lovemaking of our mother and father. Our first nine months are spent attached to our mother's uterine wall. We greet the world in undoubted terror and find comfort in parental nestling and suckling. The first and fundamental task of our childhood is to establish trusting dependent relationships with our parents. We later grow beyond the small circle of those relationships into other competencies, and yet we still depend on mother and father's love, care, and help. Adolescents don't abandon relationships; they shift focus from home to peer group. And soon, generation after generation, the messy explorations in dating and courtship begin.

"It is not good for the man to be alone." God's decision to create a partner for Adam results from the inadequacy of all other relationships to meet his need for a suitable "helper." Astonishingly, even God, though related to Adam in an intimacy that we can only wonder at, was not enough for him. Though the human person withers apart from relationship with his Creator, it is not only his Creator that he needs.

Marriage is for *companionship*. This is the first purpose indicated for marriage in the biblical record, and its centrality has long been recognized in Jewish and Christian theological accounts of marriage. This word *companionship,* however, deserves further attention. What are its components?

In the Genesis account, the term used is "helper." This word does not denote subservience but instead partnership. "The woman, 'flesh of his flesh,' [is] his counterpart, his equal, his nearest in all things . . . given to him by God as a 'helpmate': she thus represents God from whom comes our help."[9] Genesis 2:15, the preceding passage, noted that God had put Adam in the garden "to work it and take care of it." It is not insignificant that shortly after this God decides that it is not good for the man to be alone. *Companionship* in *work* is one aspect of God's intent for marriage. Marriage is a context of shared labor. Different societies have structured this work in different ways, but managing adult work responsibilities of various types is one of the fundamental purposes of marriage. Those who marry someone who cannot or will not pull his or her weight quickly discover how fundamental labor is to marriage.

It would be possible to understand marriage quite minimally as a companionship of labor and leave it at that. Some have done so. It would ask less of couples than we now do. Lower expectations would mean less disappointment. But the Genesis account points beyond work to richer realities.

Marriage has a dimension of *companionship in shared daily living*. God found that the man was in need of a partner of his own kind with whom life could be shared. Neither the divine nor the animal companions were enough.

Marriage is a context in which two adults share human experience. They simply go through life together. They rest together, eat together, take walks together, wash dishes together, talk together, learn together, weep together, laugh together, play together, and fold laundry together. Marriage is an extended human friendship, a walking side-by-side through life. It can be so beautiful as to be almost beyond description, but somehow it also can be remarkably fragile.

Marriage is a *companionship of love*. By "love" I mean mutually shared feelings of affection and attachment. Marital love means more than this, much more; but it does at least mean this, and all other dimensions of marital love mark developments of a phenomenon that begins with earthly human affections.

Our historical survey should help us see how important it is not to read modern notions of romantic love back into the Genesis account, as all too many Christian discussions of marriage now do. Notice that these passages never use the word "love." This reticence is a needed corrective. Some Christians would benefit from a sharp de-emphasis on romantic love. Expecting heights of romantic ecstasy, they become easily disappointed in marriage, even to the point of abandoning one after another "failed love." The Swiss theologian Emil Brunner put it as sharply as possible: "*Where marriage is based on love all is lost from the very outset*. . . . Even the most honest and ardent vow of love does not make a marriage. To base marriage on love is to build on sand."[10]

It is truer to Scripture's unsentimental approach to marriage to put the matter as Jewish scholar Jacob Neusner has: "Husbands and wives owe one another loyalty to the common task and reliability in the carrying out of their reciprocal obligations, which are sexual, social, and economic. . . . Out of mutual trust and shared achievements . . . may emerge emotions of affection and love. . . . But romantic attitudes do not enjoy a high priority in the value of marriage and the family."[11] In other words, love is viewed in Jewish tradition as a *result* of a successful marriage, not the *basis* of it.

In light of the chaos of romantic love in our day, some are suggesting that we abandon the notion altogether and settle for a more pragmatic understanding of marriage, perhaps embracing a premodern Christian vision in its sternest form. And yet a brief look elsewhere in Scripture can keep us from losing hope in the possibility of an affectionate marital love or from dismissing it as an unbiblical concept.

Isaac loved Rebekah (Gen. 24:67). Jacob loved Rachel (Gen. 29:17–18). Leah, in turn, wanted Jacob's love and grieved how he spurned her (Gen. 29:32). Elkanah loved his wife Hannah (1 Sam. 1:5). Michal, Saul's daughter, loved David (1 Sam. 18:20). Rehoboam loved Maacah (2 Chron. 11:21). Proverbs reminds a man to love the wife of his youth (Prov. 5:19) and not go astray from her. Ecclesiastes speaks of "your wife, whom you love" (9:9), as does Deuteronomy 13:6. The entire Song of Solomon is a racy celebration of romantic/erotic love. Hosea is a profound story of brokenhearted yet steadfast marital love. And Paul, in Ephesians 5, urges believing men to love their wives as Christ loves the church.

Of course, we are brought up short by the news that Solomon "loved" his "many foreign wives" (a thousand in all, counting concubines; he must have been a big-hearted guy!). Biblical uses of the term sometimes bewilder us; Shechem "loved" Dinah (Gen. 34:3), we hear, but "violated" her first (Gen. 34:2). Samson loved Delilah (Judg. 16:4), but she was a prostitute who happened not to be his wife. Amnon "fell in love" with his half-sister Tamar and showed his "love" by raping her, then "hat[ing] her more than he had loved her" (2 Sam. 13:15). As in our own day, in these texts the word "love" means little more than "lust."

And yet we catch enough glimmers of mature marital love in Scripture to know that it cannot be written off either as a modern idea or as lust by another name. Genesis points us in the right direction. The man is "united" to his wife and they become "one flesh." Everyone knows this text is about sex, but of course it is about more than sex. It is about the growing unity that is possible between a man and a woman. As relational beings created out of love by a God whose very being defines loving interpersonal unity (cf. 1 John 4:16), we have deep within us a drive to penetrate the barriers that divide us from others and find unity with them. The medieval mystic Catherine of Siena wrote, "The soul cannot live without love. She always wants to love something because love is the stuff she is made of, and through love [God] created her."[12]

Marriage is perhaps the premier context in which we can begin to achieve this experience of love, even with just one other human being. Two can become one, a new reality, a "we" that exists in and through the voluntary interpenetration of selves that develops between husband and wife. This "we" then mingles with the two individuals who make it up in a striking illustration of the mingled selves of the Triune God. This "community of being," as Mary Anne McPherson Oliver has put it, is the spiritual reality of marriage—when marriage succeeds.[13] When in marriage we overcome our dividedness, we experience something holy.

A Christian account of the creation purposes of marriage must include love. Perhaps it is best to say it like this: loving companionship that knits the married couple into a joyful one-flesh union over time is one of the premier creation purposes and possibilities of marriage. It is possible for a society or community to de-emphasize what Karl Barth called "simple earthly love" as a *reason* for embarking upon marriage, as the Puritans and Pietists did, but the possibility of affectionate love developing within marriage is a biblical concept that corresponds with our nature as created beings.[14] It is the very possibility of such love, and the mysterious dawning of such a love with another particular human being, that draws us forward into marriage and spurs us to continued effort within marriage, even in times when its achievement seems a distant hope or a fading memory. The presence of such love does not exclude the other purposes of marriage but brings life to their pursuit. Likewise, the absence of such love does not in itself constitute grounds for ending a marriage but does drain marriage of its joy.

Sex

Marriage is for *sex*. This is among the most obvious statements ever made. But it is no longer self-evident in our culture. It deserves a bit of unpacking.

Sex is, at one level, "just" a dimension of companionship. The love that draws us out of ourselves toward the other is a profoundly uniting force. We are attracted to the other and want to experience just as much closeness, as much unity, as much belonging, as much interpenetration as we can. Nowhere is the body-soul unity of the human being clearer than this, because we rush toward our partner seeking the uniting both of body and of soul with him or her—if body and soul are even distinguishable in genuine lovemaking.[15] As Theodore Mackin puts it, this is "the longing to 'live inside' the love-partner and to have him or her do the same with oneself; the desire to know totally and to be known totally."[16]

The sheer physical joy of sex is another of God's good gifts in creation. The church has not always been as willing to admit this as the Bible itself is. "My lover is to me a sachet of myrrh resting between my breasts.

. . . How beautiful you are, my darling! Oh, how beautiful!" (Song 1:13, 15). When linked with love, especially a trustworthy monogamous love, as God designed it, it reaches an extraordinary level of meaning and fulfillment. The richly pleasing "one flesh" act of sex becomes a "one spirit" communion of souls.

The Christian tradition has been squeamish at times about the pleasures of sex. In part this has been because the quest for this satisfaction is such a profound factor in human life that it threatens to overflow its bounds disastrously. While God's creation purpose for marriage includes sex, after sin enters the picture, the connection between marriage and sex takes on a new dimension. Now we must strain against temptation to confine sex within marriage, and the sexual fidelity of the marriage relationship must be guarded rigorously. Sex, even in marriage, always threatens to devolve into a subhuman "thing in itself" more reminiscent of animal life than anything fully human.[17] The premodern church was right in seeing marital sex as a "remedy" for lust, though not in reducing marital sex to this when it did so. But the dangers of misdirected sexuality must not mislead us into forgetting that sex is a divine purpose for marriage in creation and not just in the fall.

Children

Man and woman, drawn to each other in love and united in sexual intercourse, are God's intended means of bringing new life into the world. Marriage is—not exclusively but as one aspect of its life—for *children*. As Barth puts it: "Children are the gift of God by which the fellowship of marriage, without being terminated as such, becomes the wider fellowship of the family."[18] Marriage is for the conception, care, nurture, and education of children who are the miraculous embodiment of marital love.

As we saw earlier, modern technology made possible the weakening of the link between sex and procreation through birth control, as well as through assisted reproduction. Now we can have sex with no babies and babies with no sex and either with no marriage. But God's design in creation is not so easily thwarted, and we veer from it at great cost to ourselves.

The procreative potential of every sex act remains impossible to extinguish short of sterility. The human passion that draws men and women together in sex does not always pause for birth control. Children continue to enter the world as the product of human lovemaking, planned or not, birth control attempted or not.

God's design for marriage is intended for human well-being. To flourish, most of us need a companion with whom to share labor, life, and love. Our need is met in another, and when all goes well, there is great joy.

Likewise, God intended that marriage be the context in which children would enter the world. This also is an aspect of God's creation order and reflects concern both for personal and for social well-being. The creation mandate to be fruitful and multiply (Gen. 1:28) requires a particular context for success. That context is marriage. No one has found a successful alternative, though people are busy trying all over the world.

For children, marriage provides a context of stability, security, status, and identity. The man and woman whose sex act produced this child also raise this child, and the three of them form a "trinity of being" that links them irrevocably together.[19] The child knows where she comes from. She knows who her father and mother are and that both love each other and her. Her identity is both legally and morally clear. Her place in the human community is well established. She has a safe context in which to accomplish the developmental tasks of childhood. She is the product of her parents' love and enjoys its ongoing blessings. The fact that a minority of children now experiences this divinely intended state of affairs in our country is no argument against God's design but instead against what we have done to disrupt it.

The connection between marriage and children also has benefits for parents. Love and companionship are multiplied exponentially, growing from a private man-woman phenomenon into a riot of family relationships: father-son, mother-daughter, father-daughter, mother-son, brother-sister, and so on. The relationship between husband and wife itself is tested, changed, and grown. Men and women learn how to look beyond their shared pleasures to broader responsibilities to others, beginning with their own children. Family life becomes a school for discipleship, not just for children, but also for adults. The Catechism of the Catholic Church puts it this way: "Marriage helps to overcome self-absorption, egoism, pursuit of one's own pleasure, and [helps] to open oneself to the other, to mutual aid and to self-giving."[20]

As the married couple makes choices related to raising their children, they grapple with fundamental questions of meaning and value. The solemn responsibility of providing moral, spiritual, emotional, vocational, and social formation of their children rests on their shoulders. The decisions parents make in this sphere have profound significance, not just for the child and his parents, but also for the broader social order.

Society

This reminds us that marriage is for *society*. It serves fundamental purposes for the human community. In forgetting this, modern and especially postmodern marriage has inflicted a grievous wrong on the human community.

By structuring and stabilizing adult sexual relationships, marriage reduces social stress and frees up adult energies for constructive participation in work and community life. By clarifying paternity, marriage eliminates uncertainty about the status and identity of children. By harnessing what can become dangerous human desires for love and sex, marriage protects the social order from chaos and violence. By functioning as a context of shared labor, marriage contributes to family and community economic well-being. Marriage provides a context in which children are socialized, thus preparing them for later participation as responsible adults in society rather than as morally or psychologically ruined wards of the state.

For all of these reasons, it has long been recognized in Jewish and Christian thought that marriage is the fundamental unit of the social order. Marriage is the founding relationship in family life, and family life is the context for the nurture of children. Young men and women enter society through particular experiences in individual families. They walk out the doors of their homes into their community, both literally and metaphorically. The quality of the experiences they have had at home will have everything to do with the long-term health of the social order. Society needs a well-functioning institution of marriage just as much as individuals do. Stephen Post puts it this way: "Sex is the basis for species survival; parental love is the basis upon which moral civilization rests."[21]

Reflections and Implications

I have been arguing that marriage is an institution of creation given by God for human companionship, sexual expression, the procreation and nurture of children, and the advancement of the social good. Marriage was intended to advance God's original creation purposes even before sin entered the world and defaced it.

Human sinfulness makes the achievement of God's purposes for marriage fraught with difficulty. Tension and friction become the defining characteristics of married life. Sex spills beyond its intended boundaries with chaotic results. Children are born into instability, misery, and violence. Society pays the price for dysfunctional families, and families pay the price for dysfunctional societies.

Accomplishing the kind of marriage and family life that God designed has, therefore, always been a difficult human achievement. Every form of human expression has given voice to our failures and the miseries they have produced. How many songs, plays, movies, and television shows are about misery in marriage and family life?

But the current cultural situation presents a challenge of an altogether different order. It is a crisis of faith. It is no longer universally believed that there is a "God" or that the Bible is "inspired" or that this world is a "creation" or that we are "creatures" or that marriage is an "institution" or that any moral "truth" can be "known" at all. The quotation marks signal the end of certainty about the meaning of words at all, let alone the objects they were once thought to signify.

Dealing with *that* crisis of belief is beyond the scope of this book. It does provide its context, however, and point to its audience. I am not writing to persuade the convinced relativist that there is such a thing as "Truth with a capital T," but instead to offer a biblical account of marriage in the context of its social collapse. My primary audience is that slice of the world's population that still finds the Christian narrative compelling and seeks to orient its life around the truth claims found in Scripture—and the Truth found in the person of Jesus Christ.

If we enter that thought world, then we find a God who creates the institution of marriage for particular planetary and human purposes and wires us to desire the same thing. Or better—we find a God who wires us to seek certain goods in life and creates an institutional framework to enable us to get those needs met. We also find ourselves forced to make the audacious claim that humanity as a whole is wired to seek these goods, will search for them endlessly and often settle for second-best, but will not find full satisfaction apart from the plan God set up to meet those needs. And society will likewise not flourish if those needs are not met the way God designed them to be.

The implications of this understanding are immense.

For example, ministers and church leaders should stop being surprised when they discover, time and again, the primal drives that carry most of their parishioners toward marriage or its unsanctioned alternatives. Beginning in the middle school years, young men and women will tend to act in ways that reflect their "wiring." They will begin seeking love, companionship, and often sex (or sexual exploration). Some may even begin hungering for responsibilities with children. Christian teaching with young people should acknowledge these drives, claim them as good and God-given, and attempt to direct youth toward the fulfilling plan that God has for this area of life.

Men and women who are older but not yet married (or already divorced) will find these drives toward companionship, sex, and children even stronger. They lead many desperate men and women in our churches into unwise relationships—with married people, with non-Christians, with abusers. We have seen several twenty- and thirty-something women in our church date and marry men who, from our (happily married) pastoral perspective, are very unwise choices. The fact is that when these drives bump up against our exhortations, it is often the latter that give way. This is not good, but it must be understood and responded to with realism and compassion.

Likewise, church leaders should help young couples assess their ability to meet one another's companionship, sex, and child-related needs. Christian teaching about marriage is often so heavenly minded as to be little earthly good. Christian couples should be prayerful about marriage and intent on confirming that the prospective partner is a spiritual match for them. And Christian couples are right to try to develop a full-blown kingdom vision for marriage. There is a unique kind of possibility awaiting the kingdom-focused Christian couple. How many pastors wish that more of the couples they counsel would discover such a vision for their marriage!

But they won't achieve such a vision, however beautiful, if they can't first figure out how to be companions in work, daily life, and love. They won't hit the kingdom high notes if their sex life is discordant or nonexistent. They won't maximize ministry possibilities in marriage if they cannot manage child rearing. They won't advance their heavenly goals if they are failing at a basic level to do their earthly tasks.

Successful marriage involves achieving competency at a basic set of creation-related skills and developing the virtues associated with those skills. In the next chapter these will be discussed. Premarital preparation and marriage enrichment classes ought to involve training couples in these skills. This is one component, a very important one, of an overall Christian approach to marriage.

This approach to marriage also speaks to the pastoral response to the couple in crisis. Troubled Christian couples are often sent back to Scripture to be reminded of their covenant responsibilities. This is appropriate but not enough. A healthy theology of creation and of the goods of marriage gives us greater realism about the phenomenon of marital misery.

The fact is that grave deficiencies in marital skills threaten the health of any marriage. It may be possible to endure such a marriage—this is a moral challenge that all married Christians need to learn how to meet. But even if such a marriage can be endured in covenant fidelity, it is not possible to flourish in one. Miserable couples need to know how to develop skills that can decrease their misery, if such is at all possible. They do not just need ministers who tell them they should stay married. God's plan is for marriages, not to endure, but to flourish, just as flourishing rather than merely enduring is God's will for individual life as well.

Couples (or individuals in marriage) will begin thinking about divorce —or dreaming of death, their own or their spouse's—if their creation-rooted needs are thwarted over a long period of time. They will descend into a profound kind of misery. They will be susceptible to affairs, to alcohol or drug abuse, to a slow emotional death, to violence, or to suicide—not to mention divorce. The heartiest commitment to Jesus Christ and the most active involvement in church life do not immunize any person from this kind of misery.

A Christian approach to marriage must begin with realism about marriage as an order of creation rooted in the needs of the human person and the well-being of society as a whole. Once these creation goods are understood, practical skill development is the next step.

5

The Skills (and Virtues) of Marriage

An event to take place in my favorite Memphis bookstore was advertised in the following way:

THE 4 MAGIC QUESTIONS
You Need to Ask to Find
Your Soul Mate!

One-Time Only
Join Best-Selling Author
Dr. Bill Brown

In This Remarkable Evening, Dr. Brown will sign his books and show you how to:

- **Start a Conversation with the Man or Woman of Your Dreams**
- **Instantly identify if they're your soul mate by asking 4 simple questions**
- **Win their heart using type psychology**

You've seen the Bachelor Show on TV.
Now a Real-Life Dating Show is Coming.[1]

Though I was unable to attend this event, I did pick up one of Dr. Brown's (a pseudonym) two books, both prominently displayed in the front of the store that night. It was essentially an application of the Myers-Briggs Type Indicator, which groups personality traits along four parameters. I am an INFJ (introvert, intuitive, feeling, judging)—how about you? Brown's contribution to the love and romance scene is that "if you can speed-read the people around you" using his adaptation of these Myers-Briggs categories, "you'll be able to date smart and find your perfect match." His books promise to help you learn how to do that.

I wonder what would happen if a man and woman, each hungry for a "soul mate," met each other at the bookstore that night. What if they listened to the seminar, asked each other the four magic questions, discovered that they had matching personality types, dated and married, and then divorced eighteen months later on account of irreconcilable differences. What if they then approached Dr. Brown with this magic question—"*Why didn't our relationship work out?* After all, we did everything exactly the way you told us to, and you are an expert who has appeared on ABC, CNN, and *People* magazine. If we can't trust *you,* who can we trust?"

Love Incorporated

I do not know this author and am not trying to be unkind. It may be that his approach to love and marriage proves helpful to some people. But I am wanting to identify a trend, and this flyer makes a wonderful case study. The trend is this: love and romance consulting is a hot growth industry. These men and women travel the land selling their particular formulas for romantic happiness to a desperately unhappy and thus receptive population. Their books offer the "seven principles," "1001 Ways," "six keys," "five needs," or "eight steps" that are the "secrets to lasting love." I am looking at a shelf full of books that make such promises. I have attended marriage enrichment conferences that offer such formulas. And I am convinced that while some of the material offered is valuable, there is also something misguided about the whole enterprise.

Let's call this world "Love Incorporated" and briefly consider what to make of it.

Love Incorporated follows a well-trod American path. It offers to American consumers a product intended to be "good for what ails you." It promises access to newly discovered secrets to happiness and health through formulas created and packaged by experts recognized the world over and now available to the consumer for a reasonable price.

Much like the traveling medicine shows an era earlier, Love Incorporated offers a product that promises to solve a personally painful problem that no one else has been able to address successfully. The personally painful problem that affects tens of millions today and that no one seems able to address successfully is the collapse of the institution of marriage, indeed, our entire dating and mating system. Rushing into the gap with new nostrums and formulas is the industry I call Love Incorporated. There is no shortage of customers and no shortage of formulas. But so far, there is also no evidence that the industry is making a difference in "solving the mystery of marriage," as one book puts it.

I pity those who are seriously attempting to sort through the varying formulas offered by the various competitors in the Love Incorporated industry. Is the key to be found in asking the right "seven questions" (Parrott)? Or is it taking the "twelve steps to a lasting relationship" (Wright)? Perhaps it is identifying the "four key patterns that destroy oneness" (Stanley), or maybe taking the "seven steps to saving your marriage" (Weiner Davis). Maybe it involves focusing on "recharging your mate's needs battery" (Smalley), or "enhancing your love maps" (Gottman).

I remember attending a Baptist marriage enrichment event one year. Around me were primarily thirty- and forty-something Baptist couples, earnestly attending the various seminars, collecting the various seven-step plans, and attempting to "enhance couple communication" through various new methodologies and techniques. Many of the men looked rather miserable. I thought, *These poor guys. These are computer programmers and insurance salesmen. They're just regular guys who watch* SportsCenter *at night and go off to work in the morning. They are never going to be able to remember all this stuff. There's just something wrong about this whole thing. Marriage should not be this hard. On the other hand, marriage should not be this easy. No seven-step plan can make a marriage work.*

The Limits of Technique

Love Incorporated is an expression of the famously entrepreneurial American helping professions, especially the field of psychology. Most practitioners carry doctoral degrees in psychology, psychiatry, or counseling. In a culture that transferred its loyalty from the minister to the psychologist about thirty years ago, Love Incorporated is the natural next step. When in trouble, tens of millions of Americans now turn either to individual counselors or to the psychology industry.

The products of Love Incorporated usually focus on *techniques*. These books and seminars offer pragmatic steps or patterns that are supposed to give consumers the information, tools, even "secrets" that they need to achieve success in marriage. As such, Love Incorporated parallels what might be called Leadership Incorporated or Business Incorporated or Fitness Incorporated or even Spirituality Incorporated. Go to the appropriate sections of the bookstore, and you will find books that offer three-, five-, and seven-step plans for success in each area, offered by well-known consultants in each field. Follow the steps and find a way to your dreams.

It is a peculiarly American vision, this idea that most mysteries can be solved and most dreams achieved through the application of just the right technique. It is rooted in our pragmatism, with its tendency to embrace the notion that what is true is what works. It reflects our historic national self-confidence; rather than a sense of tragedy or of the intractability of human nature, we tend to believe that if we can just find the right technique, we can solve all the problems we face. It is also rooted in our confidence in science and technology, as well as scientists and technologists; after all, if aerospace experts can figure out how to send a man to the moon, surely psychological experts can find a seven-step plan to save marriages. Perhaps above all it reflects the endless "pursuit of happiness" that has been wired into our national soul since 1776. As Thomas Moore puts it:

> As a result of this kind of mechanization of our thinking, we've lost an appreciation for the mysterious factors that bring people together and force them apart. In the face of difficulties that have profound roots, we bring to relationships a fix-it attitude. . . . We seek out mechanical causes and solutions to problems.[2]

Here's the real secret: *There is no technical solution to marriage*. There is no five-step secret plan that can ensure marital success. Marriage is not the kind of thing to which such a plan can be applied successfully.

This emphasis on techniques tends to be devoid of historical and social context. Many marriage books fail to state that the emotionally strenuous enterprise we now understand marriage to be is a quite recent historical phenomenon. Marriage is not supposed to be this hard, and it never was this hard until about 1965. The historic collapse of the social supports that once held men and women like Robert Gachet and Almond Gushee in marriage has left all the pressure for successful marriage on the quivering shoulders of ordinary men and women—sinful, wounded, stressed, weary, not always especially sensitive or skillful men and women. The marriage cathedral has collapsed, and married couples are trying to keep the rafters from cracking their skulls while they try to do marriage. In not telling their readers this,

Love Incorporated's practitioners may unintentionally harm the cause of lasting marriage.

This combination of heightened expectations and diminished cultural support for marriage is a dreadful whipsaw that breaks the back of many couples. Successful marriage becomes a minority phenomenon, accessible only to that 7 percent of elite couples who somehow crack the code.[3] The successfully married become a kind of mysterious elite, partakers of secret techniques unavailable to others.

The problem is worsened by the rising acceptance of divorce. Mass divorce means that ordinary people, attempting to become marriage virtuosos because that's what is expected, do so in a context in which divorce can be chosen at any moment. Divorce hangs like a sword over everyone's head, always there for the taking. As Union University student Michele Bennett says, postmodern marriage paradoxically "demands a certain quality of relationship—by threat of divorce—that can only be developed in the context of the commitment which divorce demolishes."[4]

To the extent that marriage does involve skill development, it takes time and practice—just like any skill. A baseball player doesn't learn to hit a curveball overnight. It takes many years of practice. Typically, if children start hitting baseballs from the age of eight, it might take six years for the most talented to master hitting both a fastball and a curveball. At that, even the best will fail about 70 percent of the time. Yet such failure is not a crisis because there is always another try; it is part of the learning process. So young ballplayers can relax and try again another day.

But the omnipresence of divorce makes it hard or even impossible for the average spouse or couple to relax and learn the skills they need to learn. My wife, Jeanie, and I have been at this marriage business for nineteen years, and by now we have a pretty skillful, smooth-running operation. Misunderstandings are rare; fights are rarer. But nineteen years is a long time to swing and miss and swing and miss until you figure out how to get it right. It took years of patiently refining our marriage "technique" to get to where we are now, and we look forward expectantly to more joyful refining in the years to come. The clear covenantal permanence of our marriage bond created the only kind of context in which skill development could flourish. Without the confidence that this marriage was here to stay, we would not have developed the skills that make our marriage so satisfying today. I devote the next chapter to the covenantal structure of marriage, but it is important to mention it here for this reason. Skills and techniques do not stand alone; they are part of a broader context in which any marriage is undertaken.

Sometimes marriage books unwittingly worsen this problem by seeming to threaten readers who fail to learn their techniques with the failure of their marriages. Willard Harley, whose work is admirable in many ways, subtitles his widely read book *His Needs, Her Needs: Building an Affair-Proof Marriage.*[5] The implication is that, by golly, the reader better learn to meet the most important needs of her spouse or she might just find him in bed with another woman—or in divorce court. While I have already argued that creational needs are compelling, this approach risks entrenching disastrous and unbiblical patterns of thinking even further: *she is not meeting my top three needs, so therefore I have a right to look elsewhere.* Surely this is not what Harley and others want to communicate, but it is easily inferred from their approach.

This reminds us that an emphasis on character, often missing from marriage books, is fundamental to any Christian approach to marriage. Love Incorporated teaches us techniques we can try out; character asks about what kind of people we are and proposes ways of being that enable human relationships to flourish. Techniques are portable, module-like things that can be snapped into or out of people's lives as they prove helpful. But technical thinking fails to recognize that it takes a certain kind of person to actually practice the techniques being proposed.

For example, the advanced communication skills that are so often emphasized by Love Incorporated require people with the kind of character to be able to reduce their focus on themselves enough to enter into real dialogue with someone else. In other words, communication requires an unselfish spirit of servanthood that many people do not have—and that no technique will magically produce. Or consider conflict resolution, so critical a technique in marriage. Conflict resolution is actually, in biblical terms, peacemaking. Peacemaking is a New Testament command (Matt. 5:9; Rom. 12:16). It requires the willingness to initiate a reconciling conversation, to repent and be forgiven, and to accept repentance and offer forgiveness.[6] Thus, from a Christian perspective, this "technique" is a matter of moral commitment rooted in a disposition of the will developed with effort over time—and ultimately in devotion to Jesus Christ.

Such character is nurtured in Christian community. Love Incorporated, even in its Christian guise, rarely situates the couple in the context of a faith community—or any community. Reflecting the individualism of our time, Love Incorporated assumes that its audience is the lone couple wanting to prepare for or improve their marriage. Thus most marriage enrichment seminars involve a community of several hundred strangers alone together under the expert care of a seminar leader. There is little community in such a place.

As I will stress in chapter 9, any adequate Christian treatment of marriage must include an emphasis on its community context in the church. We have already seen how the collapse of any kind of national community vision of marriage has swept millions of individual marriages over the cliff. Any particular marriage is affected by what marriage is in the society as a whole, because "no man is an island." We are social beings. Our society's diseased vision of marriage infects all of us—unless we choose to carry our marriage into an alternative communal context offering a healthier vision. For Christians, that context is the church—an accountable community focused on the kingdom of God.

In the next section I turn to the basic repertoire of skills needed to meet the creation purposes of marriage. I draw on the best contributions of our society's marriage experts, some of whom do offer excellent counsel. But this extended critique of Love Incorporated has been necessary to set a context for this literature and some boundaries for what such skill development can and cannot do.

The Central Skills (and Virtues) of Marriage

One of the most widely used marriage preparation and marriage enrichment programs in use today is PREPARE. This program, founded by David Olson, a psychologist based in Minneapolis, is now over twenty years old. Olson does not make sensationalistic claims for his program, and it is grounded in solid research, clinical practice, and the results flowing in from over one million couples.[7] I have been a trained PREPARE counselor for many years and strongly recommend the program for church use. I use the categories PREPARE inventories cover as a jumping-off point for a discussion of the central skills and virtues of marriage, in dialogue with some of the best marriage enrichment literature. (PREPARE does not offer an integrated theological or moral approach to its own test results and is thus not responsible for the interpretation that I offer here.)

Remember my basic theological claim from the last chapter. Marriage was created by God to accomplish certain purposes—companionship, sex, children, and the social good—grounded in human needs. PREPARE addresses these purposes in numerous ways through its testing and discussion materials. Here I offer my own take on the skills and virtues of marriage in areas of companionship and sexuality. I have reserved discussion of children and society for other chapters.

Marriage Expectations

A central skill in marriage is to develop and maintain appropriate expectations of the institution itself. PREPARE evaluates couples concerning what they expect of the married estate they are about to enter. The test flags scores indicating a lack of realism about future difficulties in marriage; the vain hope that time itself will resolve most marital difficulties; too much emphasis on the spouse as the sole source of relational satisfaction after marriage; and the expectation that it will be possible to change the spouse after marriage so that he or she conforms to one's hopes and expectations.[8] In my experience using this test, most engaged couples' scores show inflated expectations of marriage.

Of course, these expectations are a significant and deeply ingrained aspect of our culture, which simultaneously expects more and less of marriage (more satisfaction; less permanence). Biblically, couples can reasonably expect that each partner will make every effort to meet the other's creation-based needs (companionship, sex, children, and contribution to society)—within the context of human sin, which sets limits on all our accomplishments. Yet ratcheting such expectations down—from overly hyped cultural romantic notions to more sober biblical hopes—is not so much a skill as a virtue, or a cluster of virtues. It involves humility about our own adorableness; sobriety about what can be expected of others, even the most beloved other; patience with human frailty; self-control when expectations go unmet for a season; above all, love, which is not "self-seeking . . . not easily angered," and "keeps no record of wrongs" (1 Cor. 13:5b).

It is possible to interpret the soaring hopes our culture places in marriage as a kind of idolatry. Having left God behind, all too often we worship the creature rather than the Creator (Rom. 1:25). Worshiping another human being, seeking ultimacy and salvation from her, we ask of her something that should not be asked of any person. Disappointed as we are with such inflated hopes, we then are tempted to turn against the former object of our fondest hopes with exaggerated hatred—like Amnon, who "hated [Tamar] more than he had loved her" (2 Sam. 13:15). Ask any divorce lawyer or family law judge what that hatred looks like.

Maintaining reasonable expectations of marriage is a kind of skill. But it is more adequately described as a virtue rooted in a rightly ordered way of looking at the world, ourselves, and our loved ones.

Personality Issues

Marrying someone with a suitable personality and learning to live with their personality flaws are skills suggested by the PREPARE curriculum. The test assesses the personality traits of both partners in such areas as jealousy, anger management, happiness, sociability, reliability, stubbornness, dominance, and other areas. The inventories offer helpful assessments of such issues that make good starting points for discussion.

Contemporary Love Incorporated literature pays considerable attention to temperament and personality types.[9] Most readers will have been exposed to some version of a personality test somewhere. It was perhaps an inevitable development that romance consultants would develop applications of such tests for romantic relationships. The goal is to find someone who is compatible in temperament and personality and thus avoid later trouble.

Temperamental compatibility is a valuable goal. But I cannot concede this ground to the psychologists. Conditions such as moodiness or depression may well be biochemical for many people. Depression is a medical/psychological condition that needs to be treated with skill and care. People do have personalities that mark their customary way of living in the world, and some personalities are more compatible than others. However, jealousy, anger, reliability, stubbornness, and dominance are *character issues,* not just personality issues. The categorization of such traits as personality issues can remove them from the realm of moral responsibility. They become psychological givens, which both of us must accept, rather than areas of irresponsibility to which we should apply moral effort. And, on the overly psychological view, when we run into trouble with such "personality" issues, we can be tempted to conclude that we just "married the wrong person."

Jealousy, for example, is self-assertion rooted in a fear of loss or of a bruising of the ego. If I am jealous of a colleague's success at work, it means I am comparing myself with him and finding I come up short. But such self-comparison is a vice that can be set aside if the self's value is found in something more sturdy than comparative success. Similarly, attempting to dominate or control my spouse (or being excessively stubborn) indicates that I am not being self-forgetful and exercising servanthood but instead being grasping and self-focused. If I am attempting to remake my spouse's personality, I am failing to accept her independent existence, into which I am graciously invited. Instead, I am attempting to take her over in order to remake or dominate her.

It is helpful, then, to try to marry someone with a compatible *personality,* if by this we mean those significant aspects of the self appropriately covered by this term. It is imperative, however, as a matter of sound moral judgment, to marry someone of sound *character.* But even this involves making the best judgment we can, given the available information at the time, after careful and prayerful consideration, and then living with the consequences. The only thing I can control is the development of my own character, which itself is sometimes an obstinate mule and which itself grows as I persevere through hard times and disappointed hopes (Rom. 5:3–5; see also chapter 7 of this book). The Christian should seek (and seek to be) not so much a compatible personality but a person of sound character—someone who is committed to continued moral growth under the power of the Holy Spirit.

Communication

Every marriage book emphasizes communication. Everyone agrees that communication is the lifeblood of marriage, so everyone offers a package of skills and techniques aimed at its enhancement.[10]

The PREPARE test evaluates whether couples can communicate their true feelings with each other and whether such communication is welcomed, heard, and understood. It treats as a communication problem issues of verbal withdrawal, put-downs, and dishonesty. The goal is both a high quality and a sufficient quantity of communication.

Communication is a significant marital skill that can be sharpened over time in a stable marriage. Differences in the ways men and women typically communicate are now better understood, as are the various ways that communication gets blocked and distorted.[11] My own experiences in premarital and marital counseling have given me plenty of occasions to witness badly disrupted communication, even the collapse of communication into sullen silence. Good communication is a skill that corresponds nicely with the creational goal of loving companionship in daily living. It is essential if the couple wants to ascend to the mountaintop of loving, one-flesh unity.

It remains important to draw the connections between character and communication. Consider the question of the trustworthiness of communication. A pattern of dishonesty in speech is not a technical problem but a character problem. Words are acts. They are verbal deeds that embody the spirit, values, and character of those who utter them. Routine dishonesty in speech reveals a hole in human character. That hole may have various causes; most often it is the desire to evade discovery of unwelcome truths about the self. Sometimes it is merely a bad habit, which in moral terms is a pattern of wrong moral choices reinforced by consistent practice. Though the work is arduous and requires God's help, any such bad moral habit can be rooted out over time and replaced by a new one.

Verbal put-downs are also not merely a communication problem but instead an issue of character—both of the person and of the relationship. Affectionate companionship is built upon the steady exchange of edifying words rather than destructive ones. The New Testament constantly addresses the need for Christ-followers to train themselves to offer words that build up rather than tear down (Eph. 4:29–32). Put-downs are a verbal demonstration of contempt for the person we have promised to love and honor—for that matter, they are inappropriate in any relationship by virtue of the fellow humanity of the other person. Those who have trained their tongues tend to bless those with whom they live and tend to flourish in relationships, and the inverse is also sadly true.

The advanced communication skills so often emphasized today require people to forget themselves long enough to enter into real listening dialogue with someone else. There is a kind of self-emptying in such communication that resembles Christ's self-emptying in the incarnation (Phil. 2:1–11). It is only possible for the person whose ego need not take center stage on every occasion but is able to be laid down. This is a person who is both willing and eager to make authentic human contact with another soul and who finds the concerns of the beloved at least as compelling as the concerns of the self.

The problem of verbal withdrawal is the problem of giving up on interpersonal communion with my beloved. I stop speaking to you when I become convinced that it will accomplish nothing positive in my life or our relationship. My pain and anger silence me. There are seasons in most marriages when words are not easy to come by and silence reigns. Yet love keeps trying, keeps attempting communication, because love "always trusts, always hopes, always perseveres" (1 Cor. 13:7). The character qualities needed in times of marital silence are endurance, perseverance, hope, and above all, love, which does not give up and does not withdraw into the poisonous "safety" of silence.

Conflict Resolution

PREPARE materials—every marriage book, really—emphasize the importance of discussing marital differences to the point of resolution. Differences of opinion inevitably arise in marriage. Avoiding the issue is no solution, nor is giving in too easily to avoid hurting the other person's feelings or just to end the argument. Honest communication is needed until the conflict can find a resolution that satisfies both. Both partners must take conflicts seriously and work hard to resolve them.[12]

Conflict resolution is a critical marital skill. On our best days, we will sometimes see things differently than our spouse; on our less-than-best days, we may be spoiling for a fight. However conflicts arise, couples must find ways to settle them.

At a deeper level, however, resolving conflict consistently and well requires us to be peacemakers, as noted earlier. A peacemaker is someone who desires interpersonal peace and develops the repertoire of practices that make peace. A peacemaker is humble, because humility is required if we are to acknowledge and take responsibility for our contribution to the conflict and be willing to "lower ourselves" to ask forgiveness. A peacemaker is teachable, because only a teachable person can allow the possibility that she may have something to learn about how to relate to another person, address a particular issue, or behave differently (Matt. 7:1–5). A peacemaker is courageous enough to take the first step to initiate peace (Matt. 5:21–26) despite the possible risk of rejection and humiliation. A peacemaker is forgiving in that he always stands ready to respond to the request of another for mercy, grace, and reconciliation. A peacemaker is self-controlled in speech, thus able to avoid the pattern of worsening conflicts by throwing incendiary word bombs in the heat of the moment (James 3:1–12). A peacemaker is resilient in that she is able to walk through the often painful process of repentance, confession, forgiveness, and reconciliation countless times without giving up on the relationship (Matt. 18:21–35).[13]

While the creation purposes of any marriage will be thwarted if couples are not peacemakers, Christians especially must not rest easy with the constant collapse of our marriages due to unresolved conflicts. Such a reality marks a total contradiction of who we are called to be as Holy Spirit–empowered followers of Christ. It also stands as an affront to the gospel of peace and reconciliation (Eph. 2:11–22).

Financial Management

The PREPARE test offers assessment of the couple's attitudes and plans for handling money. The test assesses how the couple spends money, whether they have developed a budget, whether debt is an issue, and whether their income will be adequate to meet expenses. It also examines the critical matter of financial priorities and the pervasive issue of power—who will decide how money is handled. Most young engaged couples have thought very little about any of these unromantic but potentially marriage-busting concerns. PREPARE, along with more specialized material related to handling money in marriage, can help in stimulating the development of critical financial skills.

There are deeper questions of character related to money, however, that are rarely placed explicitly on the table in marriage books. They are in one sense perennial—they arise in any culture—but they are also acutely connected with the collapse of marriage in our own culture with its link to the rise of American affluence.

My claim is that how we handle finances is a critical indicator of spiritual and moral health. It was critical in Jesus' own day, which is why he devoted more attention to money than any other single moral issue; and it is critical in our own consumerist culture with its mania for acquiring more stuff all the time. My own research reveals four relevant themes that Jesus taught:

- *Possessions are intrinsically insignificant beyond the basic needs provided by God.* Jesus called his listeners to trust God rather than worry about food, drink, and clothing. Having enough to eat and something to wear is not insignificant. Jesus affirms the need for such things and the obligation to help others meet such needs (Matt. 25:31–46). The spiritual problem develops when people ascribe undue significance to possessions.
- *Misreading the value of things incites us to greed.* Jesus used metaphors related to sight when speaking of the problem of "storing up treasures on earth." Misperceiving the value of possessions leads us to moral decisions characterized by an excessive love for money (cf. 1 Tim. 6:9–10) and the things money can buy. Rooted in a fundamental misunderstanding of the value of possessions, greed misleads us into ascribing inordinate value to that which is not worthy of it. It is a disorder of our affections and a kind of idolatry.
- *Greed encourages a lifestyle of luxury, pride, hoarding, even oppression*. Greed is not just a personal spiritual disorder but a temptation leading to sins against our neighbor, especially hoarding and lack of generosity (Luke 12:13–21). Many marriages have been destroyed by trying to get rich or by spending more than is earned. The end result can be a home full of stuff but empty of moral and spiritual value, or a couple buried in debt. The couple whose heart is given over to God avoids these moral distortions. They are more interested in using their money to do good for others than in buying the latest luxury item. This enables them to avoid financial overreaching and gives them a positive shared vision for financial management.
- *The deceptive allure of wealth can imperil the soul*. In the parable of the sower and the seed (Matt. 13:3–23; Mark 4:3–20; Luke 8:4–15), Jesus outlines four kinds of responses to the gospel. Both Matthew 13:22 and Mark 4:19 say that the seed sown among thorns represents the person whose growth is choked out by, among other things, "the deceitfulness of wealth." Deceitfulness involves misrepresenting

> reality, concealing or distorting the truth about something for the purpose of misleading. Wealth has a power of deceit; it can fool people into seeing in it a kind of earthly salvation that cannot be found there. It can imperil the soul of a marriage just as easily as the soul of an individual.

Money problems bring down many marriages, and money is one of the focal points of conflict in the divorce process. An emphasis on character reveals once again that money management is not just a skill to be learned but also an arena that tests the souls of individuals and marriage itself. The New Testament offers a striking vision of the place of money in life to which all are invited—and to which self-proclaimed disciples are responsible. Such teachings were not offered for our misery but for our good. They are among the most widely ignored aspects of the biblical message, with predictable consequences for marriage.

Role Relationship

The PREPARE test wades into the sex roles debate primarily by assessing practical ways in which decision making and household tasks are assigned by the couple. The test asks whether the couple will negotiate, compromise, and adjust in their relationship. It asks whether important decisions will be shared or can sometimes be unilateral. The questions of whether the wife will work outside the home and, if so, whether the household tasks will be divided evenly between husband and wife are explored in several different ways. The quiet bias of the test is toward a contemporary egalitarian vision of shared labor, shared decision making, and shared and flexible responsibilities, though the test's primary agenda is in determining whether the couple shares a vision for this area of their relationship, whatever that vision may be.

An egalitarian vision of gender roles has triumphed in the culture, at least in leading opinion-making circles. Even so, some feminists argue that marriage remains a context in which women's needs and interests remain subservient to men's, and that marriage remains an unfair deal for most women.[14] This issue remains hotly debated. It is certainly the case that when women experience marriage as a context of oppression, this leads to the greater likelihood of divorce.

A fierce debate about this issue continues to rage in conservative Christian circles between those who embrace an egalitarian vision of sex roles and those who believe a complementarian vision fits the biblical evidence better. Christian marriage preparation literature often differs sharply from secular Love Incorporated books by emphasizing distinct, gender-based responsibilities (and needs) of men and women in marriage. These authors claim that God's created order was intended to include sacrificial male leadership and joyful female submission in marriage (Eph. 5:22–33).[15] Some assert that the central skill needed in marriage is for men to learn how to be men and women to learn how to be women—for both to learn the significance of their God-given roles and differences. Let's consider both issues for a moment.

My own thinking about my leadership in family life as husband and father has evolved in recent years in some ways that have surprised me. Not only was I trained in various strands of egalitarianism, I also instinctively found typical patterns of male dominance in family life to be boorish and oppressive. I wanted no part of that, and neither did my wife, Jeanie.

However, as a couple we have come to the conclusion that our marriage and family life work best if we operate within the vision of godly, sacrificial husband/father leadership that is articulated in Ephesians 5:22–6:4. A few years ago, after many years of marriage, Jeanie essentially asked me to step up to the plate and provide stronger spiritual and moral leadership to our family. Under the impact of a desire not to be sexist—as well as various professional distractions and, I now see, some personal immaturity—I had left far too much responsibility for the direction of our family and discipline of our children to my wife.

Jeanie was asking me to be the kind of man described in Ephesians: loving, purifying, sacrificial, other-centered, fully engaged in the spiritual and moral training of our children, visionary in setting and preserving a godly family environment, and willing to make the hard and unpopular calls necessary to guard the young souls of our children. She said that if I could be the kind of man described in Ephesians 5–6, she would be more than happy to be the kind of woman described there.

This is the direction our thinking is taking. It may not be yours. But the overall issue is certainly one that every couple must settle, with clarity.

As for the issue of gender differences, every couple must learn how to navigate the real differences that often do exist between male and female ways of thinking, feeling, relating, communicating, and loving. At least they must learn to understand and navigate the differences as they show up in their own particular relationship. Even the secular marriage books these days—most famously the works by John Gray—tend to claim that there are such intrinsic sex-based differences, which makes them stand in contrast to the genderless vision that is sometimes found in feminist and egalitarian writings. Some of these claims related to intrinsic male and female differences are overblown or stereotypical. However, a carefully nuanced acknowledgment of the typical distinctive needs and relational styles of men and women fits with a creation-oriented vision that recognizes that humanity was made as an *alike-yet-distinct* male and female pair.

Further, couples must develop the skill of managing family labor effectively. As marriage is a companionship of labor, some way must be found to distribute the tasks so that they are done well and distributed equitably. Someone must pay the bills, mop the floor, wash the dishes, and earn the money. And some way must be found to determine together who will do what. The task is rendered all the more difficult today because it is not settled by the broader culture. The collapse of traditional gender roles means that this issue must be negotiated by each couple, rather than being preestablished by cultural expectations.

The issue here is actually *marital power*. Whenever the questions are "Who decides?" and "How will burdens and benefits be distributed?" we are talking about power, even in the intimate sphere of family life, which should not be sentimentalized as somehow exempt from power dynamics.[16] Here we are talking about something more than skill development and temperamental differences. We are back to issues of character and morality. Biblically, the moral norm that correlates with power is *justice*. Justice is both a moral obligation related to how we act and a moral virtue related to our character.

In biblical teaching, justice is a rich concept involving God's activity and our own toward four primary goals: deliverance of the poor and powerless from the injustice that they regularly experience; lifting the foot of domineering power off the neck of the dominated and oppressed; stopping violence and establishing peace; and restoring the outcasts, the excluded, the exiles, and the refugees to community. These four themes distill the heart of the message of the prophets and the justice aspect of Jesus' message as well.[17]

What might these themes mean for marriage? At least this: A just marriage involves a fair distribution of the financial resources of the common purse, so that whatever the financial condition of the family, its burdens and benefits are equally shared between husband and wife. It avoids any form of coercive power between husband and wife so that neither is dominated or oppressed through any kind of bullying or abusive power. It rejects any form of violence under any circumstances. And it creates the conditions of a family community in which both husband and wife (and eventually children, though in different ways) enjoy full and fair inclusion—so that neither is on the outside looking in, both have the chance to develop their God-given capacities, both have a voice, and both participate in making the decisions that affect their own lives.[18]

Notice that this understanding of justice in marriage emphasizes *outcomes* rather than *roles* or *authority structures*. I have seen couples that take an explicitly egalitarian approach and couples that take a complementarian view both succeed and fail in achieving these outcomes. The key is not so much whether a couple claims to embrace either the egalitarian or complementarian vision but whether the approach they take actually produces a mutually satisfying justice and order in their marriage.

My wife, Jeanie, and I developed a system while I was in graduate school that reflected our awareness of the need for "labor justice" in our marriage. We called it the "unit principle." At each stage in the ebb and flow of the academic year, we evaluated our joint tasks and responsibilities to be sure that they were being divided fairly. There was a baby to care for, a variety of household chores to do, money to make, and school to attend. We assigned each major task area (childcare, paid employment, school, housework) a unit value and divided up the units so that they came out even. When school was in session, I was responsible for comparatively few of the other tasks; when out of session, my responsibilities were adjusted accordingly. If we found at any point that either of us was staggering under our responsibilities, we would look once again at the "unit distribution" to see if it needed to be adjusted.

Now that life is more settled, we renegotiate our responsibilities less frequently. But even now, because we love each other, both of us seek to be attentive to the burdens the other is carrying, and we reach out to help. "Bear one another's burdens, and in this way you will fulfill the law of Christ" (Gal. 6:2 NRSV). Love *includes* justice rather than standing in contradiction to it. Love without justice to give it content and structure cannot be called love. And both love and justice are far more than skills.[19]

Sexual Needs

The sexual dimension of marriage, which is considered in most marriage books, also is covered by the PREPARE test.[20] On this issue the test's questions range widely. The focus is information and communication. The test looks back to the quality of communication about sex experienced by each spouse as a child and the level of communication that exists as they talk together about their sexual relationship. Several questions explore the link between affection and sex—whether the basic needs for touch and affection are met, how these are linked to the couple's sexual relationship, and whether affection or sex is withheld unfairly. The test also considers the varying levels of interest in sex that might exist between the spouses and the overall level of satisfaction.

Perhaps on no issue has contemporary American society turned a good gift from God into a technique more thoroughly than sex. From the covers of magazines in every bookstore screams the message: *your sexual satisfaction is critically important, and here is how you can experience it!* The former ABC news anchor Howard K. Smith once said that the media does not so much tell people what to think as what to think *about*. From every corner, we are instructed to think about sexual satisfaction.

There is a skill development dimension to marital sexuality. Growing frankness about what those skills are is a good thing, at least insofar as this communication is intended to prepare the engaged couple for marriage or to increase sexual satisfaction in marriage. Classic texts such as Ed Wheat's *Intended for Pleasure* broke new ground for Christians in the 1970s by explaining without a blush "the techniques of lovemaking." Couples were taught about the chemistry of sexual arousal, the phases of the lovemaking process, how to bring both husband and wife to orgasm, and how to solve common sexual problems such as impotence and premature ejaculation.[21] These days, many young couples receive a book like this near their wedding day from someone who cares about them.

Of course there are dangers to this new frankness about sex and especially to this emphasis on technique. One problem is the raising of excessive expectations of sexual fulfillment, especially for young couples who have waited chastely for marriage. Persistent conflict over unsatisfied sexual hopes, comparisons with former or imagined lovers, the turn to pornography for heightened stimulation, and of course the search for another lover, are all wrong turns that spouses can take if they become unsatisfied with their sexual relationship.

Sex is more than a skill. It is a central part of the human person. And it requires the development and sustaining of virtues that are rare in our age. The virtue of modesty acknowledges that even in marriage each spouse remains an individual with a certain zone of privacy that must be acknowledged. Modesty also has implications for the display of the body outside the home. The virtue of fidelity speaks not just to whether spouses have sexual intercourse with someone else but the entire pattern of how they behave as sexual beings in the world—and in their thought life.

Patient chastity is often required in marriage, as sex is not always as available as the eager young couple imagines it will be. Work-related absences, times of travel, visits with extended family, illnesses, pregnancies, even seasons of marital discord all introduce periods of sexual abstinence. The sexual dimension of marriage is played out here as well, in absence and longing, not just in presence and satisfaction.

The same kind of other-centeredness that is needed in all other aspects of marriage is needed in the bedroom. Marriage flourishes when both partners are looking for ways to please and serve each other. In so doing they find their own needs met. But this is not going to happen in the bedroom if it is not happening anywhere else. Indeed, every other major dynamic of the marital relationship is both tested and revealed in the couple's sexual relationship. Expectations, communication, conflict resolution, personality and character issues, and the level of justice in the relationship are all brought into the bedroom. When all is well elsewhere in the relationship, sexual problems are often technical and can be resolved with the kind of coaching that the sex books can offer. When all is not well elsewhere, no instruction in sexual technique will matter.

Spirituality and the Soul Mate Question

Let us end this discussion of the skills and virtues of marriage by considering one last category from the PREPARE test: spiritual beliefs. It is the least satisfying dimension of the test because its questions are so vague as to lack much power to reveal important truths about the relationship. Questions explore whether the partners agree or disagree about their spiritual beliefs, whether such beliefs are an important and constructive part of the relationship, and whether each is satisfied with the way they express their beliefs in the context of their relationship. The most concrete question asks whether the spouses think active participation in church or synagogue is important.

Perhaps it is inevitable that the diverse audience served by this test would require such thin questions about religious commitment. The nature of the questions could also lead to the conclusion that spiritual beliefs constitute just one more area in which refined techniques could be developed that would heighten relationship satisfaction. Spirituality is often treated that way in the broader culture.

I have attempted to show in this chapter that convictions about matters of ultimate concern undergird all other questions of character or behavior. Spirituality is not an optional appendage to marriage. Every human is a spiritual being simply by having been created by God as an embodied soul. What we believe (*really* believe, not just profess to believe) about God, the world, human nature, our own identity, the purpose of life, what happens when we die, what makes for a good person—these issues are unavoidable. We are all religious beings just by being human beings. The question is what god we believe in.

One basic implication is that marriage is unlikely to thrive if undertaken by two people who worship different gods—regardless of whether they might happen to attend the same religious community. Worshiping different gods, the couple will live out starkly different convictions related to the other critical questions that must be faced by any conscious human being. The test points to the possibility that the partners may hold religious convictions of different strength or of different content. This is one very practical matter to consider in marrying or in helping someone else prepare for marriage. Paul was right when he urged Christians not to be "unequally yoked" with unbelievers (2 Cor. 6:14), and in a sense the same principle applies to anyone.

In a culture in which many millions still profess a nominal Christianity while being practical pagans, those selecting marriage partners need to have the ability to sort out the wheat from the chaff. They need to know what god their prospective partner serves, regardless of the occasional foray into church. This "qualitative" approach to the religious dimension of mate selection is more significant than whether a committed Pentecostal, say, should marry an equally committed Baptist.

The goal, by God's grace, is to find someone who can be a genuine Christian brother or sister, a colaborer in living out the life of Christian discipleship. Such a person will hold a faith similar to yours in doctrinal and moral content, to be sure, but also similar in its level of passion for God and the extent to which it governs his or her life.

It might even be possible for such a person to be described as a "soul mate." This ancient phrase is dominating the imagination of those in the market for a marriage partner. According to the Gallup polling organization, over half of Americans believe in love at first sight, and finding a soul mate is now trumping all other goals among young Americans looking for marriage partners.[22] The term is making its way into the Love Incorporated literature as well. What accounts for its extraordinary appeal in our day?

As popularly employed, a soul mate is someone to whom I feel a mystical sense of connection, someone who is a match for the deepest essence of my self and thus brings me the most sublime joy imaginable in human life. For Thomas Moore, a soul mate is "someone to whom we feel profoundly connected, as though the communicating and communing that takes place between us were not the product of intentional efforts, but rather a divine grace."[23]

These days, everyone wants a soul mate. If they marry and conclude that they did not happen to find a soul mate at the altar, many feel authorized to throw in the towel and try again. This notion of a soul mate is a legacy of pagan Greek and modern Romantic thinking rather than a biblical concept. It can tempt men and women to embark on desperate quests to find that perfect match, to find that relationship "magic" they seek, and to abandon their promises to those they leave behind in their epic quest. The resurgence of the soul mate concept—and emergence of a soul mate ethic that contributes to much divorce—is a sadly fitting symbol of the disastrous confusions of our age.

And yet the concept still resonates with us. We want to find someone who is a true match for us, a partner for the journey, a companion for the soul. If so, I suggest that we redeem the concept in this way. The true soul mate should be understood as a person who serves and worships the same God as you do, who yokes her life together with yours in a shared mission, who walks by your side in a companionship of labor and love designed by the Creator, and whose covenant commitment to your marriage cannot be shaken despite seasons of conflict and sorrow. Blessed is the one who finds such a partner.

In the next chapter, we will consider the covenant structure of such a bond.

6

Covenant as the Structural Principle of Marriage

How can anyone ever bring himself to affirm that he will care for another person twenty years from now? It is one thing to promise your girlfriend that you will pick her up at eight o'clock; it is quite another to give her your pledge that you will love her for the rest of your life. The marriage vows are simple ones, but remarkable for the extremity of their loftiness.

—Mike Mason, *The Mystery of Marriage*

I have argued that marriage is an order of creation, divinely given, intended to meet some of the most significant and pressing personal and social needs of the human being. We have just considered some of the important skills and virtues that help to fulfill the creation purposes of marriage. They are critical to a flourishing marriage.

There is another dimension to marriage, however, that is best addressed by using the biblical term *covenant.* It is often said that marriage is a covenant. Recent days have seen a resurgence of the term "covenant marriage" both in Christian and secular circles. Three states have passed covenant marriage laws. So the ancient language of covenant is enjoying a bit of a comeback. But this does not mean we understand the rich meaning of the term. It does not mean we are structuring our marriages as covenantal relationships, either in church or society.

This chapter argues that covenant is the structural principle of marriage. By this I mean that just as God designed marriage to meet the creation-based needs of human beings for companionship, sex, and so on, so did God give marriage a covenantal structure. This covenantal structure is just as integral to the *nature* of marriage as the fulfillment of creation-based needs is integral to the *purpose* of marriage. Both concepts—creation and covenant—apply to every marriage. There can be no successful marriage that is not both creation fulfilling and covenantal, whether the couple realizes this or not.

The concepts of creation and covenant are intertwined in biblical thought. It is possible to argue that there is ultimately no meaningful distinction between the two terms.[1] Theologian W. J. Dumbrell asserts that from the very first covenant that God initiates, his goal is to "reestablish . . . the relationship of God to humankind and creation."[2] Covenants are God's way of organizing, sustaining, and reclaiming relationships established in creation. If this is the case, then it can be claimed, as Dumbrell does, that God and humankind already stood in (unbroken) covenant relationship in the garden prior to the first sin, as did the first man and woman. Creation and covenant in this sense cannot be distinguished.

I read the biblical evidence a bit differently. The concepts of creation and covenant are interwoven, as both are aspects of God's gracious relationship to the creatures he has made, and creation is the presupposition of any covenant relationship. But the lack of any explicit mention of covenant in Genesis until after the entry of sin into the world leads me to conclude that Scripture intends to depict God as settling on covenant as the way to structure both divine-human and human-human relationships after sin disrupts God's perfect world.

I will argue, therefore, that the creation and covenant dimensions of marriage are related but distinct. Our needs for companionship, sex, shared labor, and family partnership constitute the ends or goods of marriage. These needs, and divine provision for meeting them, are given by God in creation. Looking for a partner who can meet these needs occupies much of our time until we find such a person (or think we do).

Covenant, on the other hand, emerges after sin enters the world. Covenant exists, not as an end in itself, but as a means to creational ends. As ethicist Margaret Farley has put it, "For the sake of our love, . . . we almost always commit ourselves to certain frameworks for living out our love. The frameworks, then, take their whole meaning . . . from the love they are meant to serve."[3] I will argue here that marriage has a covenantal character in order to safeguard the bond itself, which is prior to covenant but needs safeguarding due to our fallibility and faithlessness.

Covenant is thus like a protective sheath around marriage. It makes marriage stable and sturdy enough to accomplish its God-given creation design. Or, to return to our cathedral image, the covenantal structure of marriage, reinforced in and by the Christian community, provides the support beams that keep the marriage cathedral sturdy and unshaken. Covenant holds the walls and the ceilings up, enabling all who pursue their creation and kingdom tasks within the cathedral to do so in peace, because they do not have to fear a structural collapse.

Covenant as a Scriptural Concept

The concept of covenant (Hebrew *berith*) is first introduced in the Bible in the most dramatic manner imaginable: it is depicted as God's way of structuring his effort to redeem a primeval world already spinning out of control.

How extraordinarily compelling is the history narrated in the Bible's opening pages! God creates the world in an overflow of creativity and power. God provides everything needed for his creatures, beginning with an intimate relationship with himself. A natural and unfettered bond exists between God and humanity, between the first man and woman, and between the human and nonhuman creatures.

Yet men and women turn on God and on each other in vicious rebellion. The first man and woman disobey God (Genesis 3), then blame each other for the deed. Murder tears the first family asunder (Genesis 4), eventually setting the stage for a world "full of violence" (Gen. 6:11). God sickens at the wreck his creatures have made of the world and determines "to destroy both them and the earth" (Gen. 6:13b).

And yet—Noah "walked with God" (Gen. 6:9). So the Creator decides to spare this one man and his family, as well as a remnant of animal life. Humanity, animals, and the earth will be reclaimed for a new start. God declares to Noah, "I will establish my covenant with you" (Gen. 6:18)—the first reference to the term in the canon.

The floodwaters recede. God does make a covenant with—and through—Noah. "I now establish my covenant with you and with your descendants after you and with every living creature that was with you. . . . Never again will all life be cut off by the waters of a flood" (Gen. 9:9–11; cf. 9:15). God will continue to relate to us—to every living creature—despite our rebellion and the misery we create for each other and for our Creator. God will continue to pursue his original intentions in creation but will now do so by means of a covenant with the entire created order. At the center of this covenant is humanity, which is responsible for the chaos that has engulfed the creation and thus must be the focus of this and all other biblical covenants.

If we look closely at Genesis 9, we see key ingredients of most covenants in Scripture and of the Old Testament concept of covenant:

- It is initiated by someone, often the stronger party, as here (Gen. 9:8). In this case, God establishes the covenant unilaterally; later divine-human covenant agreements often have a bilateral structure, though God always remains the "senior partner" (see Gen. 15:18). Human-human covenants are often peer documents "cut" by equal parties.
- It establishes or ratifies a relationship between two or more parties. In short, *covenant creates or restores community*. All parties to the covenant are named in the agreement, a public document to which all participants can be held accountable.
- It spells out *mutual* responsibilities on the part of all parties, in this case both God and humanity. People are called in the covenant with Noah to resume the creation mandate by repopulating and exercising dominion over the earth, respecting life, and punishing killing. God in turn promises to provide food and accountability for murder, and to refrain from destroying the world again in a flood (Gen. 9:1–11). Covenant responsibilities commonly attest both to the *goals* of the covenant and the particular *rules* that apply to the covenant makers.[4]
- It involves the freely given verbal declaration of sacred promises or sworn oaths that publicly symbolize and even "perform" (speak/enact into existence) the solemn commitments being made. Here these promises are made by God alone; in some biblical covenants the promises are explicitly made by both God and people.[5]
- It is marked by a sign or symbolic action to communicate its significance—in this case, a rainbow (Gen. 9:13). Other covenants have other signs attached to them (e.g., circumcision—Gen. 17:10; Sabbath—Exod. 31:16; offering of a sacrifice or shed blood, a shared meal, or some form of physical contact between the covenanting parties, etc.).
- It is declared to be lasting, enduring, or even "everlasting" (Gen. 9:16; cf. Gen. 17:7; Num. 25:12–13; 1 Chron. 16:17; Pss. 89:28; 105:10; Isa. 24:5). God promises to "remember" the covenant always, and to keep his end of the agreement faithfully.[6] Covenant promises are binding; they restrict our future freedom of action on the basis of our present decision.

- God is viewed both as the witness and guarantor of covenants, so any breaking of covenant promises is a sin, not only against a covenant partner but also against God.
- Therefore, God will enforce dire consequences for breaking the covenant and offer great rewards for keeping it (Gen. 9:5). In this case the consequences include an "accounting"; often covenants include a graphic list of blessings and woes (cf. Joshua 24) or vivid threats of judgment and destruction.[7]

This description should help to support the claim that though covenant is a crucial biblical concept that can be traced from Genesis to Revelation, there would be no need for any covenants apart from the existence of sin. Before sin enters the picture, God relates freely, easily, and naturally to Adam as Adam and Eve do to each other. There is no explicit covenant structure to the relationship, just unforced and innocent relating, a sublime divine-human companionship. To describe this as a covenantal relationship probably is to read back into Scripture what is not yet there.[8]

Covenant making is God's gracious response to human sin. *No sin, no covenants*. God could have responded to sin by annihilating his creatures. That is the significance of the flood narrative. A brokenhearted and angry Creator responds in judgment toward his rebellious and miserable creatures—with every good reason to do so: "The LORD saw how great man's wickedness on the earth had become, and that every inclination of the thoughts of his heart was only evil all the time. The LORD was grieved that he had made man on the earth, and his heart was filled with pain" (Gen. 6:5–6).

But God pulls back from utter annihilation and instead begins what ethicist Steve Mott calls "the long march of redemption." The approach God uses to structure redemptive relationships is covenant making. Given the turn of humankind to evil, the only way to move us to right action is to organize redemption through covenants. A covenant is in this sense quite a sad thing. It is a far cry from the easy and unforced way of relating that was possible apart from sin but that no human being since the garden has ever fully experienced.

Thus we need to have our hands held (and tied), our spines stiffened, our promises vouchsafed. Because we are untrustworthy and fickle, we need to make sacred agreements binding ourselves to promises of behaving in a certain way. We need to know what those promises are, the terms under which we are making them, and the consequences of their betrayal. We need symbols and rituals to remind us of all of this. Human beings are indeed a pathetic lot. But God in his grace chooses to relate to us on the level we need. We need the structure of covenants, so it is covenants we are given.

It is especially important to understand the similarities and differences between covenants and contracts in any study of marriage. What they have in common is this: both covenants and contracts are initiated by someone, establish or ratify a relationship, spell out mutual responsibilities, carry public status, and are a kind of promise that binds both parties to do certain things and to refrain from doing other things.

However, while contracts emphasize the precise obligations each party is taking on, covenants place more focus on the *relationships* that are being established or ratified.[9] Contracts specify an exchange of money or services and terminate when the transaction is complete, while covenants establish a relationship that transcends any particular exchange of goods. Contracts always contain escape clauses to enable people to back away from what they judge to have been unwise commitments or failed agreements, while covenants promise open-ended and permanent fidelity to the promises being undertaken and the relationship being established. Finally, contracts are purely and simply human transactions, while covenants invoke the presence of God as guarantor and trustee—even when the covenant is undertaken at the human-to-human level.

God makes covenants throughout salvation history. These covenants are all related to each other because each is rooted in a foundational promise of God's presence and relationship with people—yet each has its own distinctiveness. God's covenant with Noah is a covenant with the whole of creation and all humanity. Beginning with Abraham and Sarah, God covenants with a particular people, the Jews, promising: "I will be your God, and you will be my people" (Jer. 7:23; cf. Exod. 6:7). This covenant is then renewed through Moses in the exodus and at Sinai. It later takes a political form in the covenant with David and his family line. Through the prophets God finally promises a new covenant "written on the heart," and fulfills that promise through the blood of Jesus Christ (Jeremiah 31–34; cf. Isaiah 40–66; Ezekiel 33–39; Luke 22:20). He invites into the covenant all who would believe in Jesus and receive the forgiveness of sin won through his atoning sacrifice. Even that is not the end of the story, because Jesus himself promises a coming kingdom—initiated in his ministry but not fulfilled until the end of time.

And so all the strands come together. God creates a good world. God responds to our calamitous sin by initiating redemptive covenantal relationships. God sends Jesus to culminate all covenant making and to begin the final act of redemption in which at last "the kingdom of the world [will] become the kingdom of our Lord and of his Christ, and he will reign for ever and ever" (Rev. 11:15). All of God's covenant partners await this day with earnest expectancy.

At each successive stage, God finds human covenant partners who are willing to return his promises with some of their own. God takes for himself a people; people bind themselves to God.[10] The particular promises both make are of great significance but not as significant as the very fact of their covenant commitment to each other and the community that this establishes—and the promise that someday both God and his people shall enjoy "a realm of justice and the ultimate conquest of death."[11]

Marriage as a Covenant

It is not surprising that the biblical record is full of covenants. Covenant making becomes a central biblical paradigm for all human relationships. Individuals make vows and oaths to each other. They make sacred promises to God. They construct agreements of all types. Failure to keep various types of sacred promises is treated as punishable by the heavenly court and sometimes by earthly courts as well. Promises matter and covenants are critical. They structure workable human relationships, damaged and endangered as they are by human deceit and weakness.

There is considerable debate among biblical scholars as to whether the Old Testament defines marriage as a covenant. Gordon Hugenberger, who has written the most comprehensive biblical study on the issue, has concluded that despite rather limited direct references to human marriage as a covenantal relationship in the Old Testament, and despite longstanding scholarly objections to the claim, the concept can be found there.[12] The most important single text (some say the *only* text) identifying human marriage as a covenant relationship is found in Malachi 2:10–16, especially verses 13–16:

> Another thing you do: You flood the LORD's altar with tears. You weep and wail because he no longer pays attention to your offerings or accepts them with pleasure from your hands. You ask, "Why?" It is because the LORD is acting as the witness between you and the wife of your youth, because you have broken faith with her, though she is your partner, the wife of your marriage covenant. Has not the LORD made them one? In flesh and spirit they are his. And why one? Because he was seeking godly offspring. So guard yourself in your spirit, and do not break faith with the wife of your youth. "I hate divorce," says the LORD God of Israel, "and I hate a man's covering himself with violence as well as with his garment," says the LORD Almighty. So guard yourself in your spirit, and do not break faith.

Malachi appears to have been written in the mid-fifth century B.C., around the same time in which Ezra and Nehemiah undertook the rebuilding of Jewish life in postexilic Jerusalem. The prophet wrote at a time when much of Israel's canon had already been developed, for the book shows clear signs of referring back to works such as Genesis, other parts of the Pentateuch, and even Proverbs. Malachi demonstrates great concern for the concept of covenant (2:4–5, 8, 10, 14; 3:1), offers stern warnings against covenant breaking of various types, and claims that such moral violations profane the sanctuary of God and cause him to reject Judah's offerings (cf. 2:11, 13).

In 2:10–16, Malachi declares that Judah's men have been unfaithful to God through two offenses related to marriage: intermarriage with pagan women (2:11) and divorcing their own (Jewish) wives (2:14). Both are forms of infidelity to the covenant with Yahweh. It is possible that the offenses were related—some Jewish men may have been divorcing their Jewish wives in order to marry pagan women.[13] The threat posed by intermarriage with pagans is a central theme in the roughly contemporaneous Ezra and Nehemiah, as well as elsewhere in the Old Testament. Why God would be distressed at such practices is little debated. But why God should have a problem with "regular" divorce is much more controversial, given the provisions made for divorce elsewhere in the Old Testament (such as Deut. 24:1–4).

Hugenberger argues that God is offended by Jewish men's divorce of their Jewish wives because the relationship between husband and wife within the covenant people Israel is in fact a covenant relationship. He shows by careful biblical research that marriage *was* understood in Israel as a covenant relationship, including ratification by an accompanying oath and/or act ("oath sign") in which God was invoked as a witness (cf. Mal. 2:14). In the case of marriage, besides solemn words, that oath sign was understood to be the sexual union of the couple. Malachi's allusion to Genesis and the one-flesh relationship of marriage (Mal. 2:15; cf. Gen. 2:24) connects here as well.

Malachi appears to have been unusually sensitive to the personal significance of the marriage covenant. He points to the solidarity of male and female in creation (Mal. 2:10), alludes to the bond that develops between a man and woman over most of a lifetime spent together ("the wife of your youth," "your partner"—Mal. 2:14; cf. Prov. 2:17), and seems to suggest the additional responsibility that develops upon the birth of children ("godly offspring"—Mal. 2:15) in these ways summarizing the many binding moral obligations that marriage and family ties create. This vision of marriage means that men do a great injustice when they exploit their power over women to end their marriage covenants unjustifiably. Indeed, the section ends with a link drawn between divorce and violence, as if unjustifiable divorce (divorce on the grounds of aversion or dislike alone) is a kind of violence against its innocent victims—which it is. On exegetical grounds, Hugenberger translates Malachi 2:16 in this way: "If one hates and divorces, . . . he covers his garment with violence."[14]

Scripture—especially those works composed after the eighth century B.C., but with clear indications earlier in biblical literature—repeatedly turns to a comparison of the covenant ties binding husband and wife with those ties binding God and his people Israel.[15] Indeed this comparison eventually becomes the single most frequently used metaphor for the relationship between God and his people.

In the Old Testament the language of divine-human "marital" covenant is most frequently used as an object lesson in judgment and sometimes reconciliation (see Isa. 1:21; 54:5–10; Jer. 2:2, 20; 3:6–25; 13:27; 23:10; 31:32; Ezekiel 16; 23; Hosea 2:18–22). Israel is described as a faithless, "whoring" wife, running after other gods, breaking faith with her husband, Yahweh. God is depicted as the heartbroken and angry cuckold, in some moods pleading with his "bride" to come home, sometimes tenderly promising her his forgiveness and eternal welcome, and sometimes vowing her "divorce" (Isa. 50:1; Jer. 3:1, 8), humiliation, or destruction for "playing the harlot." The entire book of Hosea embodies these themes. The condemnations are sometimes so vivid and, frankly, so disturbing as to have aroused the anger, fear, and rejection of some readers, such as feminist Christian scholars, who see in them an incitement to violence against women perceived as faithless by their husbands, fathers, or other men in their lives.[16]

These texts need to be interpreted with great care. Christian readers today need to be aware of both the similarities and the dissimilarities in the God/Israel–husband/wife comparison, as well as the dangers of reinforcing gender stereotypes or encouraging sexual violence.[17]

An appropriate rendering of these passages, however, at least reinforces the significance of the covenant ties binding both God and his people and a man and woman in marriage. Scripture's use of marriage language to depict the God-human relationship exalts the status of marriage and helps reinforce the claim that it should be treated as a covenant. The angry and heartbroken spirit of some of these texts related to marital brokenness and infidelity should deepen our sense of the significance and binding quality of the marriage covenant and of God's intimate relationship with his people. God yearns for men and women to keep their covenant commitments. God yearns for faithless people to end their straying and come back to the Creator, their covenant partner: "In that day I will make a covenant for them. . . . I will betroth you to me forever; I will betroth you in righteousness and justice, in love and compassion. I will betroth you to me in faithfulness, and you will acknowledge the LORD" (Hosea 2:18–20; cf. Isa. 54:1–10).

Paul ascends the mountaintop of this metaphor in Ephesians when he compares the relationship of husband and wife to that between Christ and his church (Eph. 5:22–33; cf. 2 Cor. 11:1–3). Jesus had used the image of the bridegroom to speak of himself (Matt. 9:15 and parallels; cf. John 3:28–30), had compared the kingdom of heaven to a wedding banquet (Matt. 22:2–14), and had compared those ready for the King to virgins prepared to meet the bridegroom (Matt. 25:1–13). Paul extends and develops the image considerably. He not only makes the familiar comparison of marriage to the divine-human relationship (while not actually using the word *covenant*) but also specifies particular responsibilities for men and women in marriage on the basis of a "Christ is to church as husband is to wife" analogy. Husbands are called to love, sacrifice for, and care for their wives; wives are called to submit to and respect their husbands. Paul also draws upon Genesis 2:24, as Jesus did, to speak of the one-flesh marital relationship and to compare that as well to the relationship between Christ and the church. Here the concept of marriage as a sacred covenant akin to the covenant relationship between God and his people is powerfully articulated.

The image receives its culmination toward the end of the book of Revelation with the church described luxuriantly as the bride preparing for the sacred wedding to her divine Husband (19:7; 21:2, 9; 22:17), and with both preparing for a joyful wedding supper (19:9). By this point we are well beyond carefully hedged covenant language to an exultant freedom of divine-human communion much like the freedom that Adam originally enjoyed in relating to God and that Adam and Eve originally enjoyed in relating to each other. At the end of all things, God and his people will enjoy a great wedding feast, celebrating their joyful unity with one another and the triumph of God in peace, justice, and love over all forces that have opposed his rule. As Raymond Ortlund has put it, "This perfect union brings together a triumphant Lamb and a pure Bride beyond the reach of hell and sin. . . . Her faithlessness, persistent since remote times, is finally dissolved forever in the chemistry of grace."[18]

In light of the analysis of the concept of marriage as a covenant and in view of difficulties caused by misinterpretations of the key passages, I suggest that the concept should be employed carefully, as listed in the points below. Note how the structure of these seven points parallels what I said earlier about the biblical concept of covenant in general.

- *Marriage is a covenant because it is a freely entered agreement between two people.* It is initiated by someone (most often the man in our culture), but it represents the culmination of a journey that fully involves both people. Contemporary marriage covenant agreements differ from biblical ones in that marriage in ancient Israel was not initiated (solely) by the individuals but was an agreement between families as well. We would do well to recover some aspects of this concept today. But at its heart marriage is an agreement between two people to join their lives together.

- *Marriage is a covenant because it publicly ratifies a relationship between a man and a woman and subjects it to objective standards and social responsibilities.* Marriage does not *establish* the personal relationship between a man and woman, but it does *ratify* that relationship, make it public, and establish its social legitimacy.
- *Marriage is a covenant because it spells out the mutual responsibilities and moral commitments that both parties are taking on in this new form of community.* Earlier I claimed that biblical covenant stipulations commonly attested both to the *goals* of the covenant and the particular *rules* that apply to the covenant makers. The central goals God intends for us to seek in marriage were already discussed in chapter 4: companionship, sexual expression, procreation, and family partnership. The central rules embedded in marriage's sacred promises are sexual exclusivity and permanence.[19] Both goals and rules are situated in a broader context of mutual commitment reaffirmed by faithful conduct over time.[20]
- *Marriage is a covenant because it is sealed by various oath signs that publicly symbolize and even "perform" the solemn commitments being made.* The exchanged vows and rings, the promises publicly made, and consummation through sexual intercourse remain the central acts that bring the marital relationship into existence.
- *Marriage is a covenant because it is a lifetime commitment.* Marriage is treated in the Old Testament as a binding commitment that can be broken only for just cause. This message is reinforced and strengthened in the New Testament. If the promise is not a lifetime promise, it is not a covenant and it is not marriage.
- *Marriage is a covenant because God is the witness and guarantor of its promises.* This concept makes the most sense where the couple explicitly embraces God's role as witness and guarantor. But it can also be argued from Jesus' teaching about marriage ("What God has joined together, let man not separate" [Matt. 19:6]) and our overall approach to the nature of covenant that God is the witness to every couple's marriage vows and ultimately the one who empowers any couple that manages to keep those vows for a lifetime. In this sense, marriage is both an instrument and a sign of God's relationship with the world and especially with his church, as Paul suggested.

- *Marriage is a covenant because there are dire consequences for breaking its terms and great rewards for keeping them.* This is not only the case in the divine-human relationship but at the human level as well, as we have seen throughout this book. The blessings and curses of marital success and failure are visible all around us. In this sense, the blessings and curses are built into marriage and do not require an intervening act of divine judgment.

Covenant and Marriage Today

A good wedding service will be awash in covenant language, regardless of who is getting married. Listeners may find the words romantic. In light of the biblical witness we have just reviewed, we see that covenant language is far from romantic.

To speak of covenant at a wedding today is to acknowledge unattractive truths about the bride and groom—and everyone else in the room. It is to say that you can dress up this man and woman in the nicest clothes but underneath it all they are faithless sinners. There is very little that is attractive about us when the darker inclinations of our hearts are considered.

To speak of covenant is also to be terribly unromantic about marital love. This man and woman may be desperately in love—today. But even today their thoughts can turn to fantasies for someone else. Tomorrow, and a thousand tomorrows later, their bonds will be tested. To speak of covenant is to acknowledge that their love will be tried by fire—and to bind this couple to the promises they make today regardless of the screaming inclinations of their hearts on some future tomorrow. As Mike Mason has put it, "In a very real way it is the vow which keeps the man rather than vice versa."[21]

Covenant functions as the structural principle of marriage because it takes faithless people and forces them to keep faith. Covenant says: I will be sexually faithful even when my needs for sex are frustrated in my marriage. I will be emotionally and sexually faithful even when my companionship needs are frustrated. I will be faithful in my parental responsibilities even when I am bone-weary of both you and the children. I will be faithful in my communication and forgiveness even when I never want to speak to you again because you have wounded me deeply. I will be faithful in sharing the work responsibilities of family life even when I can barely put one foot in front of the other. I will be faithful in sharing a home and a bed with you even when I want to flee.

Ministers need to emphasize the *particular* covenant promises that couples make when they get married. As a minister myself, I walk through the language in the vows carefully with every couple. Do you promise to live together, love, comfort, honor, keep, and cherish each other, forsaking all others, in good times and bad, until you die? I emphasize that marriage is the public exchange of sacred promises that each partner is duty bound to keep until death. I say, "Just as you shouldn't sign a contract without reading the fine print, you shouldn't say the vows without considering in your soul the nature of the covenant promises you are making."

Historian Edmund Morgan showed how the covenantal understanding of marriage functioned effectively in Puritan New England to communicate concretely what was expected of both husband and wife. Marriage was viewed as involving the obligation to meet a fundamental set of duties. Men were required to provide for their wives financially and to offer gentle governance of their families. Women were to offer sound and frugal household management and to submit to their husbands. These gender-specific expectations were complemented by obligations incumbent on both. Both husband and wife were charged to be faithful Christians, to attend to parental responsibilities, to pay the conjugal debt (sex), to live together under one roof, to remain sexually faithful, and to do all that they could to live in peace with each other. Both were barred from striking each other or speaking harshly, and both were obligated to be kind, loving, tender, and of good temperament. Divorces were granted in rare cases when core covenantal duties were flagrantly and irreparably breached.[22]

Covenant is not all vinegar and sandpaper. The striking thing about marriage as a covenant is that it is, like every other divinely given structure, for our good.

Outside of the sturdy protective sheath provided by covenant, there is no safe context for the pursuit of the creational needs that are met in marriage. We want and need companionship, sexual intimacy, love, and family partnership. These are the benefits that marriage was designed to provide for us. But they cannot be reliably sought—let alone achieved—outside of a context of covenantal fidelity and permanence.

Our wiring as needy creatures comes first conceptually, but under conditions of sin the mandate to make covenant relationships comes first practically. If I am involved in a trustworthy covenantal marital bond with another, I can relax enough to both give and receive love. I can try and fail and try again to develop communication and sexual skills. Our mutual confidence in the permanence and exclusivity of our bond allows us to give ourselves away, and only as we give ourselves away can we maximize our progress toward human intimacy as God intended it.

One of the most corrosive effects of our culture of divorce is a vicious cycle involving the deterioration of covenant sturdiness. I see the phenomenon regularly in counseling relationships, and it was all too apparent in the interviews with children of divorce. Having been burned once by marriage, but still pursuing those God-given creational needs, a couple tries again in a remarriage. However, they are often less able to create a binding, lasting, and exclusive covenant the second time around, in part because they were so shattered by the failure of their first marriage.

They hesitate to give their hearts away because they are not sure that the investment is worth the risk—not sure, that is, that the covenant will hold. But precisely because they are unsure, they are less successful in achieving the goods of marriage. Thus the marriage never reaches a high level of satisfaction. Then one or both are inevitably tempted to betray or to end the tottering marriage covenant. Having done so before, it is easier to do it a second time. If the second marriage does end in divorce, and the individuals then pursue third marriages, the cycle is all the more likely to continue. This is why failure rates for each successive remarriage tend to increase.

For these reasons, I am persuaded that under conditions of sin, covenant making is just as natural or wired an aspect of marriage as the fulfillment of creational needs. Theologically it goes like this: because we are creatures with certain needs, we *seek* in marriage certain goods; because we are fallen creatures, we *need* covenants to bind us and keep us in our marriages.

The collapse of older moral certainties included a questioning of the concept of marital covenant. It became seen as archaic to make lifetime promises to anyone about anything. Marriage was—and still is—viewed by many as a purely voluntary relationship to be entered or exited freely, "as long as we both shall love."

The paradox is that such freedom is itself a kind of slavery. It allows the tyranny of the transient dissatisfaction to efface all commitments. The quest for true and unforced love—the "pure relationship"—led only to weaker and weaker marriages and finally to the near collapse of the institution of marriage, as if marriage itself were responsible for this noncovenantal bastardization of it. The problem is not that a binding marital covenant is a tyranny but that nonbinding marital contracts undercut the very nature of marriage itself.

Covenant Obligations to Children

Recall from chapter 3 the disastrous impact of divorce on children. The concept of covenant may be extended a bit here to help us understand at a theological and moral level what is going on with children of divorce—and help reinforce the centrality of covenant obligations in marriage.

Some scholars studying the concept of covenant today have claimed that *some covenantal responsibilities are not explicit but instead intrinsic to certain roles and relationships*. Even if I have never bound myself by sacred promises to someone, in certain roles the fulfilling of particular obligations is incumbent upon me anyway. These obligations are sufficiently serious as to be labeled covenantal, even if they lack the explicitness (and certain other elements) of covenant as biblically understood.[23]

When I was first drafting this chapter, my eleven-year-old son sustained a shoulder injury in baseball, and we had to take him to the local emergency room late at night. Many bioethicists have argued that doctors and nurses carry implicit covenantal responsibilities to their patients even if these responsibilities are never made explicit. For example, any health care provider is required to provide competent care. Hospital administrators are required to provide such care in a timely manner so as to reduce pain and suffering. Medical personnel are all required to obtain informed consent from patients or their guardians. My health insurer is required to provide the care promised under our health coverage. It is not just that these actors in the health care system are legally or contractually bound to offer these services. More deeply, all who interact with sick and hurt patients are *covenantally* bound to treat them with respect, care, and dignity. This covenantal responsibility is sensed intuitively both by the patient and by the morally sensitive health care provider. Any ethics codes that codify this relationship are ratifying something that already exists.

Palmer Robertson makes an argument about the biblical concept of covenant that supports this theme in a striking way, and in it he circles back to the question of the distinction, if any, between creation and covenant.[24] He notes that Hosea 6:7 reads: "Like Adam, they have broken the covenant." (The Hebrew translated "like Adam" is *ha-adam*, which could be translated "like men" or "like people." It is also possible that this is a geographical reference: "at Adam.") If this *is* a reference to a covenant with Adam, it can only have been an implicit covenant. If so, Hosea depicts Adam as breaking covenant with God due to his unfaithfulness and despite the lack of any formal covenant agreement. Likewise, Gordon Hugenberger argues that Malachi understood the relationship between Adam and Eve to have been a covenantal relationship despite the lack of any explicit declaration to that effect.[25] This would lend credence to the idea that we can incur covenant obligations even if we do not sign formal covenant agreements. It would also draw the connection between creation and covenant even more tightly together.

When a man and woman bring a child into the world, they incur a host of new covenantal obligations. These obligations are simultaneously to each other and to the children for whom they are now responsible. The marriage covenant expands, one might say, just like the household must, to make room for the new life entrusted to it by God. By God's creation design, parents are obligated to feed, clothe, clean, house, protect, teach, and love that child. Children don't enter the world with a "certificate of parental covenant" attached to their toes, but they may as well do so because those obligations are undeniable. They are recognized by the law. They are articulated in every human moral code. Critiquing parents who act as if they have no obligation to their children, Anna Quindlen put it this way:

> Having children changes everything. . . . The moment that little cord gets cut with those little scissors, two little people have been turned into role models instantly, whether they like it or not. Everything afterward is a process of compromise and even self-sacrifice, or ought to be.[26]

The staggering insight of research on children of divorce is that most children experience divorce as a kind of covenant violation in and of itself. By bringing me into the world as my parents, his little heart screams, "You are covenantally bound to stay together as my parents, especially while I am your dependent. The stability of my interior universe depends on your anchoring presence, *not just individually, but together*. Therefore, I perceive you as being obligated to maintain this presence in my life. If you do not do so, by your own choice, I feel that your covenant with me has been violated. You can do any number of things to mitigate the damage afterwards, but that is exactly what it is—damage control, only damage control."

Now, obviously, it is precisely this covenantal obligation to "stay together for the children" that has been rejected by millions of people in recent decades. It is at the heart of the tragic conflict of interest between divorcing parents and their children that has fueled a considerable intergenerational alienation whose full extent is only now becoming clear. In the next chapter I rethink the issue of grounds for divorce in light of the creation and covenant approach. I do not say that divorce is never morally permissible, but I do say that morally thoughtful persons must take into full account their covenantal obligations to their children when making this decision and must recognize that their self-interest, power, and pain can easily block them from doing so. The moral context for the divorce decision is radically different when children are present because of the covenantal obligations intrinsic to the parent-child relationship. This can be denied as long as anyone wants to, but its truth is written on the hearts of a million freshly bereaved children of divorce a year.

By the way, lest I be misunderstood, I must hasten to add that this covenantal obligation to children cuts two ways. Under most circumstances, it raises the threshold for divorce. I am obligated to remain faithful to my marriage covenant at even higher levels of dissatisfaction because of my covenant obligations to my children. But, likewise, if my marriage now threatens the health or survival of my children, separation and divorce may not just be permissible but even obligatory. Christian theories of the legitimate grounds for divorce have functioned as if children were invisible. Considering children's covenant rights—and parents' covenant obligations—reshapes the way we ought to think about divorce, not just marriage.

One of the striking features of Old Testament law is its attention to the powerless. God requires that the nation of Israel attend to the needs of the widow, the orphan, the alien, and the stranger (see Exod. 22:21–22; 23:9; Jer. 49:11; James 1:27; and countless other passages). To be included in this way in covenant community is to be treated as someone whose interests and needs matter. God welcomes you into the family, and so Israel must do so as well.

When my wife and I traveled to Europe a few years ago, we found it reassuring to be the bearers of American passports. This meant that if we got into trouble or needed help, representatives of the United States government had a covenantal obligation to assist us. By virtue of being American citizens, we were included within the covenant of national protection, even overseas.

Covenants protect the vulnerable. One reason for marriage covenants is because of the intrinsic vulnerability of any spouse in marriage. Covenant protects me from my spouse (at her worst) and her from me (at my worst). And covenant protects our children from us (at our worst). Marital love overflows into the birth of children, and children are automatically inscribed into the marital covenant. Any treatment of marriage as a covenant must account for the covenant rights of the children that a marriage produces.

Covenant Ripples

In chapter 4 I argued that God's design for marriage has social and not just personal dimensions. These extend beyond the children of a marriage to the broader social order.

Societies recognize the covenant ripples of the marriage relationship both in law and custom. Not long ago I signed a marriage license for a wedding that I performed. It was a legal document representing the state of Tennessee's interest in the marriage just initiated. An entire framework of laws and regulations has to do with the regulation of marriage and family life. In the final chapter, we will consider these laws in some depth.

For now the point is this: the marriage covenant between a man and a woman has a built-in social dimension. The promises that are being made are, at least implicitly, public promises. They are promises to many other people besides bride and groom.

In a Christian wedding the marrying couple is undertaking covenantal obligations to the faith community. These obligations begin with a promise to pursue the kind of marriage that conforms to that faith community's understanding of marriage. The couple is obligated to keep the promises they have made, not just for the sake of each other, but also for the sake of the church's integrity and discipline. (I will say more about this issue in chapter 9.)

In any wedding the marrying couple is also implicitly enmeshing themselves in covenantal obligations to the civic community. In keeping with the brute facts of marriage and family life as well as with God's design, they are promising to do marriage well so as to contribute to the common good rather than to be a drain on it.

Think of it: If the couple marries for life and raises their children well, the community never has to deal with that couple again other than to register births and deaths at the courthouse. But if the marriage fails, the community and its agencies will be needed. Mediation services, legal services, child custody settlements, restraining orders, police involvement, child protective services, juvenile court, and so on—all are mobilized to try to keep the alienated members of *one* family from killing each other. Likewise, at a national level, an epidemic of failed marriages has a corrosive effect on society as a whole, weakening marriage for everyone else.

Thus it is not unfair to say that marital covenant obligations extend like ripples on a lake to concentric circles of community. When a couple marries, they are undertaking covenant obligations to each other, to their future children, to their extended families, to their churches, to their local and national communities, and to God the Creator.

The Covenant Hammock

Imagine a hammock—one of those sturdy woven things, suitable for lying around on a sleepy summer afternoon.

Picture yourself building this hammock, weaving its strands together over a long period of time. At first the hammock is skimpy. It takes a while to weave together enough strands for you to feel comfortable lying down in it. But after awhile this hammock has multiple strands of increasing toughness and durability. When it's completed, not only you but your spouse and even your little kids can all rest in it together.

Covenant breaking is like one partner—or sometimes both—taking a knife to these hammock strands and slicing them, one at a time. Little acts of covenant infidelity—flirtations, small cruelties—weaken the hammock but do not destroy it. It sways a bit in the wind but hangs together. Perhaps everyone in the hammock is aware that it is not quite as sturdy as before, but still it survives.

Large acts of covenant infidelity, however, can slice the hammock out from under you altogether. Physical abuse, adultery, abandonment—any of these can cut the hammock to shreds. When it falls, even the one who did the decisive slicing falls to the ground along with everyone else, though perhaps he is less bruised because he has been preparing for the hammock's collapse. But everyone else in the hammock tumbles to the ground in great pain. Some may never recover. If they do, it becomes very difficult for any of them to consider reweaving a new hammock for fear that it too will fall apart.

Covenant helps us see that divorce is far worse than the death of a spouse. In divorce, someone takes a knife to the hammock and everyone falls down. In death, one spouse is removed from the hammock but no one cuts the hammock down. The marriage covenant is woven together over time and can become strong enough for a whole lot of people to hang in securely. Yet it can be sliced apart in an instant.

Sometimes, though, that hammock can begin to feel like a noose. What shall we do then? This opens the way to the neglected issue of suffering in marriage. We turn to this pivotal issue in the next chapter.

7

Suffering in Marriage (and Divorce)

One is the loneliest number that you'll ever do.
Two can be as bad as one; it's the loneliest number since the number one.

—From "One," Three Dog Night

Marriage was designed by God in creation to meet certain fundamental needs of the human being. When those needs are met, we flourish. Covenant is the structural principle of marriage, holding weak and fickle human beings to the promises they have made. When the marriage covenant is sturdy, it provides a stable and enduring context for the pursuit of the creational blessings of companionship, sex, and family partnership. Strong skill and virtue development in meeting creation-related needs and fidelity to covenant promises can lead to joyful marital partnerships. Such relationships reach near the pinnacle of what God created humans to be.

But as we all know, the story does not always go this way. In fact, it seems that it does not *often* go this way. Marriage becomes not a context of joy but of misery. A husband or wife wakes up each morning with heaviness of heart, saddened by the perception that the marriage is not working, perhaps even terrified by the oppression they experience. They are suffering. In some marriages, suffering is a daily and enduring reality. In almost all marriages, there are episodes or seasons of suffering.

Nobody tells the engaged or newly married couple to expect that marriage will bring suffering. Instead, the Love Incorporated books offer 1001 ways to achieve marital bliss. This leaves couples poorly prepared for the suffering that will almost inevitably come. And so, when suffering hits, the couple is bewildered. If the suffering lasts for very long or feels very intense, they may be tempted to abandon the marriage to relieve their pain. But abandoning a marriage brings its own form of suffering and creates new suffering. Yet is such abandonment in every case wrong?

Experiences in ministry and personal life persuade me that this question—how to understand and deal with suffering—may be the most significant issue to be considered in thinking about marriage today.

The Phenomenon of Suffering

We human beings are vulnerable creatures. We are a composite creation, social creatures who in our persons are an interwoven mix of body and spirit. Cut our bodies and our bodies bleed. Cut our spirits and our spirits bleed.

Pain comes to *either* body or spirit or, more often, to *both* body and spirit. Physical pain is the sensation of strong discomfort in some part of the body, transmitted from the affected nerve cells through the nervous system to the brain. Physical pain can be either acute or chronic. Acute pain is severe but generally brief. Chronic pain may be less intense but lasts longer.

Spiritual pain (sometimes called psychological or mental pain) is the sensation of strong discomfort in some part of the human spirit (the mind, heart, or emotions). Terms like distress, anguish, sorrow, misery, and grief are used to describe this kind of pain. Spiritual pain can also be either acute or chronic. Because the person is a body-spirit unity, physical pain can and often does transmute into spiritual pain, and spiritual pain is often experienced as physical pain. The Bible often links spiritual pain with pain in specific parts of the body, including the kidneys (Job 16:13; Ps. 73:21; Lam. 3:13), stomach/bowels (Job 30:27; Isa. 16:11; Lam. 1:20), and bones (Pss. 31:10–11; 42:10–11; Isa. 38:13; Jer. 23:9). Both biblical and popular uses of the term *heart* communicate this body-spirit connection powerfully (1 Sam. 1:8; Ps. 38:9, 11; Jer. 4:19; 8:18; Lam. 1:20, 22). Even today we describe people as heartbroken or heartsick or full of heartache. In biblical terms, the heart is the center of both physical and spiritual life (Matt. 12:34; 15:18–19). Because the person is "centered" there, all pleasures and pains run through the heart.

Suffering can be distinguished from pain by defining it as *the subjective human experience of pain*. It is the interaction of the individual with the particular type of physical or spiritual pain that a person is facing. Suffering is pain as experienced and interpreted by human beings in every aspect of their personhood.

Pain, especially physical pain, has a certain objective dimension. If anyone is cut deeply with a knife, they will feel pain that will be transmitted through the nervous system to their brain. Such pain is part of being human or, really, part of being any sentient creature; it goes with the territory.

However, as medical professionals long have noticed, the same level of physical pain can be experienced differently by different people. Nurses talk about some patients having a high pain tolerance, which means that they can experience more physical pain than the average person without experiencing it as suffering. Likewise, the patient with a low pain tolerance has the opposite experience. Thus health care providers orient their patient care not to the pain they think this particular malady *should* cause but to the suffering that the patient himself reports experiencing at the time.

All of this is prelude to saying the following: *the marital relationship is sometimes the source of pain*. It can be the source of physical pain, as in abuse and marital violence. It is a source of spiritual pain, as in anguish and distress of heart. This pain is experienced as marital suffering and, if severe enough, as both physical and spiritual suffering. Marital suffering, like any kind of suffering, can be either acute or chronic.

Simone Weil made the striking observation that besides the physical element of suffering, and what she called the psychological element of suffering, there is a third element: the social.[1] This is the experience of social degradation, ostracism, abandonment, or exclusion from community. German theologian Dorothee Soelle, reflecting on these themes, notes that most biblical accounts of suffering involve a confluence of all three themes. The psalmist laments the coming of illness into his life, bringing great pain (e.g., Psalms 22; 73; 81; 116). He feels a growing sense of psychological or spiritual suffering. And he feels abandoned by friends and intimates, excluded from the community of which he is a part.[2] For Weil, *affliction* is the best term to use for the combination of these three dimensions of human suffering. Marital suffering takes this potent form at times: extreme spiritual anguish, physical distress, and social isolation.

Because suffering is a subjective and personal experience, it is often the case that the spouses do not experience the exact same level or type of suffering, even though they are enduring the same marriage. Harsh words may hurt one spouse more than the other. Chronic lack of communication, or lack of sexual intimacy, or lack of spiritual partnership, could be experienced as deeply painful by one spouse and not by the other. An act of sexual infidelity or violence may be experienced as creating an unbearable suffering, or it may not, depending on the way individual spouses interpret and react to these particular painful events.

This reminds us that the suffering evoked by spiritual pain is subjective and profoundly affected by social factors. Imagine a culture in which extramarital sex is a routine and expected behavior, as in some contexts it has been. The discovery that one's spouse had an extramarital sexual relationship would evoke far less suffering than if the same event occurred in our own society. Suffering has a social dimension. The early medieval philosopher Boethius said, "Nothing is miserable unless you think it so." Where we learn to "think it so" is in society.

Contemporary Western societies are particularly averse to pain. We have developed the most advanced painkilling drugs in human history, and we use them constantly. We are, in Elizabeth Wurtzel's famous phrase, the "Prozac Nation." Some push for legalized euthanasia because of the exaggerated fear that even the best painkillers will be insufficient at the end of life. It is not too pessimistic to say that we are by now a soft people. The generation that survived the Depression and triumphed over the Nazis gave birth to children and grandchildren who often think they need narcotics or antidepressants to get through the day. In such a society, our pain tolerance is low indeed.

Less dramatically, the experience of marital suffering is linked to marital expectations or desires.[3] Short of objective physical or emotional violence, we suffer in marriage when the experience we are having falls short of our expectations. The question that must be asked is this: what kinds of expectations of marriage are appropriate to the covenant promises actually exchanged? Excessive desires set the spouses up for the perception of suffering in situations that would not have been perceived this way in earlier eras. This is an issue that keeps surfacing in this book and that will be revisited in this chapter.

One final observation is needed before moving on. As any physician or psychiatrist could tell us, the suffering person seeks relief. Whether the pain is physical, spiritual, or both, when we suffer, we want it to end as soon as possible. If the pain is bad enough, we will consider any path that can bring relief. If the suffering experienced in marriage is bad enough, people will seek relief as well. This is part of what it means to be a sentient creature, especially a human. It also speaks to the compelling nature of the needs we seek to meet in marriage. The mistake many people make, however, is in concluding that divorce is the best way to bring suffering to an end—when it may not be the best way, and it may not bring suffering to an end at all.

Sources of Suffering in Marriage

When Jesus taught that divorce is to be a rare exception and that illicit remarriages are adulterous, his disciples said, "If this is the situation between a husband and a wife, it is better not to marry" (Matt. 19:10)—and Jesus never disagreed. He only responded with a description of the various ways that people become eunuchs. When Paul reflected on marriage, he wrote: "Those who marry will face many troubles in this life, and I want to spare you this" (1 Cor. 7:28b). These are not especially romantic declarations about marriage.

People need to be taught, as they were in more sober times, that a measure of suffering is an inevitable feature of marriage. Swept away by the candlelight-and-roses vision of marriage promoted by every bride magazine on the newsstand, we have misplaced this homely truth. Even Christians, whose doctrine of sin ought to help us know better, have forgotten to teach that marriage will not just fail to prevent suffering but actually bring suffering our way. "Not only does marriage fail to mitigate the struggles of life, . . . it actually deepens them, rendering them even more poignant, because more personal."[4]

Suffering can enter a marriage through several channels. I break down these sources of suffering into two main categories: causes that are *external* to the marriage and those that are *internal*.

The traditional wedding vows reflect the awareness that every marriage is threatened by external enemies. Two types of enemies are named in the vows: poverty and illness. When the couple says "for richer for poorer, in sickness and in health," they are promising to remain loyal to their marriage covenant regardless of the trials created by poverty or illness. These particular concerns reflect the conditions of an earlier, more agrarian era. The worst thing to happen to the medieval Farmer Gachet's family was either a bad crop (threatening starvation) or illness (threatening loss of help in family labor and loss of life).

Unemployment and financial pressures remain a major source of difficulty in marriage even today. Illness or incapacitation of a spouse or child likewise creates one of the major forms of marital suffering. Most readers will know of a marriage that did not prove capable of enduring such afflictions.

Numerous other factors extraneous to the marriage itself can create marital suffering. These can include illness or bereavement in the family or extended family. Job stresses that threaten to grind up the human spirit of one of the spouses are a major issue. A move demanded by school or work can be quite stressful. This list could be extended. Suffice it to say that most marriages will face external sources of suffering at one time or another.

But improved economic and physical conditions in contemporary society mean that the *internal* sources of marital suffering are by now more significant. This is not a coincidence. Little irritations in the marital relationship don't matter when the Nazis might land on Long Island any day, or when we're not sure where the next meal is coming from. Lacking such pressures and fears, we have the tragic liberty to turn on each other or self-destruct.

Internal sources of suffering in marriage come in three primary forms. They may have to do with my partner, with me, or with the dynamics of our relationship.

Many marriages fail because of the moral, psychological, or spiritual problems of just one of the spouses. It is extraordinarily tragic but all too common—a promising marriage between two people who love each other deeply is brought down, not by any external stress, but by the immoral or sick behavior of one of the partners.

A cousin of mine suffered the failure of her marriage due to her husband's unshakable addiction to child pornography. Another marriage was brought down by a cocaine habit. A family member married a man who stole from her and opened credit cards in her name without her consent, ultimately bankrupting her. Drugs, alcohol, pornography, and gambling are among the major addictions that cause marital suffering and are leading causes of divorce.

Psychological maladies of other types cause great suffering. I once counseled with a couple whose marriage was threatened by one partner's chronic anxiety, anger, and simple inability to live peaceably. Here was a man whose wife, while not perfect, was more than adequate. However, quite tragically, he was unable to be happy; he could not receive the joyful partnership that was possible. He was not capable of living in peace with anyone, beginning with himself.

Another friend was heading toward marriage. However, her boyfriend lost his job and seemed not particularly energetic in pursuing another one. Month stretched into month, and it became clear that he was not so much lazy as incapable of functioning at a level required for minimal success in a competitive society. In this case, marriage was averted, but if this couple had been married, his inability to function fully would have created considerable suffering that might have destroyed their marriage.

It is often falsely claimed that "it takes two" to bring down a marriage. It is truer to say that it takes two functional and sound people to create the possibility of marital success. All it takes is one addicted or mentally ill or poorly functioning or morally bankrupt person to make marriage a living hell. That person might be my partner or it might just be me.

The other internal source of marital suffering can be found in the inner workings of the marriage itself. Two morally and psychologically sound people can run into trouble in managing the marital relationship, which is its own entity with its own dynamics.

One way to organize our thinking about this kind of suffering is to relate it back to the creation goods and covenant structure of marriage with which we have been working.

Suffering comes in marriage when aspects of companionship, sex, or family partnership fall far enough short of expectations as to create the experience of pain. Perhaps there is a failure to share adequately in the labor of running a household or meeting its expenses. Maybe there is a lack of time spent together in leisure. Perhaps the sexual relationship lacks passion or mutual satisfaction. The friendship dimension of marriage may have eroded. Or maybe chronic conflicts arise over how the children should be disciplined or educated. Marriage was created to meet basic human needs in these areas, and such failures will elicit suffering.

Violations of the meaning of the marriage covenant itself will also create suffering. Any crossing of boundary lines related to sexual fidelity will be painful, even if it does not involve the act of adultery. Threats of walking out or loose talk of divorce can challenge the covenant promise of permanence. Failure to care compassionately for a spouse in time of illness or bereavement or to work together in partnership during times of extra financial stress can also cause great suffering. Mistreatment of children by one spouse can threaten the marital covenant itself. Most profoundly, failure to create an overall environment of love, honor, and respect undermines the relational spirit that brings the letter of the marital covenant to life.

The success of any marriage depends on meeting the creation-based needs of the spouse in at least a minimally satisfactory fashion and on maintaining faithfulness to the marriage covenant. These basics of marriage are not merely cultural but “natural,” that is, they relate to our humanity as created yet fallen beings. We are not talking here about the relational possibilities that marriage holds when every aspect of creation and covenant is maximally fulfilled. That’s the ceiling. Here we are talking about the floor. If the basic minimum is not met, either or both spouses will suffer—and will probably look for some way to find relief.

What Shall We Do with Our Suffering?

Many Christians have joined their societal compatriots in seeking relief from suffering through divorce. Sometimes they offer little evidence that they have considered what the Bible really says about suffering itself. This is a great tragedy. It has led to the unnecessary destruction of many marriages and the collapse of Christian credibility on this issue.

The Bible is an infinitely realistic book. Coursing through its pages are dozens of references to suffering: its various types and sources, its costs, its meanings, its possibilities, and how a faithful people of God are to interpret and respond to it. Few themes receive more attention in Scripture. Let's linger over the biblical witness and see if it can speak helpfully to seasons of suffering in marriage—without in any way underwriting victimization or oppression in marriage and family life.

In God's good and perfect creation before the fall, there was no suffering. But human disobedience introduced suffering into God's good world. Sin and suffering have been linked from their very beginning.

In the Genesis account, sin introduces suffering into creation as a form of divine punishment. The serpent is punished with a lifetime of crawling, eating dust, and being feared and hated by human beings (Gen. 3:14–15). The woman is punished with great pain in childbearing and subordination to her husband (Gen. 3:16). The man is punished with uncooperative soil and arduous labor (Gen. 3:17–19). All are punished with mortality (Gen. 3:19). Adam and Eve are punished with exile from the garden, symbolizing their broken relationship with God (Gen. 3:21–24).

So in biblical terms there is an inextricable connection between suffering and sin. Sin causes suffering; suffering exists because of sin; if there had been no sin, there would be no suffering. Sin often brings judgment that causes suffering (Num. 14:33; Lam. 1:12). And yet, as Pope John Paul II has noted, "It is not true that all suffering is a consequence of a fault and has the nature of a punishment."[5]

A proper biblical understanding of sin identifies it, not just with particular acts or our propensity to do wrong, but with a broader degradation of the human condition. Sin is not just violation of God's moral order but also the disordered state of the human heart, human relationships, and human society. This disorder is the context in which we all live. It affects not just human beings but the entire creation, which also has become disordered and fallen into corruption as a consequence of human wrongdoing. As Paul put it, "The creation itself will be liberated from its bondage to decay and brought into the glorious freedom of the children of God. We know that the whole creation has been groaning as in the pains of childbirth right up to the present time" (Rom. 8:21–22).

With the entire human and global order in such spiritual travail, it is inevitable that each particular human being, and the human family as a whole, will experience suffering. Sometimes this suffering will be linked to particular sinful acts, our own or someone else's; other times it is impossible and inappropriate to draw such a connection (see John 9).[6]

Whenever we are tempted to forget this point, we would do well to return to the book of Job, for Job is the story of an innocent man's suffering. Afflicted with the loss of his family, all his animals and property, and finally his health, Job protests bitterly to God at the injustice of his fate. For thirty chapters, his three friends try to help Job make sense of his suffering by attributing it to some wrong that Job has done. Appropriately, Job denies this. He has done nothing wrong, but suffering has come upon him anyway. In misery, he seeks an explanation from God—as most of us do when suffering comes.

God finally makes his appearance in chapters 38–41. He never gives Job an explanation of his suffering; and yet the point of the passage is not so much what God says but that he responds at all. God recounts for Job the glories and complexities of the universe that he has made and challenges Job's right to "correct" him (40:2). Job ends his questioning with a kind of submissive gratitude for God appearing to him at all: "My ears had heard of you but now my eyes have seen you. Therefore I despise myself and repent in dust and ashes" (42:5–6).

God has shown up and has been with Job in his suffering. After days of questioning and challenging God, it is God's presence that finally satisfies his need, or at least ends his struggle by overwhelming him with the view from God's perspective.[7] The epilogue, in which Job's family and properties are restored, is not the heart of the story. God's response to Job's innocent suffering is, not so much to make all things right again, but simply to be present to Job in his despair.

This is the next main strand of the biblical witness about human suffering: *God is present to and with his suffering people*. God hears the cries of the afflicted. At times, though not always, God in his grace acts to rescue those who suffer, as in the exodus (Exod. 3:7) or the healing acts of Jesus toward the suffering (Matt. 4:24; 8:6; 15:22; 17:15). At other times God's activity is limited to comforting his afflicted ones (2 Cor. 1:3). God is present with sufferers as they suffer, offering care and love. This is not deliverance from the situation of suffering but merciful divine presence in the midst of suffering. Scripture is honest in recording times when God's presence seems very elusive, when God's comfort is not found. And yet believers are called to turn to God and ask for his presence in times of suffering, with the promise that God is faithful, just, and loving.

The New Testament witness about Jesus teaches that part of his mission was to suffer for the sake of the world: "From that time on Jesus began to explain to his disciples that he must go to Jerusalem and suffer many things at the hands of the elders, chief priests, and teachers of the law, and that he must be killed and on the third day be raised to life" (Matt. 16:21; cf. Mark 9:12; Luke 24:26). That Jesus must suffer to fulfill his mission was a part of the apostolic proclamation (Acts 3:18; 17:3; 26:23).

The primary Old Testament text that informed this concept was Isaiah 52:13–53:12, the famous "suffering servant" passage. Here the servant is "despised and rejected by men, a man of sorrows, and familiar with suffering" (53:3). This suffering is not an end in itself, however, but is undertaken for the sake of redemption. By enduring suffering without resistance as an innocent for the sins and wrongs of others, the suffering servant has won salvation for his people. "For he bore the sin of many, and made intercession for the transgressors" (53:12). Jesus, the Son of God, takes human suffering upon himself and therefore into the very heart of the Deity.

New Testament writers were transfixed by the vision of Jesus as the suffering servant, whose torture and death atoned vicariously for the sins of the world and whose glorious resurrection vindicated his identity as God's Son and the world's Savior. Identifying deeply with him, they promoted to their readers and faith communities a cruciform (cross-shaped) vision of discipleship in which Christians would follow the path of their master. They would, if necessary, suffer for the cause for which Jesus suffered and for the name of Jesus, even rejoicing and counting themselves blessed to have the privilege of doing so (Acts 5:41; Phil. 1:29; 1 Peter 4:13).

As suffering came amid various persecutions, the early Christians further developed a profound practical theology of what might be called the *discipleship value* of suffering. Pope John Paul II finds in the entire biblical witness, in fact, the same theme: suffering "creates the possibility of rebuilding goodness in the subject who suffers."[8] Because suffering hurts, we naturally flee from it, but New Testament writers teach that it is precisely through suffering that growth in discipleship occurs.

This is articulated in a variety of ways. Paul says that in suffering we experience God's comfort, which we can then share with others who also suffer. As we plunge into levels of suffering we never could have imagined and find God's comfort and presence there, we grow profoundly in patient endurance and dependent trust in God (2 Cor 1:3–11). Suffering also produces virtues such as perseverance, character, and hope (Rom. 5:3), which cannot be produced under conditions of comfort and ease.

The entire first epistle of Peter is a meditation on suffering for Christ. Written to Christians under severe persecution, this letter reflects deeply on the trials these communities in Asia Minor were experiencing and the meaning that could be drawn from them. Peter finds in trials an occasion for purification. Like a refiner's fire, trials test the believer's faith, showing its real quality and at the same time strengthening and toughening it (cf. 1:7).

Peter finds in suffering a morally purging power. "He who has suffered in his body is done with sin" (4:1b). The persecutor's lash, in a sense, brings people to their senses, leading them to put sin behind them with ever more decisiveness and to die to the world and its enticements (4:2–6). They now live for God rather than themselves. It is interesting that the writer of Hebrews claims that "the author of their salvation," Christ himself, was "made perfect through suffering" (Heb. 2:10).

Rather than succumbing to instincts for violence or retaliation, unjustly persecuted Christians are called to identify all the more closely with Jesus, who suffered without retaliation and died vicariously in our place (1 Peter 2:20–25). Out of gratitude to him, in obedience to his command, and in imitation of his pattern, Christians are called to "follow in his steps" (2:21), patiently enduring all persecution and awaiting a future hope that no one can ever take away because believers are "shielded by God's power" (1:5). Suffering creates a deep sense of solidarity and connection between the believer and Jesus, as many Christians have attested through the centuries.[9]

Peter, like other New Testament writers, is entranced by the glory that is coming when God will bring about his ultimate triumph in Jesus Christ. That inheritance awaits those who persevere, who don't give up or give in, who cling to the suffering Savior even as they themselves suffer. An inheritance is coming that can never "perish, spoil, or fade" (1:4). The "Chief Shepherd" will appear, and we will receive a "crown of glory" that can never fade (5:4).

At the heart of this vision of suffering is hopeful trust in a faithful God. The psalmist writes, "My comfort in my suffering is this; your promise preserves my life" (Ps. 119:50). Peter calls his readers to trust the one who "entrusted himself to him who judges justly" (1 Peter 2:23). God will triumph. His enemies will be defeated and his promises will be fulfilled (2 Thess. 1:5). Current trials can be endured because God is trustworthy and ultimately will do what he has promised, just as he has done in the past.[10] Don't be among those who collapse under persecution and ultimately must be counted among the faithless who disown Christ (2 Tim. 2:12–13). Instead, "Be faithful, even to the point of death, and I will give you the crown of life" (Rev. 2:10).

When suffering comes in marriage, the person seeking to be formed by the biblical witness has rich resources for redeeming his or her suffering or at least for making sense of it. These convictions do not resolve all issues related to particular decisions Christians must make, but they do help set the context in which they should be considered, as follows:

Suffering is inescapable in a sinful world. Therefore, I will not imagine the possibility of creating a life for myself in which there will be no suffering. I will be realistic about the boundaries the human condition sets on all human aspirations. I will consider the suffering faced in my current situation over against the suffering I would face in realistic alternative situations.

God is present to his suffering people. Therefore, I will cry out to him in my times of frustration, sadness, and despair. I will not attempt to endure my suffering apart from the presence of God. With confidence, I will turn to God and draw comfort from his presence. I will not expect to get all my questions answered or even to be delivered from all my suffering, but I will be comforted by his presence.

Jesus was a Savior whose innocent suffering brought redemption to the world. Therefore, I will be alert to the redemptive possibilities of the suffering I am now experiencing. Perhaps I can be an example to my children of patient endurance in times of trial and thus help build character in them that will strengthen them for their future marriages. Perhaps my steadfast love amid suffering will have a transforming impact on my spouse or can serve as a good example to friends who know the situation. This does not mean I will endure mistreatment indefinitely. But I will assess the situation with Jesus' example in mind.

Suffering has discipleship value for the follower of Christ. Therefore, I will look for ways in which my current suffering can deepen my faithfulness to him and enable me to grow both spiritually and morally. My focus will shift from whether I am happy, as Gary Thomas has written, to how this situation can help me become more holy.[11]

I will seek to grow in perseverance, patient endurance, and dependent trust in God. I will place my hope ever more firmly in the God who is trustworthy and draw closer to the Savior who suffered in my place. I will seek to experience this season of life as a time of intensive moral purging and growth and will be open to the changes this will bring. I will not respond with retaliation, violence, or hatred but follow Jesus by seeking reconciliation and enduring steadfastly. I will fix my eyes on the hope of eternal glory, reminding myself that my ultimate hope is not found in earthly pleasures, even marriage, as important a relationship as that is. I will cling to my marital covenant and live out its obligations rather than allowing my behavior to collapse in this time of suffering. I will do so, not just or even primarily because of my care for my spouse, but because I want to be faithful to the God who has been faithful to me.

Notice the extent to which a profound Christian hope is the key to making peace with current suffering. Vaclav Havel, the Czech writer and politician, once wrote, "Hope is definitely not the same thing as optimism. It is not the conviction that something will turn out well, but the certainty that something makes sense, no matter how it turns out."[12] As long as husbands and wives suffering in marriage are able to retain that kind of hope, they can persevere.

Responses to Suffering in Marriage: Practical Options

This stance provides a way of approaching suffering in marriage that is critical for thinking about the choices faced in such times. Still, when suffering becomes acute or remains chronic, there are sometimes excruciating choices to be made. There are only so many options available to the person who finds that he is experiencing great suffering in marriage or the couple who agree together that their marriage is characterized by much suffering. And responses to marital suffering are closely tied to the particular source of that suffering. Here I want to reflect on both what people do and what Christians should do in response to marital suffering. This will lead to the question of when divorce might be morally legitimate.

External sources of suffering, such as job loss or illness, often come into a marriage through no fault of either spouse. These are the kinds of situations that call forth and test the covenant promises that have been made on the wedding day. The morally legitimate Christian response to such suffering is to fulfill our promises—to work together to meet the crisis as partners. The suffering may be acute or it may be chronic, but the couple has no moral option but to endure it for that season. Marriage involves being the kind of people who "keep [their] oath[s], even when it hurts" (Ps. 15:4).

I am reminded of the covenant fidelity and steadfast love shown by the Mary Bailey character in the classic movie *It's a Wonderful Life*. As a young girl Mary falls in love with George Bailey (played by the marvelous Jimmy Stewart) but waits patiently for his attentions while he dreams of travel, glory, and riches. They marry, but their long-planned honeymoon must be foregone, as Mary offers the honeymoon money to prevent the bankruptcy of the savings and loan that George is attempting to save during a bank run at the height of the depression. And in the dramatic climax of the film, Mary responds to George's emotional collapse under the pressure of possible arrest, imprisonment, and bankruptcy by rallying community support and standing loyally by her man.

Such steadfast covenant fidelity requires a kind of toughness, however, that is rare in our time. Many abandon their covenants under assault from external enemies and pressures, leaving their bereft covenant partner to pick up the pieces.

Suffering caused by the addictions, poor functioning, or moral weakness of one spouse can create an acute crisis in a marriage, as we have seen. Such personal problems tend to undermine fulfillment of the creation needs of the spouse and can threaten the marriage covenant. The primary form of response to this kind of suffering is to seek help for the spouse whose problems are threatening the marriage.

Help should take whatever form needed: spiritual care, accountability relationships, psychotherapy, addiction treatment. Success requires the willingness of the one with the problem to acknowledge the issue with a broken spirit and to turn for help. Covenant fidelity requires the aggrieved spouse to undertake every effort to get help for the partner and to bear with him or her during the process of change, even if many needs go unmet for a long season of life. This assumes, however, that the offending spouse seriously undertakes an effort to change.

Where suffering emerges due to dynamics of the marital relationship, many individuals or couples now give up far too quickly. Poor communication, sexual problems, differences in financial priorities, irritating personal habits, parenting disagreements, and so on are all issues that fall within the creation-need aspect of the relationship. They are almost always problems that can be addressed through skill and virtue development. Yet many marriages end for just such reasons.

When suffering happens because of a violation of the marriage covenant itself, the issue takes on an altogether different slant. Sexual infidelity, violence, and abandonment are in my view the three central examples of covenant violations in marriage. Infidelity violates the promise of sexual exclusivity. Abandonment violates the promise to live together, which is the presupposition of the marriage relationship. And violence violates the promise to love, honor, and cherish in the most fundamental manner imaginable. Violations of covenant obligations in relation to children, such as child abuse, are also germane to the keeping of the marriage covenant and could constitute grounds for ending it. If my spouse violates her covenant with our children, threatening their well-being, it is part of my covenant with these same children to act to protect them. Here the concept of covenant very much helps us understand why abuse and other significant mistreatment of children might be legitimate grounds for divorce.

When Is It Permissible to End a Marital Covenant?

The aggrieved and suffering spouse who is loyal to the marriage covenant will not lightly end a marriage under any circumstances. Many steadfast men and women have endured the acute suffering caused by episodes of infidelity, acts of violence, and desertion and worked hard for change and for reconciliation. In some cases, hearts and lives have been changed and marriages saved. This indeed is grace and mercy.

But still we must ask the question of whether, and when, it is morally permissible to end a marital covenant. The focus of this book is marriage rather than divorce. Far too much attention has been given to trying to establish the legitimate grounds for divorce—rather than attending to what God intends for marriage. We have come a long way in this book before tackling the question of when divorce might be morally permitted. But now we have reached the point in our discussion where the question can be addressed. I will offer a brief review of the biblical evidence and refer the reader to numerous studies that tackle the issue in detail.[13]

Divorce is never formally introduced in the Old Testament. It simply makes its appearance as an existing practice, most significantly in Deuteronomy 24:1–4. This text assumes the practice of divorce, describes it and its grounds in passing, and then offers a case law application related to remarriage. This text became foundational for the Jewish rabbinic tradition, which debated the grounds for divorce based on Deuteronomy 24:1a: "If a man marries a woman who becomes displeasing to him because he finds something indecent about her." Two poles of interpretation emerged: a conservative school limiting the grounds for divorce to "indecency," and a more liberal school permitting (a man to) divorce for nearly any reason based on the language of "becomes displeasing to him."

Jesus is recorded as teaching about marriage in two primary texts that parallel each other with subtle differences. These texts are Matthew 19:2–12 and Mark 10:2–12. Small, slightly varied fragments of the teaching recorded in these texts are found in Matthew 5:31–32 and Luke 16:18.

Let's take the Mark 10 passage as our base, working from that to compare with Matthew 19 where significant differences emerge. Mark 10:2–12 has Jesus teaching about marriage in the context of being questioned by the Pharisees about divorce. The narrator tells us that they questioned him about divorce to test him; their goal was to trap Jesus in his own words, rather than to gain knowledge about God's will. This must be kept in mind or we too will ask Jesus the wrong questions.

The Pharisees want to know whether it is "lawful" for a man to divorce his wife (Mark 10:2). It was lawful in Jewish society for a man to divorce his wife; in fact, it was quite common. The rabbis debated what were the lawful *grounds* for divorce, not whether divorce was permissible. It is this sense of the question that Matthew's version picks up (19:3).

They want to ask Jesus about the legalities of divorce. In Mark, Jesus responds in the way they might have expected, asking about the dictates of Jewish law by referencing the "command" of Moses. In response, they cite Deuteronomy 24:1.

Jesus then surprises his listeners by moving the discussion to the book of Genesis. He acknowledges that the permission to divorce is (implicitly) found in Deuteronomy 24:1, but that this was because their "hearts were hard." At the "beginning of creation God made them male and female" (Mark 10:6, quoting Gen. 1:27). Thus man and woman leave father and mother and cleave to each other. "The two will become one flesh" (Mark 10:8, quoting Gen. 2:24); "they are no longer two, but one." Therefore, "what God has joined together, let man not separate" (Mark 10:9).

Jesus reclaims marriage from the divorce lawyers. He demands that the discussion of God's will for marriage return to the original intent of the Creator. He locates marriage as an institution existing "from the beginning of creation" and describes the one flesh union that exists in marriage. He intensifies the "one-fleshness" of marriage by saying that the couple is "no longer two but one," making clear that one-flesh means more than occasional marital sexual union. Then, in what amounts to new teaching, he asserts that *God* has joined together each husband and wife and demands that man not separate what God has joined.

The creation origins and nature of marriage are thus reaffirmed. But so is a strong emphasis on the covenantal structure of marriage, especially the promise of permanence. This point is emphasized in the next section of the teaching, where Jesus declares that "anyone who divorces his wife and marries another woman commits adultery against her" (Mark 10:11), and that the same would hold true for the woman who divorces her husband. The Jewish listener would not have needed to be reminded that in Jewish law adultery was a crime officially punishable by execution.

It has been noticed that the Mark and Matthew texts diverge here. Matthew has no reference to the woman initiating divorce, perhaps because if women ever initiated divorce in first-century Palestinian Jewish life, it was very rare. There was no explicit provision for it in Old Testament law.

The other divergence is the famous exception clause in Matthew. Matthew's account modifies the apparent "no divorce, no remarriage" stance with an exception in cases of sexual immorality (NIV: "marital unfaithfulness"; Greek *porneia*). This exception clause, and the fact that it is found only in Matthew, has bedeviled and distracted Christian interpreters for centuries and remains a vexing interpretive problem today.

The main point that needs to be made about the entire passage, whether in Matthew or in Mark, is that Jesus responds to a question about the legality of divorce by pushing past it to reaffirm both the creation purposes of marriage and the covenant structure of marriage. His teaching about marriage itself is best interpreted as offering an authoritative endorsement of God's will as revealed in Scripture, with a measure of intensification and a decisive shift in focus away from how we might finagle exceptions. His teaching about remarriage is best interpreted as a forceful prophetic rejection of legally sanctioned adultery; that is, the abandonment of the "wife of one's youth" in order to be with another woman. It may be legal, but it's still adultery. It was true then, and it's true now. Malachi made the same point.

Paul's largest section on marriage and divorce is found in 1 Corinthians 7. Apparently responding to a comment from this troubled Christian community disparaging marriage (7:1), he affirms that (most) believers should be married (7:2). He grounds this declaration in the creation need for sex (7:3–5, 9, 36–38) and the fear of sexual immorality. He articulates his own preference for celibate singleness (7:6–7) but notes that people are gifted in different ways. This section offers a helpful affirmation of the creation purposes of marriage related to sexuality, though what has often been interpreted as a grudging spirit here has darkened the Christian vision of sex in damaging ways.

In dealing with the issue of divorce, Paul reaffirms an oral tradition of the teaching of Jesus that corresponds with the passages in Mark and Matthew. Believers are not supposed to divorce one another. If they separate, they should abstain from marrying someone else and instead be reconciled (7:10–11). Here Paul is reaffirming the covenant permanence of marriage, with the extra note emphasizing the central Christian focus on reconciliation.

Then Paul deals with a situation arising with some frequency in Corinth—the religiously mixed marriage. A Christian is unhappily married to an unbeliever. Should she initiate divorce, perhaps in order to remain pure of the taint of being joined with an unbeliever, even a worshiper of pagan gods?

Paul says no. The covenant of marriage is sufficiently binding, in the view of this rabbinically trained Jewish Christian, that even marriage to an unbeliever is not enough to justify ending it (7:10–14). Contrary to the decision for mass divorce of pagan partners mandated in the period of Ezra and Nehemiah, Paul has hope that the unbelievers (and their children) will be changed by the believers, not the other way around.

However, in a final twist, Paul does open the door to divorce (and, apparently, the morally justifiable prospect of remarriage) if the unbeliever "leaves" (7:15). In such cases, the believer is not "bound" to the marriage (7:15, 27–28). Though the believer cannot initiate a divorce, he or she may be forced to accept it as a fact if initiated by an uncooperative and hostile partner. Why? "God has called us to live in peace" (7:15) and "How do you know . . . whether you will save your [spouse]?" (7:15–16).

How shall we interpret these cryptic comments? Paul is doing three things here. First, he is acknowledging that peace in marriage has significance. This is a way of saying that the creation good of companionship matters, and that its opposite, constant conflict, is a dismal way to live. Second, in view of his earlier comments about marriage as a context for safe and sanctioned expression of the sexual drive, permanent separation without possibility of divorce or remarriage would also violate the creation good of sexual fulfillment (and open both people to the likelihood of sexual immorality). Finally, in noting that it is not always possible to win over a spouse to faith in Christ, Paul is recognizing that the covenant of marriage is deeply threatened by conflicting "religious" covenants on the part of the spouses. All three of these issues have surfaced in historic Christian treatments of divorce.

These texts have been relentlessly parsed for legalistic justification for and against divorce and remarriage for Christians. But that misses the point. Neither Jesus nor Paul wanted to emphasize when it might be permissible to divorce or remarry. Instead, they wanted to call believers to keep their marriage covenants and fulfill God's creation purposes in marriage.

Combing through the texts and the history of their interpretation leaves me convinced that the best summary of a moral standard related to divorce is this: the covenantal structure of marriage is so binding that *only a fundamental and irreparable breach of the marriage covenant* can morally justify divorce.

Jesus, at least in Matthew, notes that sexual infidelity in marriage is a sufficiently grave violation of covenant that divorce might be permissible. Paul adds another possibility—desertion by an unbelieving spouse. This text can be interpreted somewhat more broadly to encompass other covenant violations, and it has been read that way in Christian history. The church father John Chrysostom, for example, interpreted "desertion" in 1 Corinthians 7:15 to include situations in which an unbelieving spouse demands that a believer participate in pagan religious rituals or else part ways. In the same verse he interprets the reference to "living in peace" as speaking to the issue of violence: "If day by day he buffet thee and keep up combats on this account, it is better to separate."[14]

We have already seen that grave violation of the parental covenant in relation to a couple's children raises the serious possibility that covenant obligations to children may override covenant obligations to a covenant-breaking spouse. In short, it is impossible to offer any definitive list of covenant-destroying marriage misdeeds.

As for remarriage, here the history of legalism has had devastating consequences. Jesus linked remarriage and adultery in order to warn men that legal niceties do not cover over the reality of adulterous covenant violating. If a man leaves his faithful and well-intentioned wife to go sleep with and eventually marry his secretary, he is adulterating his covenant with his wife (and his children), regardless of whether he can get a judge to give him a divorce decree. This is the point of the remarriage/adultery teaching, and it makes sense. Close reading of Paul's treatment of divorce in 1 Corinthians 7 helps us see that Jesus did not intend to bar all remarriage or classify all remarried persons as adulterers. He did intend to stop his hearers from finding false comfort in legal procedures that enable covenant breaking.

Philip Turner has pointed out that the root metaphor of a marital language of covenant is "relation." The Catholic tradition has employed a root metaphor of "substance" or "being."[15] For historic Catholic thought, marriage is indissoluble because a metaphysical entity has supernaturally come into existence that literally cannot be destroyed. In shifting to the biblical language of covenant, the Protestant Reformers changed metaphors. For them, marriage is a human relationship with particular ends and particular obligations. Though the marriage covenant is solemn and binding, it is still relation-based—that is, it can be destroyed by the misdeeds of those human beings who participate in it. Divorce under such circumstances can be understood as the legal acknowledgment that the marriage covenant has been irreparably broken.

Does this mean that the marriage covenant was conditional rather than unconditional? If so, how can it be said to be a covenant? If not, how can it be ended? This vexing question cannot easily be settled with reference to the Bible, because Old Testament covenant language can be both unconditional ("I am making between me and you and every living creature a covenant for all generations to come" [Gen. 9:12]) and conditional ("If you obey me fully and keep my covenant, then out of all nations you will be my treasured possession" [Exod. 19:5]).

Margaret Farley has proposed a very wise answer to this dilemma. God's covenant promise is unconditional in that "it cannot be undone or withdrawn." Especially in light of the decisive act God undertook on the cross, it is clear that "God's love is not pledged conditionally." But on the other hand, the nature of human response to God's unconditional love does matter, because the *goal* of God's covenant efforts is to establish and maintain relationships with people, and there can be no relationship that is not mutual, not two-sided. God reaches out to people in love and implores them to love him wholeheartedly in return (Matt. 22:36–40). God's goal in doing this cannot be reached unless people freely respond in love. And this God will not compel, indeed cannot compel, if he would respect their freedom as persons.[16]

The same thing is true in marriage. The covenant promises made on the wedding day are unconditional in that they are not revocable at will. They cannot be withdrawn. However, the nature of the covenant partner's response does matter. If you respond to my covenant love with rejection, hatred, and infidelity, it does not affect the nature of my promises to you. But it does break my heart, because it annihilates the possibility of achieving the very goals to which we both once promised to give our lives. And if it becomes clear that the relationship the covenant was intended to establish, the goals we both committed to, the sacred vows we took, and the rules that were stipulated to achieve those goals all stand in ruins, then even the most faithful covenant partner may have to acknowledge that the covenant is damaged beyond repair.

One puzzle remains: whether frustration in getting creation-based needs met might also constitute grounds for divorce. The case of fundamental covenant violations directly addressed by Scripture, like adultery and desertion, is clear. But what about problems that go to the heart of the creation purposes of marriage: companionship in labor, life, and love; sexual relations; and family partnership?

My response remains a covenantal one. Part of what spouses promise to each other is to devote themselves to meeting one another's God-given sexual needs, bringing new life into the world together and raising that new life responsibly, sharing in the labors necessary to support a family and providing for one another a measure of good-willed companionship. In other words, a good faith effort to meet one another's creational needs is itself part of the marital covenant.

Because human beings are imperfect sinners, we all fall short of fulfilling such promises in all their potential. Falling short in a way that can be expected of normal sinful human beings is not grounds for divorce. However, situations emerge in which a pattern develops of willful and repeated violations of both the letter and the spirit of such promises. Remember that covenants don't just stipulate behavior, but they also establish a kind of marital community. This covenant-formed community hinges on a good-faith effort on the part of both parties to live out the relationship promised at its inception.

It is obvious that a pattern of physical and emotional abuse, the steady refusal of conjugal relations, the willful mistreatment or abuse of the couple's children, the refusal to contribute any effort to shared family labors either paid or unpaid, and the creation of an environment of unremitting hostility or hatred are all examples of violations of the covenant promises made on the wedding day. The circumstances in which such promise breaking could create sufficient suffering to morally justify divorce cannot be determined by way of a general statement, but such circumstances exist.

Covenants protect valuable relationships from harm. In Margaret Farley's words, "They take their meaning from the love they are designed to serve. They are relative in meaning and in value to the substance they help to frame."[17] Biblical prohibitions against divorce support marital covenants and are aimed at protecting the innocent, especially women and children, from abandonment and harm. A certain measure of suffering is a reasonable price to pay to preserve a marriage covenant. But when a marriage relationship itself becomes fundamentally and irreparably harmful and oppressive, then it is probably the case that the marriage, rather than a divorce, poses the greater threat to the well-being of the most vulnerable.

The spouse suffering in such a marriage will likely consider divorce. But the Christian spouse in such a situation should not attempt to determine alone whether the state of affairs in his or her marriage constitutes a fundamental and irreparable breach of the covenant. One key role of the Christian community is to stand in the gap with suffering spouses and help them discern the nature of their moral obligations in times of great suffering—rather than turn away from them in their sorrow. In so doing, the community must take seriously both the marriage covenant and the current suffering. Mike Mason says that the marriage vows ask this question: "How dark a night are you prepared to pass through" with this person?[18] In the middle of such a dark night—in the midst of a marital nightmare—no believer should find herself alone.

Suffering in Divorce

One reason to hesitate before any decision to move toward divorce is that it does not necessarily provide the pain relief that people hope it will offer.

Looking at her situation in an unhappy marriage, an individual often thinks that anything would be better than the current suffering. Regularly, people write books and say that their choice was divorce or insanity; divorce or murder; divorce or suicide; divorce or a long, slow emotional demise. *The suffering will seek relief*. Divorce is often the medication chosen.

In some cases divorce improves the lives of those who choose it. Many profoundly miserable men and women have found an end to their suffering through divorce. However, recent studies of the divorced and especially children of divorce show that, for many, divorce creates at least as much pain as it resolves. We have already discussed the consequences of divorce for children. Let us briefly relate that discussion now to this issue of suffering.

Divorce can intensify the suffering of the divorcing person in numerous ways. The divorce process itself stirs up emotions and passions that sometimes spiral out of control. Many men and women who never acted violently during their marriages become violent during the process of divorce. Divorce involves considerable cost and often a great deal of legal hassle that complicates life for months or years. Divorce most often blocks fulfillment of any of the creation-based needs we have been discussing.

Unexpected emotions are frequently generated when the divorced begin to date and remarry. Jealousy sometimes emerges as one spouse looks on at the other's new love interest and sexual involvement. Remarriage itself involves all parties in complications, especially where there are children. The ex-spouses are generally forced to relate to each other, and now they must relate to the new live-in or new spouse. There may be ongoing custody and financial disputes. Life gets messier and messier. It turns out that in fleeing the suffering close at hand, the divorced couple has ended up running right into the arms of a suffering that is just as bad, or worse.

A divorce involving children may bind the ex-spouses together more tightly than ever before, despite how much everyone wishes for the reverse. They may have managed to live as virtual strangers in their house while managing life's various responsibilities. Now, divorced, they have to relate to each other constantly. Divorces involving children are like tar paper; the ex-spouses are stuck with each other and can't get loose, however much they may hate it. This is one reason why so many divorced people are still actively angry years after their divorce.

Of course, children suffer deeply during divorce, even justifiable divorces. It is fair to say that divorce does not so much end suffering as redirect it. If there are children, what might be called a *suffering force* that exists in the struggling marriage is redirected their way. They deal with its effects for years, even when the ex-spouses relate amicably to each other but especially when they do not. The complications of managing turbulent custody and visitation arrangements are almost intrinsically suffering producing. I argued earlier that children tend to experience divorce as a covenant violation in and of itself, and thus the experience creates for them great suffering.

Bye Bye Love, a mid-'90s movie about divorce, climaxes with a main character saying, "It never ends. It never gets better, and it never ends." Where there are children and neither parent abandons them, the marriage and the divorce never end—if that means the end of having to relate to the other person. No—the ex will very likely be in the other's life until one or the other passes from the earth.

Children are the one-flesh physical embodiment of what was once the one-flesh bond of their parents. *Children cannot be dissolved, even if marriages can.* (The fact that this is sometimes inconvenient poses a real threat to the physical survival of some children.) Children will always be living incarnations of a covenant that once existed. And unless one or another parent is to perform the most grievous covenant violation of all toward his children (total abandonment), he will always have to be reminded of the marital covenant that once was the context for the birth of this child.

Children are not explicitly mentioned in biblical teachings against divorce, though perhaps it is not coincidental that both in Mark and in Matthew the teachings about divorce come right before teachings about treating children as they ought to be treated. It is true that in the Jewish context, every couple hoped not just for a child but for a quiver full of them. The rabbis were the first to interpret the one-flesh teaching of Genesis 2 as, at least in part, representing children. It may be, then, that it is precisely the disastrous impact of divorce on children that underlies the strict biblical teachings against it, even though the connection is never explicitly drawn.

In light of these truths, those who are working with couples in ministry settings would advance the cause of marriage by:

- teaching couples to have reasonable biblical expectations of marriage;
- helping couples understand the creation goods of marriage so that they can best work to provide these for their spouse;
- preparing couples to expect seasons of suffering in marriage when at least some of these needs go unmet and to grow in endurance as they think theologically about the meaning of their suffering;
- reminding couples to learn to be happy and to get many needs met outside of the marital relationship by developing a range of nonromantic relationships and other interests and joys;
- strengthening the couple's understanding of the permanence of the marriage covenant so that when suffering grows intense, they have the steadfastness to endure;
- leading couples to receive the good and joyful moments of marriage as grace, holding lightly to them as gifts rather than entitlements;

- drawing couples to look to God for companionship, to rediscover the self before God and the joy available in the most basic relationship there is—with the Creator;
- strengthening the church's understanding of itself as a context for both supporting marriage and holding its members to their marital covenants.

A Personal Word

I said in the introduction that everything I know about marriage is through my own marriage. I also noted that Jeanie and I had experienced our own harrowing journey before coming out in a healthier place on the other side.

While drafting this chapter, I discovered a fragment that I wrote at perhaps the worst moment of our own marital crisis. I was in what seemed to me unbearable pain and was trying to think my way through it.

At the top of the page I wrote, "Status of a Marriage." Under this heading, I listed eight options:

1. Ecstatic union
2. Intimate partnership
3. Cordial friendship
4. Peaceful coexistence
5. Tense silence
6. Active hostility
7. Full-scale belligerence
8. Irreconcilable brokenness

Finally, at the bottom of the page, I jotted these thoughts: "A marriage's status can vary over time. What to make of our swings between ecstatic union and active hostility? Should I seek to narrow the range (say, options 3–4) so the swings are not so intense? Right now I just want to move from 7 to 5 and perhaps to 4 for a goal."

I record these words publicly because they teach better than anything else a very important truth: *Suffering comes in marriage, but if we endure, if we hold true, it does not necessarily stay*. Darkness may come with the night, but joy comes in the morning.

As I write these words, I would place the status of our marriage at a 1. For many months, we have had the joyful experience of living at 1 or 2. Of course, these numbers are symbols and approximations. But they symbolize and approximate something very important. Seasons of suffering in marriage push individuals and couples to levels of endurance they may never have imagined having to reach. Such seasons test the strength of the marital covenant beyond what the blushing bride and groom ever could have envisioned on the day they took their vows. Those who have not (yet) gone through this vale of tears have no idea what it is like.

Mike Mason was right in saying that we don't keep vows; the vows keep us. When covenant structures our marriage relationship, that covenant sometimes is the *only thing* that holds us. When our spouse for a time becomes enemy, and none of those lovely creation needs are getting met well, still we have our covenant. Unless that covenant has been fundamentally and irreparably breached by our spouse, we have no moral right to breach it either, despite a time of misery. That remains my best statement of an ethic for divorce. Our covenant held, the crisis passed, and today we delight in a joyful marriage. Thanks be to God.

8

The Kingdom Possibilities of Marriage

> Love does not consist in gazing at each other but in looking outward in the same direction.
>
> —Antoine de Saint-Exupery

Thus far we have explored with some thoroughness two of the four pillars of a Christian theology of marriage: creation and covenant. Grounded in the human needs wired into us by God in creation, marriage exists as a divine gift to enable us to flourish in our most intimate relationships. Structured as a covenant relationship, marriage gives us the context of stability, accountability, and trust needed to achieve God's creation intent for marriage and family life.

I have been careful to argue that in both of these senses, marriage is not a specifically "Christian" institution. It was not introduced in the new era inaugurated by Jesus Christ but instead at creation. Thus the creation and covenant principles outlined so far are applicable to any human being who marries. They point the thoughtful married person to God, or ought to do so—this is one of the tasks of the effective Christian minister who gets involved with a non-Christian couple moving toward marriage. But whether the couple comes to see the traces of God's handiwork in marriage or not, marriage succeeds or fails based on the ability of the partners to meet creation needs adequately and to maintain covenant fidelity.

But this approach to marriage begs the question: What is distinctive about *Christian* marriage? Did Jesus add anything to the Old Testament witness on marriage? What about other leaders of the early church?

A review of the New Testament teachings in various places in this book has revealed that little new content was offered by Jesus or early church leaders related to marriage itself. Jesus did not need to reinvent marriage, but he did need to call his listeners back to God's intent for this pivotal institution. Key elements in Jesus' teaching included his emphasis on God's design for marriage in creation and his reaffirmation of the binding nature of the covenant promises made in marriage, over against the use of Deuteronomy 24:1 to enable men to slither out of their marriages all too easily. Jesus' concern for the well-being of women and children in a situation of misused male power is noteworthy. His adoption and adaptation of bridegroom and wedding imagery is significant, as well as the way the image courses its way through the New Testament until its climax in the book of Revelation.

We have also considered Paul's teachings on marriage and have noted his explicit endorsement of the celibate single life and its implications in Christian tradition. His emphasis on marriage as a context for the harnessed expression of sexuality is significant. In teaching about divorce in 1 Corinthians 7, Paul adapted Jesus' "no divorce" teaching both to emphasize the significance of reconciliation and to make reluctant provision for the possibility of divorce in situations of an unbeliever's desertion in a mixed marriage. Paul's comparison of the Christ/church and husband/wife relationship in Ephesians 5 has also been noted.

I want to argue in this chapter that the most distinctive contribution of the New Testament to our understanding of Christian marriage is not found in any of the above. What the New Testament does offer that is unique is a focus on the kingdom of God. Christians who are looking for a maximized, ceiling-scraping, distinctively Christian marriage can find what they are looking for here. In tandem with a skillful achievement of the creation purposes of marriage and a faithful keeping of the covenant promises of marriage, a Christian couple can find extraordinary fulfillment in giving their marriage and family over to the kingdom of God.

The Kingdom of God

"Now after John was arrested, Jesus came to Galilee, proclaiming the good news of God, and saying, 'The time is fulfilled, and the kingdom of

God has come near; repent, and believe in the good news'" (Mark 1:14–15 NRSV). Biblical scholar Gordon Fee has written, "The absolutely central theme of Jesus' mission and message was 'the good news of the kingdom of God.'"[1] Jesus taught his followers to "seek first the kingdom" (Matt. 6:33). If we want to be followers of Christ, we must seek the kingdom, even in marriage.

But what is the kingdom of God? The answer to this question has proven elusive. Is it a place? If so, where is it to be found? Is it a time? If so, when was it/is it/will it be? Is it a vision or ideal? If so, what does this vision include? Is it a state of affairs of some sort? If so, what characterizes it?

Each of these questions implies further questions related to God's activity and our human response—and responsibility. If the kingdom of God is a place, what must we do, if anything, to gain admission? If it is a time, is there anything we can do to hasten it (or delay it)? If it is a vision, or ideal, or state of affairs, what role do we have in bringing it about?

Let us dispense with the time dimension first. I say "dispense," because Christians tend to get fixated on the "when" question rather than the "what" question when thinking about the kingdom. Clearly, in Jesus' teaching, the kingdom is "both a future event and a present reality."[2] Jesus celebrated the fact that in himself God was initiating the long-promised salvation of the world, beginning with the covenant people Israel. Jesus was the bridegroom, and the wedding party was under way. However, it is also true that Jesus pointed to a future time when this salvation would be fully consummated. So the kingdom is a reality that has been initiated but not yet finalized or consummated. We now live in the time between the two events.

This begun-but-not-completed kingdom is not a place, either on earth or in heaven, as many suppose. It cannot be equated with the church or with heaven itself. Nor is it a vision, as in a utopian dream of a better world. Nor is it some kind of internal human attitude, as in Tolstoy's "the kingdom of God is within you," which is a mistranslation.

Instead, the kingdom of God as Jesus taught it is *that state of affairs in which God reigns*. It is rooted in the most significant fact about our world: the earth is a place created and sustained by God yet characterized by the rebellion against God of those creatures intended to be the pinnacle of the Creator's efforts. Thus the fact of the matter is that God reigns and yet he doesn't. God is king, and yet his kingship is rejected—in deed and often in word as well. When you see a bumper sticker that says, "Jesus is Lord over Louisville" (or Miami, or wherever), you are reading a statement that is both true and false at the same time.

The Old Testament is achingly familiar with this horrendous contradiction. The sacred writings of the covenant people Israel, especially after their history collapsed in war and exile, are full of grief over the violation of God's reign and the promise of its future consummation. Jesus did not spin the concept of the reign of God out of whole cloth. Instead, Jesus' proclamation of the kingdom of God must be understood, as biblical scholar W. D. Davies puts it, "In light of the expectations expressed in the Old Testament, and in Judaism, that, at some future date, God would act for the salvation of his people."[3]

For hundreds of years, faithful Jews all around the world had nurtured the hope that God would intervene decisively for the salvation of his people. Some hoped that this salvation would extend to the whole earth. In entertaining such hopes, Jews had ample biblical material to ponder. In our book *Kingdom Ethics,* Glen Stassen and I argue that it was from the prophet Isaiah that Jesus seems to have drawn his understanding and proclamation of what the kingdom looks like.[4]

Close study of Isaiah reveals a basic picture of the kingdom or reign of God in which seven things happen.

- God will act decisively to deliver his people from their suffering.
- God's justice will prevail over current injustice.
- God's peace will bring an end to war and violence.
- God's presence will be acutely felt and experienced (the language of God's Spirit is used frequently).
- Healing of the broken and the ill will take place.
- Outcasts and the exiled will be restored to covenant community.
- God's people will respond with great joy to all that God is doing.

It is clear in Jesus' teaching that the kingdom is something that *God* is doing. God initiates the kingdom; in a sense, God *performs* the kingdom. It is not a human work. Like a mustard tree, it grows from a tiny seed even while we sleep (Matt. 13:31 and parallels).

However, the kingdom is a divine action that human beings are called to participate in. Almost all kingdom teachings emphasize *both* God's activity *and* the call to human response and participation. Thus the fact that the kingdom is being initiated by God demands of people some kind of response. Either we are on board or we are not. Either we are part of the advance of the reign of God or we are part of what hinders it. A fundamental life decision is thus required: Am I or am I not a kingdom person? Do I believe this story, and am I willing to live accordingly?

Jesus' moral teachings take their proper context in this light. Jesus is the trailblazer for the reign of God. He both demonstrates and teaches kingdom practices. Followers of Jesus—Christians—are those who imitate the kingdom practices of Jesus and obey his kingdom teachings. We do so, not because we want to go to heaven or be decent people, but because we have made the reign of God the purpose of our lives and want to participate in it.

Therefore, we work for justice and righteousness. We teach and practice the way of peacemaking in relationships. We experience the presence of God and help others do the same. We facilitate healing of bodies and spirits. We restore outcasts and lonely ones to community. We live joyfully in the Spirit of God. And, in general, we give our lives over to participating in the delivering salvation that God has brought to the earth in Jesus Christ. This kingdom agenda becomes what our life is about. We live for God by practicing kingdom values.

Marriage and the Kingdom

If a Christian is a person who lives to advance the reign of God, what are the implications for marriage? Almost by definition, it would seem that the marriage of two Christians ought to become a context for the vigorous practice of kingdom living. Marriage transitions from being about the *couple* to being about the *kingdom*.

In one form or another, this is now a claim that is common in some Christian circles. It is said, "Marriage is not about love and romance but about the kingdom" (or the gospel, or the church, or the Bible, or missions, or whatever). Thus the Christian person seeking a mate is supposed to look for someone with a heart for the reign of God, and the Christian couple is supposed to turn their attention away from themselves.

To this we must say a surprising no before we say yes.

There was a time when I was among the most enthusiastic in claiming Christian marriage is about the kingdom, not about the couple. But I am coming to see that the creation origins and purposes of marriage, in particular, are stubborn. They are not so easily bypassed for a higher purpose.

Let me be quite blunt. The godly man, afire for the kingdom, who denies his wife the basics of good communication or tender nurture will not find a partner in fruitful kingdom work for very long. Likewise, the godly woman, afire for the kingdom, who denies her husband sex or respect will not find a partner in fruitful kingdom work for very long. The creation goods I have named could be reversed; I am not trying to stereotype gender. The point is that the frustration of the creation goods of marriage renders the pursuit of other goods, even the highest good—the kingdom—extremely problematic.

The same is true about the covenantal structure of marriage. Almost by definition, a marriage with a shaky covenant foundation will not thrive as a context for advancing God's reign, regardless of the couple's fondest and most pious hopes.

An unwillingness to acknowledge the demands of nature, of our basic humanity, is a denial of the doctrine of creation. It is all too common among Christians today. Jesus inaugurates the kingdom in order to restore creation to what God originally intended for it, not to bypass creation and move us to some reality in which we stop being flesh-and-blood-and-spirit human creatures. How many well-intentioned ministers have responded to marital problems by calling the couples to pray more, to be more spiritual or more holy, rather than working with the couple to help them meet one another's primal human needs, as God intended? How many devout men and women have said, "I tried to do the right thing, but after five years of no love, no sex, and constant fighting, I couldn't take it any more"?

A better approach is to say that the successful Christian couple will attend first to solidifying the binding quality of their covenant promises to each other. They will establish clearly and without equivocation that this will be a marriage characterized by sexual fidelity and unshakable permanence, as well as a good-faith effort to meet every other marriage covenant promise with energy and love.

Then the successful Christian couple will work hard to become skilled in meeting the creation needs of each other and exhibiting the virtues necessary for a flourishing marriage. They will work at communication, conflict resolution, household labor, financial management, sexuality, child rearing, and every other area of their life together. They will work hard to untangle snagged areas and to move ahead with growth in intimacy.

On the basis of these two commitments, and in tandem with their successful and ongoing development, the Christian couple will then be in a position to turn their hearts more fully to a kingdom vision. The mature and maximized Christian marriage will become a context in which the resources of the couple and of the family more broadly get turned with great passion to the kingdom of God.

This is not to say that successful Christian marriage itself is not part of the kingdom. If the kingdom is God's reign—which includes peace in relationships, the experience of joy and God's presence, and an end to violence, suffering, crying, and pain—the happy Christian marriage is a major participant in the reign of God. Those who have suffered the brokenness of marital misery and divorce know viscerally that their experience is not part of that reign. And those who even touch the hem of the garment of joyful Christian marriage would be among the first to attest that here heaven meets earth. This is one reason why marriage and family life receive the exalted attention they do receive in Scripture. One might say that they are the first battlefield where the kingdom of God is contested, and when victories are won, they are sweet indeed.

Even so, however, the concept of a kingdom marriage cannot be confined to the joyful pleasures of marital bliss and family harmony. Christian marriage books reinforce our tendency to turn inward in this way. I am aware of many couples who are quite happy but do not extend themselves beyond the boundaries of their front porch. This reflects the split between public life and private life that was so characteristic of the economic transition to the modern period and so fateful in its consequences for marriage, as we saw in chapter 2. The public selves of those engaged in this kind of marriage serve the world insofar as they must when they leave the house to go to work, but their private selves and the home they live in are reserved for each other. This marks an enormous waste of resources for kingdom advancement and is not a biblical vision for living.

One way to think about this issue is to employ Mary Anne McPherson Oliver's contrast between marriage as a "community of purpose" and a "community of being."[5] As a community of being, the married couple's gaze is directed at one another, and their primary goal is the relationship itself. As a community of purpose, on the other hand, the couple turns their attention from one another to the world, and their primary goal becomes the accomplishment of particular tasks in the world and the advance of a particular vision for the world.

At a theological level, we must claim that marriage ought to be both a community of being and a community of purpose. Keeping these aspects of marriage in balance involves, in our own time, constantly correcting an imbalance in the direction of emphasizing the marital community of being—that is, the health and happiness of the marriage relationship—which became the crux of the meaning of marriage during the modern period and is now all that survives of it.

Instead, at the creation level, marriage is a divinely ordered community of purpose with great potential to develop into a rich community of being. When that marital oneness of being occurs, energy is released and attention is turned to an even fuller pursuit of divine purposes in the world. A kingdom person is concerned for a suffering world that God is acting to redeem. A kingdom marriage takes the overflow of marital joy and uses it as fuel for serving the neighbor and advancing God's reign. Marriage becomes a place where love is experienced, learned, and expanded: "Success in true conjugal love is an educational foundation for the love of humanity," as Stephen Post puts it.[6]

Marital Capital

Decades ago sociologist Glenn Loury coined the term "social capital." The term is now in widespread use. In a free-market economy, capital is wealth, which in various forms can be used to produce more wealth. Land is capital, cash is capital, skill is a kind of capital. *Social* capital, by extension, is a kind of resource that is produced by a social system. It is a kind of wealth because it advances the well-being of those fortunate enough to enjoy its benefits. It often produces actual financial wealth as well.

A good example of social capital is *connections*. Not long before drafting this chapter, I found myself in need of a particular judge's signature on an important legal document. The judge was to be out of town, however, on the day when I had to have that signature. My wife, Jeanie, remembered that I had made a contact with another judge in town through a conference event in which this second judge introduced me. In desperation I called her and politely asked for some help. She managed to track down the judge on vacation and, on the basis of her warm relationship with him, coaxed him to come back from his vacation and sign the needed document. No money changed hands. But my social capital enabled a very concrete benefit to come my way.

Loury applied the concept of social capital to point to its relative lack in the African-American community compared to the white community. He argued that black Americans lack the social capital that white Americans take for granted and that generates enormous advantages for them in navigating the American economy. This was a significant contribution to understanding continuing patterns of economic injustice in American life.[7]

One could argue that a thriving marriage produces social capital. Let's call it *marital capital*. The marriage's happiness creates (rather than drains) energy. In chapter 7, I talked about a tragic suffering force that gets produced in a collapsing marriage and in divorce. Its inverse is this *happiness force* I am calling marital capital. This energy, always renewable as long as the marriage is thriving, becomes available for loving each other better and better and for loving the children of that marriage with excellence. But there is still more energy to go around. Thus the marital capital can be employed to do good outside the family.

The church needs to produce more marriages healthy enough to generate marital capital. Then it needs to help couples figure out how best to invest that capital, and to celebrate well when the kingdom is furthered.

Those suffering in miserable marriages or in the throes of divorce are the first to say that it consumes all their energy. One reason for the drying up of so many voluntary organizations, the paucity of school chaperones and volunteers, and the reduced voting rates and participation in civic life is that everyone is so busy trying to make sense of their soap opera lives that there is nothing left over.

But marital capital is a resource for advancing God's work in the world—the reign of God. It energizes couples for raising their own children well and perhaps including lonely, outcast, and abused children and adults into the community of their household. It frees up emotional resources for working for justice in such causes as the fight against abortion or racism. It empowers families to invest in their local neighborhoods in a time when neighborhood community has all but disappeared in many contexts.[8]

Marital capital has other benefits. It gives emotional space for a vigorous prayer life, in which the needs of hurting people near and far can be brought before God. It gives people energy for working in the church nursery or on the pastor search committee to facilitate the work of the kingdom-advancing church. It gives resources for peacemaking at work or in the community—or in the world. It brings a peace of heart that can be of great comfort through counseling with hurting people in the neighborhood or at church. It leaves room for evangelism in the marketplace or on the airplane. As the social gospel theologian Walter Rauschenbusch put it, "The love for [family] . . . widens out into the love of many and weaves more closely the web of social life."[9] The family becomes a household open to the world in hospitality and extended into the world in service.

Marital capital also frees the blessed children of such a bond from worrying over the survival of their family or from constantly adjusting to postdivorce family arrangements. This empowers them to play, to enjoy a real childhood, and to dream their own dreams for the future. As we have already seen, this puts them at a stark advantage over their peers not similarly favored.

The kingdom marriage can become a sign of the full redemption of divine-human and human-human relationships that was initiated in Jesus Christ. Out of the overflow of his triune love, God made humanity. There was more than enough love to go around, and there has been for century upon century and billions upon billions of people. In the maximized kingdom marriage, there is more than enough love to go around. It gets poured out in the bedroom, at the kitchen table, at the church, in the neighborhood, and everywhere God calls the couple to serve. This is marriage at its highest.

Florence Nightingale, the pioneering nurse who chose not to marry due to the constraints her culture's understanding of gender roles and marriage would have placed on the pursuit of her vocation, wrote this:

> For two to marry because they can do together the work of God better than each can do it alone—for a family to unite to do together their "Father's business" better than any can do it alone—this would indeed be a marriage, this a home.[10]

When Jeanie and I were going through the most difficult times of our marriage, I found that I could barely get up and face each day. I had to teach classrooms full of college students, but I was so miserable that I could hardly brush my teeth. Those who knew me knew that I was suffering and that it was, inevitably, reducing my energy for my work. I soldiered on, but it was tough.

Today, after the healing of our marriage, I find enormous reserves of energy are now available for kingdom work—by both of us and by us as a family. We are actively engaged in hospitality ministries, premarital counseling and our marriage enrichment ministry, various forms of service at church, volunteering at the kids' school, personal evangelism, and so on. We also have more energy for play and instruction of our own children. We understand that this marital capital is a rare gift, to be used for God's kingdom. How we yearn that more Christian couples had both marital capital and a vision for its kingdom use. The Christian home, as Rodney Clapp has said, is a "mission base."[11] It exists not as a haven from the world but a mobilization center for active service to the world.

The kingdom possibilities of Christian marriage are endless. The question every church must face is how to minister to couples in such a way that those possibilities can be realized. To this question we now turn.

9

The Church as Marriage Counterculture

We will walk together in brotherly love, as becomes the members of a Christian Church, exercise an affectionate care and watchfulness over each other and faithfully admonish and entreat one another as occasion may require.

—Church Covenant, Capitol Hill Baptist Church, Washington, D.C.

In the wistful 2002 movie *About a Boy,* Hugh Grant plays Will, a lonely, miserable, fatherless, bored, forty-year-old Englishman whiling away his time doing . . . nothing. However, by "chance" an equally lonely, miserable, fatherless, bored, ten-year-old boy comes into his life. Will tries to shake him off, but the boy's desire for a man in his life ultimately exceeds Will's desire to reject him. In a nicely drawn character study, Will begins to care about, not just the boy, but also the boy's depressed mother—and others in their motley collection of friends and acquaintances. The final scene of the movie shows Will and his first real love interest, the boy, his mother, and a variety of other friends gathered for a holiday dinner. The final voice-over has the boy saying, from painful personal experience, "I don't think couples are the future. You need more than that. You need backup." *About a Boy* is actually about *community*.

Western society is now coming to understand, once again, that it does take more than two to make a marriage. It takes a community. Samuel Johnson puts it quite trenchantly: "It is so far from being natural for a man and woman to live in a state of marriage that we find all the motives which they have for remaining in that connection, and the restraints which civilized society imposes to prevent separation, are hardly sufficient to keep them together."[1] In the historical development which we traced in chapter 2, we saw that the "restraints" imposed by "civilized society" have dropped off almost entirely since the eighteenth century, when Johnson penned these words. What remains as the foundation for a pivotal social institution is the most fleeting of phenomena: one partner's perception of the current level of affection and satisfaction that exists between two sinful human beings in a sinful world.

There is another social institution, however, that still has the potential to impose the restraints Johnson mentions. That institution is the church. This chapter explores what it might look like—and even now, sometimes does look like—when the church of Jesus Christ becomes a community context in which marriage is strengthened.

After creation, covenant, and kingdom, community is the fourth pillar of our marriage cathedral. In this chapter, the community we consider is the church. In the next, we consider the possibilities still available to the broader civic community to strengthen and protect marriage.

What Is the Church?

At a basic sociological level, a church is any organized group of human beings who profess belief in Jesus Christ. *The* church (or *Church*) is the aggregate of all organized bodies of believers anywhere in the world. Missions scholar David Barrett has estimated that as of mid-2002 there were 3.55 million Christian congregations in the world and just over 2 billion Christians. In North America, 215 million people are official members of Christian churches, out of a population estimated at 316 million. Christianity remains the largest living world religion, claiming the professed allegiance of a third of the entire human population and two-thirds of North Americans.[2] One would, on the face of it, have reason to hope that such a massive social institution would have a significant national and global impact as it pursues its mission.

A theological definition of the church would, of course, raise our hopes all the more. The New Testament abounds with exalted definitions of the nature and purpose of the church. The church is that community "in which the gospel is proclaimed, believed, and obeyed."[3] It is the communion of the saints, the corporate assembly of those who are being saved (1 Cor.

1:18; 2:15) through the atoning sacrifice of Jesus Christ (Rom. 3:21–26). The church is a "new humanity" (Gal. 3:28; Eph. 2:11–22; Col. 3:9–11), serving as a "holy priesthood" (1 Peter 2:4–7). The church is that body of human beings in whom Christ dwells and who in turn are "in Christ" (Rom. 8:1; 1 Cor. 1:30; 2 Cor. 5:17). We are the very "body of Christ" (1 Cor. 12:27; Eph. 4:12; Col. 1:24), in a way the focal point of God's presence in the world—God's "household" (Eph. 2:19; 1 Tim. 3:15) and "temple" (1 Cor. 3:16–17; 2 Cor. 6:16; Eph. 2:21). And in a particularly important image for our purposes, as we have seen, the church is the "bride of Christ" (Rev. 19:7–9; 21:2; cf. Eph. 5:22–33), expectant, lovely, and pure, preparing herself for her coming great wedding day with Christ the bridegroom.

My own understanding of the church focuses especially on its role in the kingdom of God. As discussed in chapter 8, the kingdom is the dawning reign of God, the reclaiming of creation by its rightful king. This reclamation, initiated in the incarnation, will come to consummation at the end of time. Between times, the church is that pioneering community of human beings who devote their lives to the joyful work of the kingdom. They (we) proclaim and enact the shape of the coming reign of God in obedience to the teachings of Christ, the inaugurator of that reign (Matt. 28:19–20). In every area of life, we blaze a trail for others to follow. We say: watch us; join us; participate in the good things that God is doing in a broken world.

One of those good things is the reclamation of marriage. The church is called to bear witness to the creational purposes of marriage, the covenant structure of marriage, and the kingdom possibilities of marriage. That witness will take many forms, and different local churches will pioneer different strategies. However, what the church is not permitted to do is to fail to bear that witness. And that is what has happened in a large number of churches. The problem is so widespread that it is often said that the church has failed to be the church when it comes to marriage. This reminds us that the exalted reality of our existence in Christ is met with the far less exalted reality that we are still sinful. We live in the excruciating tension between being both a community of saints and a community of sinners.[4] At times our "life in the Spirit" is joyfully visible; at other times our fallenness is all too apparent. This is a chapter for those who have not given up on the church, however, but believe instead that the church is the hope of the world.

Five Patterns of Church Response to the Collapse of Marriage

The story of the church's response to the collapse of marriage is much more complex than a simple condemnation can indicate. I would suggest that five primary patterns of church interaction with the divorce culture of North America can be identified. As these are discussed, you might find it instructive to place your own local congregation somewhere along this spectrum.

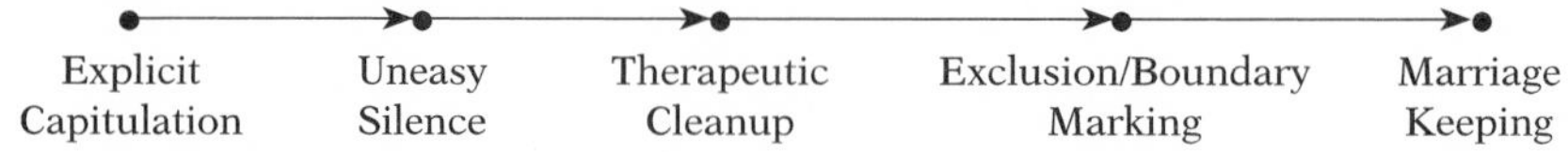

Explicit Capitulation

The most scandalous response of a church to the collapse of marriage is this one—explicit capitulation. There is nothing stealthy or hidden about this capitulation—it is publicly trumpeted. Here the pastor and other church leaders give up core biblical principles related to marriage. They say, "We know the Bible speaks negatively about divorce (or extramarital sex, or out-of-wedlock birth), but after all, this is a new day. We must keep up with the times. We must keep the faith relevant to modern people. We don't want to seem judgmental. We must be about grace rather than law." Biblical teaching about marriage and divorce is abandoned.

An interesting example of this spirit could be seen in an August 2002 *New York Times* story about the phenomenon of "secondary virginity"—situations when individuals or couples who have been sexually active decide to refrain from further sex until they are married. This often happens on the basis of biblical teaching, sometimes because of an intuitive sense that sex belongs in marriage and that the boundary between marriage and any other estate must be guarded. One minister, not enthusiastic about the idea, told the paper, "I assume that most every couple who comes to me is sexually active. I don't advise them about sex—more marriage problems are due to money. I'll talk about the importance of communication."[5] The fact that the Bible teaches that sexual intercourse is reserved for the marriage bed appears to be irrelevant to this minister.

The same thing happens in the internal life of congregations. Consider the true case of a man who initiated an affair while his wife was pregnant with their third child. Throughout the long course of the pregnancy, he laid plans to end his marriage just after the baby was born, which he did—*he told his wife while she was still in the hospital*. Several months later, he asked his pastor to bless his union with his new bride—in the very church where his aggrieved and brokenhearted ex-wife (and very young children) still attended. When questioned about this, the minister declared publicly that he would in fact perform the wedding and would not attempt any intervention in the case at all, because making judgments about such matters is not the role of the minister—or the church.

If a church merely tells its congregants what they could more easily and entertainingly hear on the radio or at the movies, why not just close up shop? Explicit surrender to damaging and unbiblical ways of life within the church subverts the church's mission as that community devoted to participating in the kingdom's advance and to standing under the authority of the Word of God.

Uneasy Silence

The most prevalent approach to the collapse of marriages in churches today is uneasy silence. When confronted with divorce, many ministers and church people fall into a paralyzed speechlessness.

That silence has many roots. At one level, those who bear preaching and teaching responsibility are confronted with the practical challenge of speaking to congregations filled with the divorced, the remarried, and the children of divorce. A basic pastoral sensitivity leaves the minister afraid of offending or hurting his congregants, and so biblical texts speaking to issues related to marriage are evaded.

It is easy to lampoon the spineless minister here, but the challenge is real. On a recent Father's Day, one of the teaching pastors on our team addressed the issue of divorce as one part of a broader sermon. He called men to remain true to their marriage covenants and spoke to the pain of divorce for children. Sounds simple, but the ripples were felt in some unexpected ways. Some children of divorce were not comforted but reminded of their pain, especially on Father's Day. Some once abused and now divorced women were not sure that their particular situations were considered (while others felt quite comforted). Some divorced and remarried members felt that they were being condemned. Ours is a peaceable church, and no one called for a vote to fire the pastor. Pity the minister with less security, seeking to be faithful to biblical truth, navigating these minefields. Uneasy silence is all too often the result.

Intervening in individual situations is also rejected for some of the same reasons. Consider the lay leader who gets involved in an affair and plans to leave his wife and family. Most churches do not have a culture, customary practices, or constitutional principles authorizing someone to challenge the behavior of a member who stands in clear violation of biblical teaching. The lack of any structures of accountability leaves uneasy silence (and lots of gossip) as the standard response to gross misconduct in the church. We are embarrassed that we have no response; we wish we could do something, but we are struck dumb. Such uneasy silence solves no problems, saves no families, and does nothing to advance God's reign.

Therapeutic Cleanup

Many churches have taken the laudable step of initiating divorce recovery ministries. Ministers and concerned laypeople are attempting with this approach to make the church a place of healing and recovery for the broken. Increasing numbers of churches are participating in such national ministries as DivorceCare.[6]

These kinds of ministries represent a good fit with an aspect of the Christian moral vision in that they focus on grace and healing, second chances, and fresh starts. It is hard not to miss these themes in the New Testament. Jesus repeatedly emphasized that his Father is a God of grace, of second chances and fresh starts for the broken and repentant sinner: "There will be more rejoicing in heaven over one sinner who repents than over ninety-nine righteous persons who do not need to repent" (Luke 15:7).

However, a church that offers only therapeutic strategies like divorce recovery ministries can succumb to a broader accommodation to culture, perhaps despite its best intentions. If God's will for marriage is not taught and if egregious marital misconduct within the congregation is met by uneasy silence, purely therapeutic approaches may communicate the wrong message: "You can live however you want, even if you proclaim yourself a Christian, and when your (and your victims') pain level gets too high because of your disastrous moral choices, we will help you feel better. We will shoulder the responsibility for your choices." The church must be more than a cleanup crew. Sweeping up the shards of broken lives, broken marriages, and broken families is important and laudable work, but it is a rear-guard action. It is not enough.

Exclusion/Boundary Marking

For some pastors and churches, the primary strategy for responding to the collapse of marriage appears to be exclusion and boundary marking. Here the church attempts to draw clear lines between biblical and unbiblical behavior and, if necessary, to exclude from good standing those who fall on the wrong side of the line. This approach extends far back into the history of the church.

It is easy to dismiss any strategy that draws clear behavioral lines with the pejorative label of "legalism"—the application of stringent laws or rules to situations regardless of circumstances, often in a harsh spirit. There are many legalistic churches in North America—though far fewer than there used to be. Sometimes such churches are stricter than Jesus and carry a spirit more reminiscent of some of Jesus' adversaries than of the Savior.[7]

Sadly, some ministers are fired or permanently barred from ministry because their spouses abandon them. Biblical scholar Craig Keener tells the story of Stephen, a minister whose wife ran off with another man and abandoned their marriage despite her husband's best efforts to win her back. Stephen's denomination refuses to allow divorced people to serve as ministers under any circumstances, so his wife's betrayal meant the end of Stephen's ministry in that faith community.[8] The fact that Stephen was not the adulterer, and that he had made every effort to save his marriage, meant nothing.

Boundary strategies more often affect church leaders than laypeople. While divorced and remarried persons are often welcomed in churches, church leaders are held to a higher standard and are thus excluded from service. Here two kinds of boundaries are being marked: that between laypeople and church leaders, and between the married and the divorced.

The New Testament teaches that church leaders will be held to account for their stewardship of their calling and for the conduct of their lives and provides several lists spelling out the demanding requirements of the ministerial office (1 Tim. 3:1–7; Titus 1:6–8; cf. Acts 20:20–28). James states explicitly that teachers in the church will be judged "more strictly" (James 3:1). It is appropriate that churches expect their leaders to live according to these criteria; and ministers need to create accountability relationships in which their character can be encouraged and examined.

Committed efforts to hold onto biblical principles are far preferable to capitulation or silence. However, exclusion and boundary strategies do not save many marriages. They rarely affect the decisions of those poised to initiate divorce. They often function more like clubs than scalpels; unable to make the right kinds of distinctions, they wound innocent people all over again. They are an *ex post facto* strategy. They chase the horses long after they are out the barn door.

Marriage Keeping

With growing urgency over the past two decades, some church leaders have concluded that a different approach is desperately needed. This brings us to our fifth approach: *marriage keeping*.[9]

I derive the term *marriage keeping* from the many biblical uses of concepts translated by the English term *keeping*. The first uses of the term in Scripture are found in the early chapters of Genesis. In Genesis 4 we hear that Abel *kept* (Hebrew *ra'ah*) flocks, the offerings of which pleased God, inciting his brother Cain's jealousy. Here the term is associated with the work of shepherds, with a broader meaning of looking after something or someone with care and concern. After murdering Abel, Cain is questioned by God and responds with the famous words "Am I my brother's keeper?" (Gen. 4:9—Hebrew *shamar*). The Hebrew term here is widely used in the Old Testament and means guarding, watching, observing, or looking after. The implicit divine answer to Cain's question is yes.

The term recurs again in Genesis 6 and 7, when God commands Noah to prepare for the coming flood by taking animals on the ark and *keeping them alive* (Gen. 6:19–20; 7:3). The Hebrew term *chayah* is used here, with the meaning we find in English translation—preserving life. The other major use of the term in the Old Testament has to do with keeping covenant obligations before God (Exod. 20:6; Deut. 8:2; 11:1). Again the term is *shamar,* now with the additional meaning of faithfully and carefully obeying, observing, and performing these covenant obligations.

The New Testament retains the language of "keeping" as well. Sometimes it is used as in the Old Testament with reference to obeying the Law and its obligations (Mark 10:20; 1 Cor. 7:19). We are similarly to keep Jesus' word (John 8:51), keep the unity of the Spirit (Eph. 4:3), keep the pattern of sound teaching (2 Tim. 1:13), keep the royal law (James 2:8), keep our moral purity (James 1:26), and keep a clear conscience (1 Peter 3:16). In these and other places, the meaning includes preserving, guarding, holding onto, obeying, and fulfilling.

The heart of the biblical concept of keeping is this: we are called to preserve, care for, and honor something valuable that God has entrusted to us. Abel did not create his flocks but kept the flocks God entrusted to him. Cain did not create his brother but had a responsibility to him nonetheless. Noah did not create the various animals but was called to preserve them—as all of us are called to preserve the creation. Israel did not create the law but had an obligation to keep it.

In the same way, the church did not create marriage but is called to preserve, care for, and honor it. Neither does the couple create marriage. Nor does the state create marriage. God creates marriage. Those who enter this estate enter something holy by virtue of God's authorship of it. The role of the church is to preserve, honor, protect, and strengthen marriage. Some churches have come to see that they have a marriage-keeping mandate. What follows in the next section is one model for how to fulfill that mandate.

A Holistic Marriage-Keeping Strategy

I have spoken with many pastors and church leaders who are tempted to despair in the face of the constant collapse of marriages in their congregations. They just begin to stanch one wound when a new one is inflicted. They know that slapping bandages on the wounds is not enough, but they do not know what to do instead. They are perplexed.

A comprehensive strategy is needed. Church leaders can begin by declaring their intent to make their congregations oases of healthy lifetime covenant marriage. Governors of three states have made cutting the divorce rate a central goal of their administrations. If secular leaders can proclaim and work toward such goals, church leaders can do the same thing—and do it better.

A wise strategy will begin with four assumptions. First, congregants have already been taught something about marriage, for good or ill, mainly the latter. Disastrous patterns of thinking and living characterize many couples, even those who make their way into church. Thus the church will need to undertake a considerable project of resocialization—identifying untruthful and damaging approaches while instilling and incarnating a new vision of marriage (and life).

Second, a holistic strategy will require creative and committed employment of all that is known about how behavior and thinking are changed. Various learning theories are helpful here in identifying ways that different kinds of people learn, change, and grow. Motivation, reward, correction, modeling, and apprenticing all need to be considered.

Third, the church's instructional ministry must be complemented by ongoing pastoral care and recovery ministries. It's like trying to teach a teenager to drive with the car still moving and accident victims littering the roadways. We have to tend to the wounded while we try to prevent further wrecks, which is no mean feat.

Finally, the church will not be able to address marriage and divorce in an adequate manner without clarifying the relation of the individual congregant to the community. The church and all its members must be clear on whether accountability and correction are a part of the church's repertoire of resocialization tools or whether church leadership is confined to instructional and therapeutic ways of ministering. It must be determined whether the church is a purely voluntary community, in which congregants sift through teachings and partake of ministries they perceive as beneficial, or instead a community in which the members are covenantally bound to accept direction, correction, and discipline.

In light of these assumptions, if a minister or church wants to declare marriage keeping a central goal for the congregation, the strategy for getting there should involve the elements I outline below. They encompass a mix of proclamation, education, pastoral care, church policies, and congregational polity. Consider advocating or implementing elements of this strategy in your congregation.

1. Preach, teach, and model with the goal of nurturing whole, healthy, morally sound, committed Christian disciples. We saw in chapter 5 that success in marriage hinges on the development of both skills and qualities of character; and in chapter 7 we considered how suffering in marriage is often brought on by the character flaws of just one of the spouses. A presupposition of a healthy marriage is two morally and psychologically healthy people. Many marriages fail today because of the flaws in character and conduct of one or both of the participants. In other words, there is nothing specific to the marriage *relationship* that causes the failure of that relationship, but instead the internal *crumbling of a human life* drags spouse and family down with it.

Immoral or criminal behavior brings down thousands of marriages each year. Healthy people abuse neither substances nor each other's bodies and do not participate in wantonly immoral behavior, whatever the temptation. A man who is stealing his wife's jewelry and selling it in order to buy drugs (a true story) makes successful marriage impossible. Addicted, dysfunctional, violent, and deeply immoral people create a climate that poisons marriage. Churches need to develop the capacity to intervene and help men and women struggling with such disastrous problems, as well as their victims.[10]

I am reminded of the mid-1980s movie *St. Elmo's Fire*. In that film a freshly minted college graduate (played by Rob Lowe) marries his college sweetheart because she is pregnant with their child. He turns out to be a completely faithless and uncaring husband, carousing most evenings, sleeping around, staying out all night, using drugs, getting fired from every job, and so on. In this case, the marriage is doomed to failure because of the immorality and desperate immaturity of one of its partners, which is the source of their unending conflict.

At the heart of a joyful lifelong Christian marriage are two healthy, whole, committed Christian disciples. Their commitment to living "in a way worthy of the saints" (Rom. 16:2) animates their daily lives. They study the Scriptures, seeking guidance for that way of life. They repent before God and each other when sin affects the relationship. Their daily behavior reflects the normative Christian virtues of love, joy, peace, patience, kindness, goodness, faithfulness, gentleness, and self-control (Gal. 5:22–23). They seek diligently to meet each other's creation needs while viewing their marriage and family life in kingdom perspective. Jesus says that a good tree produces good fruit (Matt. 7:16–20). The people we have in mind here are not perfect, but they are good trees producing the fruit of a good marriage. The great challenge of lifetime marriage is that it genuinely requires two such people; one is not enough. Perhaps nowhere is the overall spiritual health of a congregation more apparent than in the fruit being produced in that congregation's marriages.

Thus the first stage of a church's marriage-building and divorce-prevention ministry should be an educational and preaching focus on discipleship and character formation, beginning with children. Imagine a children's educational ministry that consciously emphasized training in those character traits and behaviors—responsibility, promise keeping, covenant fidelity, peacemaking, sobriety, discipline, and love—that are necessary for successful marriage keeping. The church need not necessarily tell the children that they are being trained for marriage, for marriage is quite remote from an eight-year-old's experience. Yet a comprehensive marriage-keeping strategy begins here. The adults might just benefit from a similar emphasis.

2. Preach, teach, and model a reoriented moral vision related to the nature and purposes of marriage. Part of moral and spiritual health related to married life is a radical reorientation of moral vision. The current cultural approach to marriage sounds like this: Marriage is the setting in which I can have my relational and sexual needs met most securely (by my "soul mate"), and marriage is the best environment in which to raise a family. So I marry someone whom I care about, who can meet those needs at least for now, and who I think will make a good family partner. Because of its links to the creation needs of the human person, this vision is not completely bereft of truthfulness.

But it falls far short of a biblical vision of marriage, which would be this: Marriage is the institution God established for creation purposes. I marry someone who will share with me a full covenant commitment to fulfill those purposes and who will make our marriage a useful instrument in God's hands for the accomplishment of kingdom goals. Together we will trust that as we commit our marriage to divine purposes, God will bring us a sense of joyful partnership.

The difference between these two visions of marriage should be quite clear: One is centered on God; the other is centered on self. One seeks to fulfill God's purposes for marriage with happiness as a by-product; the other seeks personal happiness as its primary end. When dealing with issues of divorce, the first approach considers the place of divorce in the purposes of God for marriage; the other looks at the impact of divorce on my own personal happiness. The first is always aware that a third party—namely God—is a participant in this marriage; the other lacks that sensibility.

The search for happiness as an end in itself usually leads to its opposite. As Jesus said, "Those who want to save their life will lose it, and those who lose their life for my sake will find it" (Matt. 16:25 NRSV). If marriage is not primarily about my happiness but instead God's purposes, then I am free to receive its regular joys and personal benefits as God's gracious and unmerited gift. Churches need to create a climate in which this joyful paradox is understood and lived. As the ethicist Vigen Guroian has written,

> Marriage need not be reinvented by Christians. Its character and intentionality, however, must change from selfishness, carnality, and possessiveness to being married "in the Lord." Marriage must be reconnected with the divine purpose through its full integration into the sacramental life of the church.[11]

3. Preach and teach a biblically sound approach to divorce and remarriage. Churches must end their evasion of direct teaching about divorce and remarriage. The biblical evidence related to the legitimate grounds for divorce was reviewed in chapter 7. The texts are complex enough that divergent interpretations circulate among Christian scholars and ministers. Congregations will have within them members who have been exposed to a wide range of views. Thus church leaders dare not assume any natural or easy consensus on what the Bible teaches about divorce and remarriage. There is no substitute for careful biblical study before declaration of a church policy or interpretation.

My own view, as indicated, is that divorce is permitted in Scripture as a rare exception to the norm of lifetime marriage. It is a concession to human hard-heartedness and can never be celebrated or treated as a good in itself. The best summary of the teaching of Scripture is that divorce is permitted in cases of fundamental and irreparable breach of the marriage covenant. Two clear examples of such a breach are named in the New Testament: sexual infidelity and desertion (by an unbelieving spouse). Violence toward spouse or children also violates the marriage covenant as well as the parental covenant, and should be included in any summary list of legitimate grounds for divorce, though no list can exhaust the many diabolical ways in which men and women destroy their covenants with each other.

As for remarriage, Jesus linked divorce, remarriage, and adultery in order to prevent his listeners from thinking that they could hide behind the legal provision for remarriage as moral justification for abandoning their wives for someone more appealing. That is nothing other than sanctioned adultery—then or now. But not every remarriage occurs in this kind of context. Remarriage is thus not categorically ruled out for Christians. Those seeking remarriage in the church—and the remarried who enter the church—should be treated on a case-by-case basis, which is only possible where the congregant's relation to the church involves sufficient honesty and accountability for the necessary kind of conversation to happen.

Whether or not you agree with this statement of concrete moral teaching and church practice related to divorce and remarriage, one aspect of a marriage-keeping strategy must be to address the issue in the local congregation.

4. Employ the resources of the youth, college, and singles ministries to offer sound instruction related to dating, sex, and courtship. Primary responsibility for the moral instruction of children and youth rests with the family. However, those families who covenant with local congregations are entrusting their children to church leaders for instruction in the way of Jesus Christ. Congregations thus have an extraordinary opportunity to begin the resocialization process with teenagers and college students before (and while) they make the choices that will determine the course of their lives.

The issue of how Christian young people should think about courtship and dating has attracted extraordinary attention in recent years. What began as a quiet emphasis within conservative Christianity on sexual abstinence has broadened into a national conversation about the American way of mate selection and sexual behavior. This national attention reflects the sad recognition that whatever we are doing is just *not working.*

So everything about courtship and dating is up for grabs. Authors like Joshua Harris have instructed teens to "kiss dating goodbye" altogether; instead, they should trust God to send a spouse their way at the right time.[12] Others have embraced older courtship approaches involving a sharply heightened role for parental involvement and careful control of private time for the couple. Most evangelical churches that deal with dating teach an abstinence model; more sophisticated approaches in recent years reflect the recognition that young people need to be taught a vision for their sexual and relational future (and present), and not just self-denial.

The growth of programs of age-appropriate instruction in a Christian approach to dating and mating is a significant and constructive development in recent church life.[13] The patterns that youth develop related to meeting their creational needs, making and keeping covenants, and learning to seek the kingdom first have a profound impact on their ability to construct a successful Christian marriage.

5. *Require premarital testing and counseling before participating in any wedding or permitting any wedding to be performed in your church.* It is by now clear that no one should be married by a Christian minister or in a Christian church without extensive premarital preparation. The best premarital preparation process will include a mix of biblical instruction, relationship assessment, and skill development, all offered in a prayerful spirit that helps to communicate the solemn purposes of marriage.

I have already indicated that I use the PREPARE material for my premarital counseling. I interweave biblical and character instruction into the discussion of the various issues raised by the relationship inventory. This mix of instruction and assessment takes anywhere from six to sixteen weeks. The material can be used in individual counseling with a couple or in a group setting; I have participated in both approaches, and either can work. Couples who have walked through PREPARE with me report high levels of satisfaction with the test and the insights gained. Of course, a number of other relationship inventories and materials are now available. There is no excuse for not using one of them. Even the busy pastor can find the time to gain competency in one of these tests and then to see to it that others are trained to offer them and to guide couples through the counseling.

Premarital counseling policies must include the clear understanding that the minister is free—even morally obligated—to refuse to perform a wedding for a couple who is unprepared for a lifetime together. This policy is rooted in the minister's sacred responsibility to keep watch over the flock and guard its members from obvious spiritual and moral error (Acts 20:28; Heb. 13:17). It is an important part of marriage keeping—preserving and honoring the institution (and protecting individuals as well) by guarding its boundaries.

A church's stance on premarital preparation is best solidified by establishing it as a church-wide policy rather than as the preference of an individual minister. It may be best for the church to discuss these policies and approve them in business session to ensure the maximum level of support for them and to protect against a minister being bulldozed by a powerful church member who wants to bend the rules. They should be in writing.

While we have not yet pursued this in our community, I also support the development of *community marriage policies,* innovated by Michael McManus, in which churches in a local area agree on a common set of standards related to premarital preparation.[14] These standards include a four-month waiting period and substantive premarital counseling. The benefit of such a community marriage policy is that it prevents a few irresponsible ministers from serving as the "marrying Sams" of a community whose ministers are otherwise trying hard to prepare couples for marriage. Over 190 American communities have now established such policies.

6. *Offer marriage enrichment, instruction, and mentoring programs.* Of course, as cynics often note, couples don't understand much about marriage until they get into it. Premarital preparation cannot be seen as the end of the church's involvement in working with couples.

One way to begin to address the needs of couples is to structure the premarital counseling program so that periodic follow-ups are built in over the critical first year of the new marriage. These sessions can be a time of great celebration and much laughter but might also prove occasions for serious discussion of snags in the young relationship.

More systematic instruction should also become a part of the educational program of the congregation. If statistics are correct in estimating that less than one-tenth of marriages are experienced as genuinely satisfying, there is considerable room for ongoing relationship assessment, biblical instruction, and skill development.

Our church leadership team decided in 2002 to launch a Marriage-Keepers ministry as part of our overall discipleship program. My wife and I have developed the curriculum and taught several twelve-week classes involving six to ten couples each. We mix instruction concerning the issues covered in this book with the best insights of the contemporary marriage enrichment literature. The class is taught in a two-hour small group context, along with private conversations with couples as needed.

It is also possible to steer couples in the direction of regional and national marriage enrichment events rather than to run a congregational ministry. These events take the form of weekend conferences. The oldest such ministry is the often transformative Marriage Encounter, but a variety of denominational and parachurch programs are available.

At our church, we have chosen to emphasize in-house instruction to make clear that marriage keeping matters to us as church leaders. We also see it as an important way to stay in touch with our couples in order to provide the best possible ministry for them, rather than "farming them out" to traveling conferences. However, we do publicize marriage enrichment conferences for those who are interested.

Though this is not the direction we have taken, many churches have found great success with the use of lay couples as marriage mentors, both in premarital preparation and in marriage enrichment. The most common approach is to assign a young couple to an older and wiser couple. They meet regularly to discuss dynamics in the young marriage and learn from those who have been around the block a few times. This is another strategy recommended by Michael McManus.[15]

The use of mentors reflects an important truth about how people learn a new skill, whether baseball or baking. First, the new skill is demonstrated by the mentor while the student observes. Then the student tries it while the mentor coaches him through, step-by-step. Next, the student tries the skill without coaching but under the mentor's observation, with correction if necessary. Finally, the student is ready to perform the skill on his own. Though it involves more than skills, marriage is a context in which certain key skills must be developed. Many individuals approach marriage lacking any semblance of such skills. Someone will need to coach them.

7. *Offer crisis counseling ministries and a network of referral services for some of the most serious cases.* Sadly but inevitably, every church will include couples who run into significant crises in their marriages. Surely one of the fundamental aspects of a congregational marriage-keeping ministry is to offer quality counseling to such couples. Such counseling bears with it the hope of bringing healing, restoration of covenant, and growth in marital satisfaction. It can be used by God to save marriages, thus sparing both adults and children enormous pain. Crisis counseling also presents a great opportunity to serve those who are marginally connected to the church and invite them into a life of discipleship.

Church leaders must be realistic, however, about the extent of their competency and the time they have available for counseling. Local church ministers rarely take more than a handful of counseling classes. I was reminded in seminary that ministers are best trained for spiritual and moral instruction, the brief pastoral word of comfort, and short periods of crisis counseling. If a problem is beyond the pastor's knowledge, it is an aspect of professionalism to refer the person to someone with more expertise. Ministers must also be aware that counseling can consume the greater portion of the workweek, thus causing neglect of other duties, including the sermon preparation that feeds the spirits and helps direct the lives of the whole congregation. For both of these reasons, referral should be seen not as a brush-off but as an act of ministerial responsibility and genuine pastoral concern.

A final note is needed here with reference to referral and to the church's own counseling ministry. Not everyone who hangs out a shingle as a marriage and family therapist offers counseling according to biblical principles. Nor is every "Christian counselor" as strong an advocate for marital preservation as he or she should be. The ideology of personal self-actualization and a vision of the counselor as someone whose role is to advocate such fulfillment sometimes cuts against the mandate for marriage keeping that is the church's responsibility. Both the church's own counseling ministry and the referral list that the church develops should support, not undercut, a biblical vision of marriage.

8. *Offer a divorce recovery ministry or information about how to find one in the community.* Sometimes people suffer divorce in their families and find themselves being divorced by their church as well. This experience surfaced repeatedly in my interviews with children of divorce. More commonly, uneasy silence prevailed, along with gossip and implicit social rejection. This drove many out of church altogether at a time when the healing balm of Christ's love was needed more than ever.

Divorce is devastating. The church needs to be in ministry with all those who suffer the scourge of divorce. The particular shape of that ministry depends in part on the role of each person in the divorce itself. The children of divorce have intense needs that do not go away after six months or a year.

One fundamental contribution a divorce recovery ministry can and must make is to help prevent hasty and ill-considered second and third marriages (or cohabitation relationships). As the healing process begins and a sense of community is developed, those whose world has crashed down around their heads can find comfort and hope. They can also become equipped to reflect deeply on the failure of their marriages, learn the appropriate lessons, and prepare carefully and slowly for the possibility of another chance at marriage.

Remarriages of bride, groom, or both constituted just under half of all marriages conducted in the United States in 2001. Successive remarriages also fail at progressively higher rates. Any marriage-keeping strategy realistically addressed to this kind of culture must offer access to divorce recovery and remarriage preparation services, including informed instruction about stepparenting and blended family dynamics. There is a place for therapeutic cleanup if it is one part of a broader church strategy and does not reflect a compromise of biblical principles.

9. *Establish and maintain the kind of faith community in which relationships of intimacy, trust, and accountability can grow.* One of the most elusive commodities in contemporary church life is accountability and honest intimacy within the church family. Far too frequently church is experienced as a place that individuals or families attend once or twice a week or less. Here individuals rub shoulders with other individuals for a brief time. But when it comes to honest communication concerning heartfelt needs, hurts, trials, and temptations, it is nowhere to be found. When churches get past this superficiality and reach more authentic corporate intimacy, it is a wondrous thing to behold. But it is all too rare.

A man once told me this story. In a former church he attended, there was a young adult Sunday school department bursting with happy-looking young couples. The department was an important part of the church. But then after awhile the marriages started dropping like flies. No one knew what to do about it. No public discussion of the problem was possible either at the level of the whole church or in the department, though there was of course plenty of gossip. No intervention was apparently attempted. Everyone just looked around at each other, silently wondering whose marriage would be the next to fall apart. The department collapsed in uneasy silence.

In a society that does nothing to restrain us from divorce, each marriage needs to be undergirded by a strong support structure.[16] Lacking an overall social climate that supports lifetime marriage, we must create such social contexts for ourselves within our communities of faith. Every Christian needs at least one person with whom he or she is comfortable speaking with brutal honesty about his or her behavior and marriage. Every Christian needs at least one person whose no to a possible course of action he or she is considering has real significance, even authority.

It is clear that a biblical faith community functions to provide structures of accountability, of saying yes and saying no in the interests of the body and of the individual involved. Of course, abuses of church discipline, changes in cultural values, and the omnipresent "don't tread on me" individualism have weakened the accountability dimension of church experience. Thus marriage breakdown, infidelity, divorce, and serial remarriage (among other problems) are all witnessed silently by an impotent congregation rather than wrestled through alongside an engaged and caring community of fellow disciples. The starting point for creating such a community is found in these relationships of trust, intimacy, and mutual servanthood. For our church, these relationships are nurtured in our small groups, which we require every member to join.

10. Establish clear policies and practices related to confrontation of sin, accountability, restoration, and church discipline. Many churches stop where I just left off. They seek community and celebrate it when it happens. But they do not structure their churches to build accountability into the marrow of church life. However, exciting experiments are under way in many churches in reclaiming biblical accountability. Church constitutions are being amended or drafted so as to include binding practices of accountability.

The starting point for such change involves a rethinking of the meaning of church membership. At our church, potential members must go through a lengthy membership class that explains the philosophy of the church and the requirements for membership. These requirements include, not just a profession of faith and baptism, but also specific behavioral commitments. Foundationally this consists of "living according to biblical standards." Members also commit to "participating in the ministries of the church," including regular attendance in worship, involvement in a small group, financial support of the church, prayer, and service in a ministry area. The constitution is explicit that members "agree to remain accountable to God and the Northbrook family for their fidelity to these membership commitments once they have been freely promised." No one has an obligation to be a member of our church. But those who choose to covenant with us sign on to specific commitments, including a willingness to be held accountable.

This requirement has teeth. Each December our leadership team leads the church through a process of reviewing membership commitments and renewing individual memberships. Some choose not to renew, and sometimes church leaders must undertake conversations with members who are not keeping the covenant promises they have made. These are not easy conversations, but they frequently reveal needs we can address—and they maintain our integrity as a covenant community. Not often, but a few times, it has led to the ending of the membership relationship with our church. At other times it has stimulated fresh recommitment.

An approach like this clarifies whether church leaders have the standing to initiate contact with members whose lives are about to jump the tracks or have already derailed. It is a striking kind of paradox in our postmodern culture—adults voluntarily covenant to restrict their own freedom and to invite reasonable scrutiny of their own lives because they believe that it is the best way for them to find true freedom in Christ. They would not do so if they did not trust the community and its leaders. It is a fragile trust because it is so countercultural and so contrary to fallen human nature. But it is a church practice that provides the only kind of adequate context for moving from uneasy silence to marriage saving.

I once knew of a Christian woman who had become involved in a sexual liaison and was considering abandoning her marriage (including her small children). On the brink of a decisive breach in her marriage, her church family intervened. They surrounded her with clear, direct, passionate rebuke. They called her to be true to her commitments. They reminded her of her children's well-being. In contemporary context, it was an almost unthinkable intrusion into what most would consider her private life. In the end, though, the woman came to her senses, ended the affair, and returned to her marriage. The church family welcomed her back with open arms; she in turn was grateful to her church family for their clear, caring, and biblical intervention.

Such intervention is indeed ill-suited to our age. But it is well-suited to New Testament practice and continues a long tradition of mutual accountability in Christian discipleship. Churches need to explore ways to recover this kind of intimate accountability among brothers and sisters who are committed to the way of Jesus Christ. Keeping silent with one another while we blow our lives apart does no one any favors.

11. Find ways to honor successful models of healthy marriage. One unfortunate consequence of the divorce epidemic has been the disappearance of models of joyful lifetime marriage. Increasingly, young people have to look back to their grandparents, or stories about their great-grandparents, for any exposure to a marriage that lasted, say, fifty years. They cannot find in their current world *anyone* to look to for a model of marital permanence. We are, all of us, caught up in a cycle of divorce that no one planned and that no one wants. Couples find their marriages falling apart and they do not know why. This cycle feeds upon itself, divorce producing more divorce, all the time producing a social climate in which lifetime marriage is increasingly rare. This is social evil and the systemic thwarting of God's will.

Yet it is still the case that long-term marriages can be found. They are to be found in healthy Christian congregations. There are many communities where only in churches can you stumble upon anyone whose marriage has lasted twenty years or more. The church may become one of the very few cultural bearers of the tradition of lifetime marriage to be found anywhere in Western culture. As the church regroups and puts marriage building strategies into place, our public witness will be even more striking. This is the church at its best!

It is incumbent upon churches to lift up these model marriages and bring them to the attention of those who have not been married as long. One church I know has a prominently displayed "Marriage Wall of Fame" in their foyer. There they post pictures of couples who have been married fifty years or more. The use of mentor couples is another way to offer practical help to younger couples and to honor those who have succeeded at marriage. Part of creating an ethos of lifetime marriage is to increase the visibility and eventually the proportion of such marriage giants among us so the feedback loop the younger generation experiences reinforces permanence rather than transience in marriage.

12. Nurture a radically countercultural church ethos in which congregants are accustomed to doing things differently than the world. Undergirding all of the suggestions I have made is a broader proposal. In an increasingly post-Christian culture, the only way for Christians to live the way of Jesus is to form themselves into a tightly committed counterculture whose very existence is a sign of contradiction to the broader society. This was a common theme in the early church, was picked up by minority churches during the Reformation era, and has resurfaced heavily in contemporary Christian thought.

Yet the concept is completely foreign to most American churches, which tend to reflect the patterns of the broader society. This capitulation to culture represents a tremendous failure both of Christian leadership and of training in the way of Christ. Perhaps nowhere is the problem more obvious than in relation to marriage.

Once again we see that merely focusing on when it might be permissible to get divorced cannot begin to scratch the surface of the problem. A renewed moral climate is needed in which Christian moral convictions of all types are held with clarity and practiced with fidelity in rigorous covenant communities and in which resistance to broader cultural currents is understood as fundamental to Christian identity and discipleship. Only this kind of ethos can create the climate in which radical change is possible. Only this can nurture joyful marriages that last a lifetime and are useful for the work of the kingdom. And only clear evidence of success within the body of Christ will give us standing to offer a witness to the broader society, its laws, mores, and media.

To that broader public witness, we now turn.

10

Marriage and the Law

> Other contracts may be modified, restricted, or enlarged, or entirely released upon the consent of the parties. Not so with marriage. The relation once formed, the law steps in and holds the parties to various obligations and liabilities. It is an institution, the purity of which the public is deeply interested in, for it is the foundation of the family and society without which there would be neither civilization nor progress.
>
> —U.S. Supreme Court, *Maynard v. Hill,* 1888

I have argued throughout this book that marriage is a God-given institution intended to meet the creation-based needs of human beings and human communities. It is designed to be covenantal in its structure, which is also a provision made by God for our good and which is equally essential to the proper functioning of the institution itself. Marriage belongs to the entire human family and is not an exclusively Christian institution. The health of marriage should be of concern to all thoughtful people. The obvious current decline of marriage in Western societies affects people of all faiths and of no faith, especially the most vulnerable among us—our children.

For all of these reasons, it is appropriate for Christians to consider strategies to strengthen marriage that extend far beyond the boundaries of the church. Our first task is to get our own house in order. However, we must also articulate a vigorous public witness about marriage in every venue we have available to us. As a part of this effort, it is appropriate for us to press our representatives in government to take steps that may have the potential to strengthen marriage as an institution. We have already seen the key role historically played by the law in relation to marriage: first in limiting the possibility of divorce, then in flinging the door to divorce wide open. The law undoubtedly matters a great deal in establishing the community context in which people undertake marriage and consider divorce. The law guards entry to, and exit from, the marriage cathedral, either strengthening that cathedral or undermining its very foundation.

Thus my goal in this final chapter is to consider legal changes that may strengthen marriage and prevent divorce. The reader may be surprised at the many proposals already being considered and implemented in the fifty states. Careful examination of the options can help each of us catch a vision of what our own citizenship responsibility may require in terms of advocacy and action in the years ahead.

Entry Points for Legal Reform

Christians who are interested in the reform of divorce laws tend to concentrate their fire on the legal regime known as no-fault divorce. This focus is much too narrow. No-fault divorce, as we will discuss in more detail later, has to do with the issue of how and on what grounds an individual or couple may enter into divorce. Yet if we want to think coherently about addressing the divorce problem through legal means, we must look at the entire marriage and divorce law system. As with the rest of this book, the fundamental issue is marriage, not divorce.

Marriage is a relationship governed by state law. Each of the fifty states offers a comprehensive system of laws governing the full range of activities related to marriage. The federal government relates to marriage primarily through welfare and tax policies. But the most important arena for actual policy change remains with the states. In each state:

- The *entry into marriage* is regulated. Laws govern who has the capacity to marry, what makes a marriage legally valid, and how licenses are obtained.
- The *conduct of marriage* is regulated. Laws govern the status of premarital agreements ("prenups"), property rights, legal liability, and the treatment of spouses and children (violence, abuse, etc.).

- The *entry into divorce* is regulated. Laws address residency and jurisdiction, grounds for legal separation and divorce, the process of divorce, mandated counseling or waiting periods, and the handling of property and child-related issues during the divorce process.
- The *postdivorce relationship* is regulated. Primary issues include child custody and visitation, family support duties, and final terms for any financial and property settlement. (I will allude to these issues briefly, though tragically they consume the great majority of the legal system's attention.)
- Finally, in its shaping of laws related to each particular pressure point in the marriage and divorce process, as well as in its broader approach to marriage and divorce, government communicates values that cannot help but have an impact on public attitudes and practices. This "bully pulpit" dimension of public policy response must also be considered when thinking about divorce law reform.[1]

Public Policy Levers

Laws have a logic to them, hard as that may be to believe sometimes. Think of it as a system of levers and pulleys. Policy makers try to accomplish certain social goals. They embed these goals in laws and regulations. Political debate involves not only argument about which goals to pursue but also how strenuously to pursue them. The more vigorously a goal is pursued, the more pressure is put on people to adjust their behavior. Levers and pulleys are attached to laws in order to increase the pressure to conform to them.

Essentially, with regard to any particular social practice, whether marriage or fly-fishing, policy makers can do one of the following:

Remain neutral. Policy makers can decide that there is no governmental interest in either encouraging or discouraging a particular action. Or they can conclude that any attempt to interfere with this action would exceed the boundaries of their jurisdiction or limit freedom too much.

Create (or permit) options. Policy makers can choose to open up a range of options to citizens for the accomplishment of a particular social goal while remaining neutral concerning which options citizens avail themselves of. For example, government has a legitimate interest in seeing that its citizens receive an adequate education. But government permits and sometimes creates a diversity of options for accomplishing that goal.

Offer incentives or disincentives. Government can create incentives and disincentives by which it can encourage or discourage behavior. The incentive set that government has available to it is impressive. Most compelling is the power of the purse. Government can create incentives by offering money to those who perform the behavior government seeks. These dollars can be delivered via the tax system in the form of direct cash grants or through the reduction or waiver of licensing fees. Likewise, government can create financial disincentives in similar ways.

Government also has the ability to create and offer nonfinancial incentives or disincentives. It can offer public honor or dishonor, praise or blame. It can, for example, publish a list of the fifty companies in the state that are doing the best job of putting former welfare recipients to work and then hold a press conference that honors them. This kind of approach is a major feature of the most recent state initiatives to strengthen marriage.

Regulate access (or exit). Another policy lever available to government is its ability to regulate access to some product or benefit—or to regulate the exit from a status or responsibility. Thus, while cigarette smoking is permitted in our country, access to cigarettes is limited to those over a certain age. The same holds true of access to alcohol or R-rated movies. These examples immediately bring to mind the limits of law, for each of these is routinely violated. Yet access regulation is an important policy mechanism. It is especially important with marriage and divorce, because both are "products" that you actually get from the government.

Mandate or prohibit. Finally, policy makers can decide that an action is of sufficient importance that it must be either prohibited or mandated. Because mandating or prohibiting certain behaviors limits personal freedom, a higher burden of proof must be met to justify it. The social benefit gained must exceed the cost to personal freedoms. Most often the move to this level involves a prohibition rather than a mandate, with a punishment attached. We are required not to kill, not to rape, not to steal, and so on. However, it is easy to think of things we are required to do, such as wear our seat belts.

Public policy signals its level of seriousness on such matters through the harshness of the consequences for violations. The same principle holds true with all policy mechanisms—they can be employed with various degrees of intensity depending on their public significance.

In the ongoing debate about marriage and divorce law reform, variations of each of these public policy levers have been proposed. Those who are passionate about particular issues tend to move immediately to the "mandate or prohibit" level. Quite frequently, however, such demands are inappropriate to the issue under consideration, politically infeasible, or a violation of personal freedoms or church/state boundaries. We must remain open to less dramatic measures.

Entry into Marriage: Reform Options

Let us turn now to particular legal reform proposals and possibilities, as well as to two proposals that might be viewed as systemic reforms. We begin with the entry into marriage.

Most states currently regulate the entry into marriage very lightly. Those seeking marriage must obtain a license by filling out a brief form and paying a small fee. There is sometimes, though not always, a very brief waiting period, which the American Bar Association legal guide says is intended "to give a brief cooling-off time during which the parties can change their minds if they wish."[2] This might be viewed as a modest access regulation strategy—as are provisions restricting the marriage of close blood relatives. Those marrying must have the legal capacity to do so, in terms of mental and psychological competence. Most states also regulate access to marriage by age, generally requiring both parties to be eighteen years old (sixteen with consent of parents). Some states lower the age if the woman is pregnant and the parents consent. Sometimes judges are brought in to help determine competence to marry. Currently, all states prohibit same-sex marriages, though that is under intense debate nationally, and Vermont permits gay "civil unions."

One reform option is to attack the problem of marital quality and divorce through more vigorous regulation of the entry into marriage. A number of different strategies have been proposed.

First, some are proposing either the *requirement or the encouragement of a program of premarital preparation, including some combination of testing, counseling, and education*. Such an initiative could be undertaken in tandem with another measure, *the strategic use of extended waiting periods and fees related to obtaining a marriage license*.

In 1998, Florida became the first state in the nation to pass a law—the Marriage Preparation and Preservation Act—with precisely this approach. Couples who take a four-hour marriage preparation class can get a $32.50 discount on their marriage license and can marry with no waiting period. Those who choose not to do so must wait three days and pay the full fee.[3] My own state, Tennessee, passed similar legislation in 2002 that added $62.50 to existing county license fees, which is waived if the couple can certify that they have taken a four-hour marriage preparation class. Minnesota legislators passed a similar bill involving twelve hours of premarital counseling, but it was vetoed in April 2000 by Governor Jesse Ventura. Maryland's Governor Parris Glendening signed a bill similar to Florida's into law in 2001. No state has *mandated* premarital counseling—only voluntary or incentive-based approaches are currently under consideration. Florida's procounseling lawmakers discovered that any mandated plan ran into bipartisan opposition on libertarian grounds.

Another strategy related to the entry into marriage is to address the *age* issue more carefully. States could choose to use one or another lever to try to increase the age at which couples marry, reasoning from all relevant data that teen marriages are likely to be less stable and enduring than those begun later. In March 1998, a Missouri legislator proposed an incentive-based law along these lines. Representative Pat Kelley's bill would have the state offer a $1,000 bonus to any couple that delays marriage until both are at least twenty-one.[4]

Close kin to this kind of approach would be a strategy aimed at encouraging longer courtship.[5] States could offer incentives to those who have known each other at least six months and discourage impulse marriages. One minimal way to move toward this goal would be to impose a longer waiting period from the day of application for a marriage license; this could perhaps be waived upon proof of receiving premarital counseling.[6] Again, such an approach would reflect the recognition that marriages are more likely to succeed if preceded by a significant courtship period.

How are we to evaluate these kinds of proposals?

There are practical administrative concerns, but in my view these are solvable. Such policies could require states to create a new or expanded bureaucracy. If the state provides premarital counseling, there is the question of the expansion of state payrolls to accommodate hordes of official marriage preparers. There is the issue of whether state funding would be provided for those couples unable to pay for counseling. There is the question of possible abuse through the filing of false affidavits.

More deeply, some argue that premarital counseling is ineffective because such couples rarely view their relationships realistically. Coerced premarital counseling might be even less likely than voluntary counseling to have a positive impact on the couple involved. And yet these arguments have been answered by solid data indicating that well-designed premarital inventories and counseling programs have had a positive impact both in strengthening marriages and in preventing certain foolish marriages from taking place.[7]

Some see this kind of regulation as an intrusion of the state into the private sphere. This libertarian-type objection will doom any mandatory measures. As Illinois Republican James Durkin said, "It's not our place to dictate how people will enter into the sanctity of marriage. For the state to mandate premarital counseling is just going too far."[8] This was Governor Ventura's objection as well—even to a *voluntary* plan!

Even those who support the basic concept here must be aware of the "iron law of unintended consequences." Given the rising rate of cohabitation in our society, it can be argued that nothing should be done to increase its frequency—but that putting speed bumps in the path of marriage could lead some couples to live together instead, thus making the cure worse than the problem.

Despite these concerns, I support an incentive-based, voluntary approach focused on significant premarital preparation tied to a waiting period. Such an approach does not violate the boundaries of the state's jurisdiction. The administrative time and costs are worth the trouble and can be limited through the use of streamlined procedures.[9] The state should not be in the counseling business itself. Instead, it should accept the counseling offered by any certified counselor. This includes religious-based counselors—church/state issues on this front should not be seen as a problem, and the state must not restrict the religious content of such instruction. County clerks could keep a list of providers on hand and would make this list available to all applicants for marriage licenses (or divorce petitioners).[10]

To sharpen the incentive all the more, states should offer tax breaks for couples who undergo premarital counseling in any given year, unless the counseling is free. States should not establish some kind of entitlement to premarital preparation, but they could use surplus funds from the federal TANF program (Temporary Assistance to Needy Families, popularly known as "welfare") to provide vouchers for low-income couples to take marriage preparation classes. This approach was pioneered by Arizona in 2000.

I would broaden the difference in the way counseled and noncounseled couples are treated. To be bold, how about a sixty-day waiting period and a $200 fee for those not receiving counseling? This would raise the level of incentive to undertake the premarital program. It would require experimentation to see how high a fee and how long a wait could be employed without negative side effects. A state could defend higher fees and longer waiting periods by spelling out the stark social costs of divorce and the state's legitimate interest in discouraging it, as many states are now doing. All fees could be officially designated for the massive divorce-related government expenses that are a daily reality. Tennessee's legislators did this by designating all extra license money to the Department of Children's Services and other agencies whose time and money are spent dealing with divorce-related issues.

Religious leaders, congregations, or denominations could contribute mightily to the rate of participation in a state-encouraged premarital preparation process by offering high-quality programs themselves and refusing to marry anyone who won't participate in them. This should be the stance of ministers and congregations with regard to premarital preparation in any case, regardless of state law.[11] But where states move in this direction, the churches can happily partner with government.

The Conduct of Marriage: Reform Options

Current state laws regulate the conduct of marriage in three basic arenas: finances, children, and domestic violence.

In terms of finances, a maze of regulations covers all aspects of the financial partnership that is marriage: property, debt, and taxes are among the issues that garner the most attention. The decision concerning whether or not to have children is left to the couple, as are most decisions concerning how to raise children. The rights of children themselves are also the subject of law. Domestic violence statutes prohibit murder, assault, rape, or robbery between spouses or against children.

Besides this, the states tend to demonstrate no particular interest in the well-being of the marriages within their jurisdiction. This section of the law is almost always the briefest in state codes. The state remains neutral or, as Milton Regan puts it, "agnostic" about behavior within families.[12] While it is true that states must not micromanage relationships between husbands and wives, it is no less true that states have a compelling interest in marital harmony and permanence.

States should move from neutrality to a clear public stance of encouraging high-quality, just, and lasting marriages. As Sylvia Ann Hewlett and Cornel West have put it, "Government should get back into the business of fostering the value of marriage as a long-term commitment."[13]

I suggest the following modest initiative: states should use incentives to encourage married couples to undertake marriage enrichment and marriage counseling activities. There would be no need for states to develop such activities or programs themselves. They would offer a modest tax incentive to couples that could certify their participation in such a program (as proposed in New Mexico in 2001). Church/state and funding issues raised by this kind of approach were discussed above. The real policy debate here is not whether such programs would benefit marriage, but whether public will exists for investing tax dollars for this purpose.

At a much broader level, states need to consider a wide range of measures that would offer public policy support for stable and permanent marriages. Hewlett and West have proposed a "parents' bill of rights"—a set of measures that would demonstrate societal support for the honorable, sacrificial, and absolutely critical work of parents. They group their proposals under the following categories: time for children, economic security, a pro-family electoral system, a pro-family legal structure, a supportive external environment, and honor and dignity.[14] Other analysts and advocacy groups have for years been constructing entire public policy programs around the vision of strengthening families, though particular proposals vary widely along ideological lines.[15]

To pursue this issue further here would take us outside the focus of this chapter, but I concur with the basic claim that public policy has a legitimate role to play in offering broad support for strong and healthy marriage and family life.

Entry into Divorce: Reform Options

Today most states approach the regulation of entry into divorce with the same agnostic neutrality that marks state laws related to the entry into marriage. All states require residency of one or both parties to the divorce in the state in which the divorce is being sought. Residency requirements range from six weeks to one year. There are fees and court costs. This could be seen as a very modest access regulation strategy, but in general states have not attempted to impose significant burdens here, in keeping with a Supreme Court decision that barred states from setting unaffordable filing fees.

All states specify the permissible legal grounds for divorce. Here we find two basic but very different patterns: no-fault and fault-based grounds. Since 1985, all states have had no-fault statutes; some have fault-based grounds to go with no-fault approaches; others only have no-fault divorce; some now have "covenant marriages" as well. There is an important history behind the rather strange current structure of our divorce laws.

Through most of our nation's history, legal separation or divorce was available only to a husband or wife who could demonstrate that his or her spouse had committed an offense that was serious enough to merit the relief of separation or the dissolution of the marriage. The presupposition of the law was that the marriage relationship was a matter of significant public interest that extended well beyond the feelings of either husband or wife. Marriage was viewed as a status that imposes a permanent set of obligations on all who are embedded in the relationships that marriage creates.[16] The law legitimately held people to those obligations, releasing them from these only when one partner's behavior constituted a fundamental offense against the marriage. This legal theory was closely tied to the legacy of the Western Christian tradition, with its understanding of the covenant permanence of marriage. But it was also realistic about the social significance of marriage as an institution.

Early in American history the list of offending behaviors, or grounds for divorce, tended to be short and closely tied to a reading of biblical teaching. Thus, for example, the premier ground for divorce has always been adultery. Over time those grounds expanded incrementally, with great variations across the fifty states.[17] But what these codes held in common was the view that the dissolution of a marriage was a grave act that should be limited to particular offenses against marriage.

Quietly and with relatively little fanfare, a revolution in divorce law was successfully undertaken in the 1970s. The first to take the plunge was the state of California in 1969. Marking a clean break with the entire history we have been outlining, non-fault-based divorce (popularized under the label "no-fault divorce") became the new benchmark for divorce law. It swept not only the United States but most of Western Europe as well.

The framers of no-fault divorce were not intending to argue that no one is ever at fault when a marriage collapses or that the end of a marriage is not morally significant. However, they did believe that no one's interests were being served by an adversarial system in which divorcing couples had to go to court to prove to a judge that each other was to blame for a marriage's problems. They believed that the adversarial nature of this structure only aggravated conflicts and was particularly hard on children.

They were also aware that as the demand for divorce began to increase in the 1960s (before the laws were changed), current divorce laws were creating an environment of duplicity in the legal process. Couples genuinely and mutually wanting to divorce were pretending that one or the other was guilty of some particular marital offense. These "disguised mutual consent" divorces generally involved offering perjured testimony under oath. Further, the demand for divorce was leading some judges to stretch the permitted grounds beyond recognition; for example, "cruelty" as a ground for divorce now became "mental cruelty," which could be recognized whenever one or the other partner appeared miserable.[18]

The reformers' idea was to eliminate all of this by waiving the requirement of showing fault. Much like no-fault auto insurance, which was introduced at the same time and influenced the public perception of this divorce law reform, no-fault divorce would remove the legal system from the role of sorting out blame and guilt for a marital "crash."[19] We might say that the legal fiction of a marital offense as cause of every divorce was replaced by the legal fiction of *no* offense as a cause for *any* divorce. The public interest consisted not in keeping troubled marriages together but in enabling their dissolution to be as painless as possible.[20]

Of course these legal changes were driven not only by legal logic but also by profound cultural shifts occurring at the time. Marriage was becoming precisely that consensual, always-up-for-review relationship that the Supreme Court rejected in its 1888 decision cited above. Because my "unhappiness" or "failure to thrive" or "lack of sexual satisfaction" does not necessarily involve fault on my spouse's part, there should be no need to prove that she did anything wrong. I should be free to leave as I continue that search for personal fulfillment that is every American's birthright. Thus the entry into divorce was almost entirely deregulated.

The no-fault vision, if implemented in pure form, would have eliminated all fault grounds from legal codes. However, not all states were willing to go this far: a majority has retained both fault and no-fault grounds. Yet the fault grounds are at this point mere vestiges; their primary use appears to be in the postdivorce financial settlement process where state law still permits fault to be considered at all. Our actual divorce laws permit divorce to be initiated by either spouse for any reason at any time in the marriage. By claiming "irreconcilable differences" or "marriage breakdown," refusing counseling or mediation, and waiting out the legal process, a spouse can find a way of escape from marital commitments in most states.

Today there is much discussion as to whether this thirty-year-old experiment in legal reform should be reconsidered or even abandoned. I believe that it should be modified profoundly, though not abandoned. The argument for some kind of rollback of no-fault divorce can be made in at least the following ways:

Legal considerations. Milton Regan and others have argued that marriage was once understood as a status relationship but now has become contractual in nature. Yet under no-fault what we have is a very flimsy contract. Contract law regulates the entry of parties into a binding legal agreement, specifies the means by which such contracts may be ended, and metes out punishments to those who violate contractual agreements. But no-fault divorce allows a person to abandon the marriage relationship unilaterally, without penalty, and without recourse by the offended contract partner. In legal terms, this is a "terminable at will" relationship. The state's continued participation in the supposed regulation and licensing of marriage is revealed as a sham, little more than "notarized dating." As Bryce Christensen writes, "No fault divorce put[s] the state . . . in the absurd position of requiring a license for the pronouncing of public vows which the state subsequently regards with indifference."[21]

Moral considerations. The law is a teacher, even if at times we might prefer not to notice this. If it is a teacher, no-fault divorce teaches all the wrong things. It teaches men and women that marriage can be casually entered and exited. It teaches that contracts can be violated with impunity. By its very name, it teaches that no one is to be faulted for offenses against marriage such as adultery and abandonment. It permits gross injustices against spouses and children without penalty—indeed, by its structure, no-fault divorce allies the state with the irresponsible party.[22] It teaches that marriage itself is not of particular social significance. It thus contributes to the weakening of personal character, relational stability, public justice, and social virtue. It further contributes to weakened links between American law and our common moral heritage.

Economic considerations. The ease with which anyone can obtain a divorce places the economically dependent spouse (usually the wife) in a precarious situation. If she is abandoned, the fact that no-fault is claimed tends to reduce the value of the property settlement she obtains during the legal process of divorce. Given that 90 percent of divorces leave custody with the mother, she and her children are at risk of impoverishment.[23]

Despite considerable unease related to no-fault divorce, no state has done away with it, nor does it appear that any state is likely to do so in the near future. Not every antidivorce analyst is convinced that the return to a fault-based system would be constructive.[24]

Speed Bumps on the Road to Divorce

But is there something short of a rollback of no-fault divorce that we can propose?

I suggest four "speed bumps" for consideration: enhanced waiting periods, a more vital role for mutual consent, stronger counseling and education requirements, and modest judicial discretion in granting divorces.

1. Waiting periods. When states require substantial waiting periods from the time in which a plaintiff files for divorce until a divorce can be legally granted, they communicate a public interest in preventing unnecessary or rash divorces. In Virginia and several other states, marriages in which children are present cannot be legally dissolved without a one-year period of "living separate and apart without cohabitation."[25]

I suggest the possibility that each state should adopt waiting period requirements at least this rigorous. Amy Black suggests that these waiting periods should be extended to the two- to five-year range, as is the case in some Western European nations.[26] In thinking about this issue, we need to be realistic about what waiting periods can accomplish, as well as the chaos that emerges when the next relationship begins during a spouse's court-enforced waiting period (as happens frequently now). We must be especially concerned with protecting the interests of abused spouses and children. Exceptions can and should be made in these cases. Yet clearly a substantial waiting period is called for under most circumstances. Such legislation is being considered in several states.[27]

2. *Mutual consent.* There is much ferment concerning the entire issue of consent. The legal fiction that a marriage has broken down or suffers from irreconcilable differences even when both parties do not share that view is under withering assault. Some argue for the reinstatement of mutual consent requirements at every stage of the divorce process in every case. This proposal would be unworkable and is politically infeasible. However, proposals are surfacing, such as one in Virginia, that would eliminate unilateral no-fault divorce.[28] This is already standard practice in my home area, Madison County, Tennessee, according to judges here. Other proposals would eliminate no-fault divorce without mutual consent where children are involved. Various proposals have surfaced that would permit unilateral no-fault but would treat the process differently than where there is mutual consent. William Galston has proposed eliminating unilateral no-fault where there are children with the alternative of a five-year waiting period.[29] The principle at stake is important: the decision to divorce is of a fundamentally different nature where there is mutual consent and where there is not, and where there are children and where there are not, and the law should almost always side with the nonconsenting partner when it can.

3. *Counseling and education.* A focus of considerable attention in recent divorce law reform efforts has been the strengthening of counseling and education requirements. This is to be heartily endorsed.

Some states require a period of counseling prior to granting a divorce. Others have no such requirements or limit them to the requests of one party or the discretion of a judge. Here I support a mandatory sixty- to ninety-day period of counseling for every divorcing couple.

Education efforts should be an integral part of any counseling or instruction obtained during the divorce consideration process. Several states have launched recent initiatives requiring divorcing parents to receive some sobering education concerning the effects of divorce on children. Some, including Tennessee, require the couple to write and have approved a child custody and parenting plan. This education or counseling process should also include a prior emphasis on marriage building practices such as communication and conflict resolution. The bias should first be toward the resolution of marital conflict with the goal of preventing unnecessary divorces. Of course some angry, alienated, or irresponsible ex-spouses will resist compliance with such programs. But to the extent that even a percentage of adults and children are helped, the social good is advanced.

4. *Judicial discretion.* While nearly every state involves judges in the divorce process, generally they have very little discretion in their decision making, and those who do have some discretion rarely seem to employ it. They do not normally take the time to undertake a real inquiry into the circumstances facing the couple, but instead the process is generally little more than a summary administrative procedure.[30] Some states permit them to require counseling, and they are heavily involved in postdivorce financial and custody issues. Being a family court judge seems to be deeply dispiriting work. My suggestion here is that judges should be given the leeway to at least delay the granting of a divorce where it is fundamentally frivolous or unnecessary; my hope is that more of them will make use of the discretion they are given. As Carl Schneider writes:

> Many laws now make divorce available where there has been an "irretrievable breakdown" of the marriage. In practice, however, this standard is essentially ignored in favor of divorce on demand. Revitalizing that standard might . . . allow courts to, in effect, send some divorce petitions back for reconsideration.[31]

Mary Ann Glendon has pointed out that several European countries include hardship clauses in their no-fault divorce laws. For example, a 1976 West German law permitted judges to deny divorces "if dissolution of the marriage would impose severe hardship on the unwilling spouse" or if preventing divorce was "exceptionally necessary" for the well-being of the children.[32] This extremely sensible provision—which apparently was never used—would be one way of limiting divorce on demand and holding people accountable to the obligations they have taken upon themselves in marriage. Judges should also have the freedom to assess the circumstances of marriage breakdown, especially egregious fault, in determining divorce settlements. States that have stripped such considerations out of their law should think again.

In summary, then, I support the following steps in relation to the entry into divorce:

- Retain the possibility of mutual consent, no-fault divorce for couples without children.

- Retain and use fault grounds where appropriate both for the entry into divorce and for the just determination of divorce settlements.
- Require substantial waiting periods prior to divorce—longer where there are children.
- Eliminate unilateral no-fault divorce, at least where children are present.
- Require counseling and education prior to granting of divorce, in specialized and more extensive form where children are present.
- Enhance judicial discretion to deny divorce, especially in hardship cases.[33]

Systemic Reform 1: Covenant Marriage

Let us consider two systemic reform options. These attack the divorce problem through an overhaul of the entire marriage and divorce system. We will look first at what has come to be known as "covenant marriage."

The 1997 passage in Louisiana of the Covenant Marriage Law (and similar laws in Arizona and Arkansas) has created considerable public interest. Covenant marriage is best understood as an effort to create *an optional fault-based marriage covenant as a supplement to the current no-fault regime*. It uses the public policy lever of option creation as an expression of public values related to the importance of marriage.

The covenant marriage idea can be traced back at least as far as a 1990 article by Elizabeth Scott, a law professor at the University of Virginia, who employed the language of "precommitments" to discuss the possibility of a couple making an advance commitment to marital permanence, or of the state requiring couples to do so.[34] The first legislative proposal related to covenant marriage surfaced in Florida, also in 1990.[35] The influential communitarian Amitai Etzioni wrote a *Time* magazine article in 1993 in which he proposed the use of "supervows," premarital contracts committing couples to do more than the law requires to keep their marriages together.[36] Since that time the idea has picked up momentum, so that by now it is the leading divorce reform concept in the nation. Bills have been passed in Louisiana, Arizona, and Arkansas and are being considered in many other states. Let us look at the pioneering Louisiana law.

As of August 15, 1997, married couples in Louisiana can choose voluntarily to enter into a covenant marriage. The language of the law implicitly recognizes that a covenant marriage contract is a different kind of arrangement than the typical current marriage, and it is to be treated as such by the legal system *at every stage*—this makes it a systemic reform. Note how each aspect of the marriage law system is addressed in the following provisions:

The Entry into Marriage

- The couple must execute a formal declaration of intent to enter into a covenant marriage. The declaration in Louisiana reads as follows:

> We do solemnly declare that marriage is a covenant between a man and a woman who agree to live together as husband and wife for so long as they both may live. We have chosen each other carefully and disclosed to one another everything which could adversely affect the decision to enter into this marriage. We have read the Covenant Marriage Act, and we understand that a Covenant Marriage is for life. If we experience marital difficulties, we commit ourselves to take all reasonable efforts to preserve our marriage, including marriage counseling.

- This declaration must accompany an application for a marriage license.
- The marriage certificate also indicates whether this is a covenant marriage; witnesses to the marriage must certify that this is the case.
- Those seeking covenant marriage must be able to certify by a notarized affidavit that they have received premarital counseling; the law specifies in detail the key elements of the content of this counseling, which includes discussion of a pamphlet from the state attorney general's office concerning the nature of a covenant marriage. The counselor must also offer a notarized attestation of the counseling.

The Conduct of Marriage

- The declaration of intent to enter a covenant marriage *requires* the couple to seek marital counseling if they experience difficulties.

The Entry into Divorce

- Divorce or separation in a covenant marriage is intended to be fault-based; adultery, imprisonment for a felony, desertion, physical/sexual abuse of child or spouse are listed as fault grounds.

- Otherwise the couple has to show that they have been living separately without reconciliation for two years, longer than is typical in state divorce laws.

How shall we evaluate this innovative legislation? Covenant marriage is an attempt to encourage rather than mandate a return to pre-1969 divorce law. The mechanism it uses to offer this encouragement is solely the creation of an optional "marriage deluxe" legal structure. No incentives or disincentives, mandates or prohibitions, are employed. That is one reason why the law was passed: it could be presented in the language of choice rather than mandate.

Even so, a close reading of the law reveals its clear intent to encourage a return to older ways of looking at the permanence of marriage. The state wants to encourage couples to believe that marriage is a lifetime commitment. It is prepared to help them do so by structuring its marriage laws to make it more difficult to end a marriage if couples contract to play by those rules from the outset. The net result is the creation of a two-tier marriage system: intentionally permanent marriages governed by the covenant marriage laws, and other (implicitly impermanent) marriages governed by no-fault laws. Louisiana and other covenant states hope that the number of the former will grow and the latter decline.

Criticism of this approach could come from two directions: that covenant marriage is going too far, or not far enough. Already there are critics who argue that lawmakers have no business enshrining their moral convictions about marital permanence into law. Even the vocabulary, with its biblical overtones, signals the religious and moral convictions that helped motivate this legislation. The fact that the legislation first emerged from the South heightened the suspicions of some. A predictable chorus of despair concerning the influence of the religious right could be heard.

On the other hand, this law can be seen by serious advocates of divorce reform as not going far enough. Louisiana's law does not abolish or even modify no-fault divorce but seeks to supplement it with an optional fault-based alternative. It can be questioned whether a purely optional system communicates public values in a sufficiently vigorous manner. A set of incentives, such as reduced license fees and tax breaks, could be added.

More broadly, it is reasonable to ask whether a two-tier legal system related to marriage is coherent. It is hard to think of any other area of the law in which citizens can choose from two sets of rules. Here lawmakers are attempting to articulate a public valuing of marital permanence but without requiring or even using incentives to encourage anyone to act in a way that accomplishes that goal. It is as if they are saying, "We want you to stay married but only if *you* want to. If you do, here's a legal option that can help. That's all we'll do for you, but we hope you're interested." That approach may be too weak. Yet it appeals to our preference for freedom of choice. Indeed, some are now arguing for a totally deregulated free market in marriage contracts—not just two options, but the freedom to make whatever marriage contract we want to make.[37] In a sense, this is what prenuptial agreements already do.

Early returns from Louisiana indicate that requests for covenant marriage have trickled rather than flowed in. It is hard to know whether these numbers will increase in the years ahead. The law has encountered a distressing lack of cooperation: from court clerks, from the state's media, and even from many key religious leaders and groups in the state. This includes the influential Roman Catholic Church in Louisiana, which in a devastating decision chose to remain neutral on the law because it requires counselors to discuss divorce as a legal option.[38] (A clear example of the best being the enemy of the good.) Some thought that what one Internet wag called "the diplomacy of love" would lead courting couples to agree to covenant marriages rather than admit in advance that they wanted the low-octane variety. So far this hasn't happened.

It may turn out that citizens will prove unwilling to voluntarily bind themselves to laws that are stricter than those that apply to their neighbors. Can you imagine people doing so in any other area of the law? It may not work here, either, despite the legislature's good intentions. My suggestion is that covenant marriage approaches be strengthened through the intentional use of incentives and, despite discouraging responses thus far, this experiment should continue to be attempted wherever feasible. And yet I do not consider this voluntary, optional regime the most important divorce reform strategy being discussed today.

Systemic Reform 2: A Child-Focused Two-Tier Approach

The concept of a two-tiered divorce law could take another form: a mandatory system hinging on the presence of children. I believe that this is the main direction that divorce law reform should take.[39] The presence of children should automatically transform the legal status of marriage and raise the guardrails against divorce.

Society has a strong interest in supporting marriages that endure and that are worth enduring, and among the most persuasive supports for this claim is divorce's lasting impact in the lives of children. And it is children whose interests are most frequently the last to be considered in our modern culture of divorce.

What would our family law system look like if those interests were taken seriously?

First, a strong case could be made that because roughly two-thirds of all divorces do involve children, the kinds of "entry into marriage" reforms we have already considered should ultimately be mandated for all couples. When we consider the engaged couple, we should see not only who they are now but also the children they will very likely bring into the world—and the predictable impact of divorce on those children. Those impacts are becoming clearer and clearer to the generation of children who have suffered the serial monogamy of their parents.[40]

But let us bracket that proposal and now consider the couple that already has children, either through out-of-wedlock birth or through a prior marriage. A two-tier marriage law system that takes the needs and interests of those children seriously would *mandate* rather than merely encourage a course of premarital testing and counseling and a lengthy waiting period prior to marriage. The freedom of the couple in this case should give way to the well-being of the children involved and to society's stake in that well-being.

The same basic principle applies when it comes to the entry into divorce. When children are involved, states should require lengthy waiting periods of perhaps as much as two years or more. (As in Virginia, these waiting periods should be longer when children are present—and of course abuse situations should always be treated differently.) Couples with children who are considering divorce should be required to attend classes related to the impact of divorce on children as well as all child-related postdivorce issues. The educational process at this pivotal point should operate with a bias toward preserving the marriage and should require reconciliation counseling. Judges should have the discretion to delay or discourage unnecessary or frivolous divorces when children are involved.

Amy Black has argued that mutual consent should be required in divorces involving children, even if it is not required for other divorces.[41] Galston agrees but would leave a five-year waiting period as an escape clause.[42] While I can see needed exceptions to this approach, I do believe that it is appropriate to return to a modified fault-based system for divorce where children are present. In such a system, the presence of children in the home would raise the state's threshold for permitting divorce to something approaching the older fault-based standards that prevailed in American law until 1969. Child or spousal abuse should always be one of the permitted grounds. But a unilaterally initiated divorce for the purpose of personal self-fulfillment or career advancement (or whatever) should not be permitted when children will be affected. Or, if an escape clause is required, the person seeking the divorce should be required to pay dearly for the privilege in terms of both a waiting period and a financial settlement.

With this final proposal, I may have stepped over that line of personal liberty that must be carefully guarded in our political system. However, I do believe that a mandatory two-tier divorce law system that takes into account the well-being of children is morally justified and could be politically feasible. Such a proposal would constitute a systemic reform that includes most of the specific incremental proposals outlined above. It is stronger than covenant marriage in that it would be mandatory rather than voluntary and would apply to at least two-thirds of all marriages. Indeed, it would constitute legal recognition that once children enter the picture, every marriage is, and must be, a covenant marriage, because bringing children into the world imposes covenantal obligations on parents that they must not be permitted to evade in the quest for personal fulfillment.

The Bully Pulpit—and Federal Efforts

One of the most exciting recent developments in this arena has been the use of the "bully pulpit" by both governors and the executive branch of the federal government. Recognizing that leadership involves defining which issues are worth a constituency's attention, the governors of Utah, Oklahoma, and Arkansas in 1998 and 1999 publicly declared reducing the divorce rate to be a goal of their administrations.

Their proposed strategies for accomplishing these goals varied. They included raising the profile of the issue by making it a priority; establishing statewide commissions designed to study ways to strengthen marriage; paying consultants to offer conferences for marriage enrichment and divorce prevention; designing pamphlets aimed at encouraging marriage and preventing divorce to be given to couples in county clerk's offices; instituting marriage skill programs in high schools; using a portion of excess federal welfare money to promote awareness of the value of marriage and to fund other ways to prevent divorce; and encouraging community marriage policies across the state.

President George W. Bush used the occasion of the 2002 debate over federal welfare law to press for $300 million in funding to promote healthy marriages. The background of this proposal is that when welfare was reformed in 1996, Congress reconceived its goals so as to explicitly encourage two-parent families. Federal welfare dollars flowing to the states could be used for marriage-enhancing programs. However, until 2000, not one state devoted a single penny to such programs.

Then, in March of that year, Oklahoma Governor Frank Keating announced his intention to use $10 million from these federal block-grant funds to encourage healthy marriages and help reduce divorce, out-of-wedlock childbearing, and welfare dependency. Wisconsin, Arizona, and New Mexico are among the states that have followed his lead.

President Bush's spring 2002 speech on this matter reviewed the clear evidence that "children raised in households headed by continuously married parents fare, on average, better than children growing up in any other family structure." He reminded listeners that Congress recognized this fact and responded in its 1996 welfare reform legislation, but that states had done very little to follow up. Thus he proposed a variety of initiatives to call the states' attention to these available funds and to highlight effective marriage-building programs. These initiatives include:

- clarifying the encouragement of healthy marriages as a welfare goal
- funding marriage-strengthening research and demonstration projects
- creating a competitive matching grant program for state initiatives to strengthen marriage
- requiring states to describe their efforts to promote marriage as part of their state plan
- encouraging states to provide equitable treatment of two-parent married families in their state welfare programs.[43]

This proposal was predictably opposed by those who believe that the federal government has no business encouraging any particular form of family life. The combination of libertarian (don't infringe on my freedom) and liberal (marriage is not an unalloyed good) objections will make progress on promarriage initiatives more difficult, but the evidence of this chapter is that the great need of the hour is being felt across the country, and that change is on the way.

Conclusion: The Limits of Law

Policy makers can do much to encourage marital permanence and discourage divorce. However, it is important to close with a note of realism and of admonition. The note of realism is this: law cannot produce people of good character, of sound relational skills, and of the mental and psychological health required to make a lifetime marriage work.

Neither can the law force a couple to live out the meaning of the marriage covenant or, ultimately, to live as married persons. Law always has its limits, and those limits are most obvious here. James Fitzjames Stephen is perhaps a bit more pessimistic than I am when he writes, "To try to regulate the internal affairs of a family, the relations of love or friendship . . . by law or by the coercion of public opinion, is like trying to pull an eyelash out of a man's eye with a pair of tongs. They may put out the eye, but they will never get hold of the eyelash."[44]

Thus a word of admonition must go to individuals, couples, and churches. The future of marriage and the well-being of children rest in our own hands. Government can encourage "the better angels of our nature," but we must be willing to live accordingly. Churches, in particular, must do more to exercise their own leadership in this area. What government cannot mandate or prohibit for citizens, churches can for their members. And what we mandate, we can supply—marriage preparation, marriage enrichment and counseling, divorce prevention tools—an entire vision of the creation purposes, covenant structure, and kingdom possibilities of marriage.

Real progress in this area of the law is most likely to result from a partnership of individuals, families, churches, government, and other spheres of society.[45] Change must begin with renewal in our hearts and lives of what once were shared values among us. These values must then find creative expression and incarnation in the preaching and programming of churches and other religious organizations. Then and only then can Christians legitimately seek to employ the limited power of government in this sphere of life to enhance public justice and serve the common good.

Epilogue

Why Christians Divorce "Just like Everyone Else"

The question I most often receive when speaking with various groups about divorce is this: why do Christians divorce *just like everyone else?* Why is it that our divorce rate is the same as, or worse than, the national average? Trying to provide an answer to that question seems like a good way to pull together the various strands of this book.

I have attempted to be very careful in all statistical claims. People trying to make an argument often throw statistics around far too casually, repeating something someone told them who got it from they don't quite remember where. So let's first consider the claim itself and its source.

Most people who make a statement like this are referring, intentionally or not, to a study released in 2001 by the Barna Research Group, an evangelical Christian polling company based in Ventura, California. In that study of divorce, the Barna Group's precise claim was as follows: "Overall, 33 percent of all born again individuals who have been married have gone through a divorce, which is statistically identical to the 34 percent incidence among non–born again adults."[1] Interestingly, and undoubtedly related, when the nation is broken into four regions (Northeast, Midwest, South, and West), the South has the second highest divorce rate, expressed as the percentage of adults who have been married who have also been divorced (35 percent).

The Barna Group's statistic hinges on the term "born again." This is how the research firm describes their use of the term:

> In Barna Research Group studies, born again Christians are not defined on the basis of characterizing themselves as "born again" but based upon their answers to two questions. The first is "have you ever made a personal commitment to Jesus Christ that is still important in your life today?" If the respondent says "yes," then they are asked a follow-up question about life after death. One of the seven perspectives a respondent may choose is "when I die, I will go to Heaven because I have confessed my sins and have accepted Jesus Christ as my savior." Individuals who answer "yes" to the first question and select this statement as their belief about their own salvation are then categorized as "born again."[2]

In the most recent Barna statistics, by this definition 41 percent of the American population is born again.

This bit of research offers the clue needed for responding to the question so often posed. Christians divorce just like everyone else if Christians are defined as born again, which in the terms used in the Barna study consists of one past experience, one current feeling, and one belief about the future. The one experience is having once "made a personal commitment to Christ," the one feeling is that this commitment is still personally important today, and the one belief is that this one experience has guaranteed entry into heaven.

With all due respect to an excellent research firm, I believe that this definition of what it means to be a Christian is theologically inadequate. The problem, however, does not rest with the research firm—it rests with the churches themselves. A great majority of Christians would agree with this fundamental distillation of Christian identity, even if they would not know that this qualifies them as "born again." Christianity is widely understood as some combination of experience, feeling, and belief. Indeed, in a February 2002 document, the Barna Group reported that the greatest percentage of Americans based their moral decisions on feelings rather than absolute moral truths, which is a concept increasingly unfamiliar or rejected in American life.[3]

So now we see that the problem is not so much that this distinct group of United States residents called "Christians" is somehow failing to act distinctively in the area of marriage but instead that there may not be a distinct group of people by that name at all. In a society marked by remnants of Christian cultural influence, including tens of thousands of churches, not to mention TV preachers, bookstores, and radio ministers, with many millions of people drifting in and out of churches off and on at various points in their lives, "Christianity" is all too often a cultural phenomenon that reflects and fully participates in American culture, rather than standing in any way apart from it. In looking at the reports and books offered by George Barna over the years, I am confident that he would agree completely—it is one of his deepest concerns.

I am therefore claiming that to say Christians (as defined by Barna and by most believers) divorce at the same rate as everyone else is to say that Americans who have had a handful of core religious experiences, feelings, and beliefs that are spoken of in American culture divorce at about the same rate as other Americans who do not report those same experiences, feelings, and beliefs. At this point, Christianity dissolves into the cultural morass, which is exactly, in most respects, what it has done.

In this book, we have reviewed the long historical journey that has taken us to this point. Our topic has been marriage, but the broader significance of this study should be fairly obvious. What has happened to the marriage cathedral has in many respects happened to every other institution and to every other aspect of historic Christian moral teaching, because the collapse of the marriage cathedral is in fact the result of the collapse of the Christian worldview and its theological and philosophical underpinnings.

In the premodern Christian marriage paradigm, marriage and divorce were governed by a stern rule-based ethic, emphasizing who may and may not legitimately marry, divorce, or remarry. Divorce was basically impossible. What survives of that approach now is primarily a remnant of quite conservative churches (including the Catholic Church) attempting to enforce their understanding of biblical and church rules, where necessary through exclusion and boundary marking. Though this emphasis extends deep into the history of Christianity, it was never an adequate reading of the full biblical witness about marriage, and it is being routed in contemporary American culture.

Uneasily grafted onto that tradition in the Western church after the coming of the modern era was the *affectionate marriage* ethos that emerged in the eighteenth and nineteenth centuries. This approach grounds marriage in the love relationship that develops spontaneously, and is maintained voluntarily, between a man and a woman. The norm of affectionate marriage that swept Western culture eventually came to pervade the Christian understanding of marriage as well. In the culture, the victory of affectionate marriage ultimately left the door wide open to mass divorce in the postmodern period as the inevitable answer to the question of what happens when one or the other partner no longer *feels* or *wants to be* affectionate.

In the church, the affectionate marriage ethos has eroded but not completely eliminated the original biblically based, rule-oriented paradigm onto which it was once grafted as a minor addendum. The vision that prevailed for perhaps two centuries (say, 1760–1960) was this: "As a Christian you are allowed to marry for love but only once, come what may." But where the erosion has penetrated most deeply, we find pure capitulation to mass divorce and, sometimes, therapeutic cleanup. Thus: "You are allowed to marry for love as many times as you want to, and we will support you every time, solemnize your various unions, and perhaps help you sweep up the broken pieces along the way." Where affectionate marriage has only partly eroded the older approach, there tends to be uneasy silence, as the two aspects of the paradigm cancel each other out, leaving paralysis.

It is the uneasy *combination* of a remnant of the premodern, rule-based approach with the modern affectionate marriage ethos that still survives as the primary (though not exclusive) existing paradigm for marriage and divorce in North American church life. It is a paradigm that does not work, either in its component parts or as a combination. Its inadequacy helps to account for the impotence of the churches in responding to the waves of divorce that have washed over our heads since the 1960s.

This paralyzing clash of perspectives manifests itself in many venues. An October 2002 segment of ABC's *Primetime* profiled the musicians Amy Grant and Vince Gill. Both Grant and Gill were married to other people and both were parents of children at home when they experienced "love at first sight" (Grant's words). For several years they struggled to determine whether they should remain faithful to their marriage covenants or follow their feelings into divorce from their current spouses and marriage to each other.

To their credit, it was at least a *struggle* that was not immediately resolved in favor of divorce. The struggle was both personal and professional for Amy Grant, whose committed Christian faith had been the subject of her lyrics for the largest part of her career. She had become perhaps the best-known female Christian musician in the nation. But now, as the *Primetime* narrator put it, "Her faith and her Christian fans told her marriage is forever. Her heart told her something else." Grant and Gill were asked on camera, "What do you do when you find your soul mate, and it is not your spouse?" Grant paused, said that there were many options in such a situation, but that she had obviously made her choice. She went with the soul mate.

Grant was asked if she believed in "fate" and whether her relationship with Gill was "meant to be." She agreed that she did in fact believe in fate, but "with a whole lot of mercy all over it." Neither Grant nor Gill asked the viewing public to endorse their choices, nor did they unequivocally endorse those choices themselves. However, Gill probably spoke for both of them when he mused about his long and winding journey to get where he is now. He said his life was his own and he need not defend it to others. They both carried themselves with a thoughtful dignity.

I hope only the best for Amy Grant, Vince Gill, their ex-spouses, and their children. They have embarked on the blended family path that is now the American Way, and the God who goes with them, as with all, is gracious. I write not to judge them but to observe that here we have a very visible example of the phenomenon that has been the focus of this study. The redefinition of marriage, of divorce, of moral obligation, of how we know what we are supposed to do in this life, indeed, of the meaning and purpose of life itself, are all here to see. The displacement of the biblical language of covenant permanence with the pagan language of fate and destiny is particularly telling. Covenants are freely made and bind their makers for life, short of some fundamental and irreparable violation. They are the products of human choices and are held together by those same choices and by a faithful covenant God. Fate and destiny are, on the other hand, things that happen to us that are beyond our control. No one can prevent them; no one is responsible; no one is to blame.

Amy Grant would, almost definitely, fit Barna's definition of a born-again Christian. But in a culture so deeply penetrated by modern and postmodern ways of thinking, it doesn't matter that she fits that definition. That pivotal born-again experience, current feeling, and core belief about eternity are not enough to make any real difference in how most Christians actually make their decisions in this culture now.

I have offered an alternative vision of marriage in this book and of the beliefs that undergird that vision of marriage. Given to his creatures by a good God, marriage exists to fulfill pressing creation needs for companionship, sex, and family partnership. Marriage is a lifetime covenant, structured as such to advance its creation purposes and protect all who participate in it, both adults and children. For Christians, marriage should be explicitly understood as directed toward the advancement of God's reign in this world torn asunder by sin. This thirst for God's reign creates a new context for the pursuit of the good gifts of marriage itself. For Christians, and for all who are married, marriage requires a context of community support—not just the soft emotional support of the friend who will bless whatever you choose to do but the sturdy support of the church family and maybe even the civic community that helps us hold true to our covenants when, in times of suffering, we most want to abandon them.

Christians are people who gladly submit to the sovereign authority of God the Father, gladly receive the delivering love of God the Son, and gladly reshape their lives through the empowering presence of God the Holy Spirit. Christians are people who believe that they are not free to follow their hearts or live as they choose but instead have found a new and better kind of freedom in giving themselves with full commitment, in repentance and faith, to Jesus Christ. Christians are people who marry on God's terms, conduct marriage on God's terms, and divorce only on God's terms—and so are unlikely to divorce at all. Finally, in resisting the core worldview commitments of the culture with such ferocity, Christians are people who know that they cannot sustain such a life alone. Together with other disciples of Jesus Christ—the One through whom the world was made, the One who suffered for our redemption, the One who will come again to establish his kingdom in glory—they pursue the path he established in marriage as in all of life.

Appendix

The Divorce Interviews

I began conducting more or less formal interviews with children of divorce at Union University in 1997. I conducted the first thirty interviews personally over the next two years, using an identical printed questionnaire in every case. Select Union staff members and student workers transcribed these interviews from audiotapes. The other thirty interviews were conducted by students in an upper-level class on marriage and divorce that I offered in 1998, 2000, and 2002. I made my own interview questionnaire available to student interviewers and most followed it rather closely. Some students exceeded my questionnaire in terms of the extensiveness of the questions, while a handful were not quite as rigorous as I suggested. Students generally, though by no means exclusively, interviewed fellow students they already knew personally. Student interviewers were responsible for transcribing their own interviews.

For the 2000 and 2002 classes, I permitted students to interview divorced adults, couples they perceived as happily married, or children of divorce. Six interviews were conducted with divorced adults, seven with the happily married. The data from these interviews has not been employed in any statistical compilation in this book.

Both interviewers and those interviewed knew that the interviews were to be used for this book on marriage and divorce. All who were interviewed signed a release form granting permission to tape, transcribe, edit, and publish the interview, as long as no names were divulged. Details mentioned in the interview that might unintentionally reveal the identity of particular individuals were altered to preserve confidentiality. Originally

I had planned to publish entire interviews in a book that would be built around the theme of "voices of the children of divorce." Eventually I decided on a different approach and am thus using these interviews more narrowly, which helps to preserve confidentiality all the more.

The consent form closed with an expression of appreciation to those interviewed for opening their lives up for scrutiny in this way. While those who were interviewed responded with varying levels of visible emotional intensity during the interview, undoubtedly the 90–120 minute discussion was quite difficult for most. I am deeply grateful to these men and women for their willingness to share their stories. They did so because of their desire to bring some redemptive value out of their pain—and because it seemed meaningful to many of them to have their stories told. Once news of my project spread in 1997–98, students actually began approaching me, asking for the opportunity to speak for the record about what they had experienced. The voiceless sought a platform.

I make no pretense here that these interviews or the data collected thereby meet the strictest standards of social scientific research. Perhaps these sixty conversations are best understood as a rather carefully organized collection of anecdotes. Even as such, however, they prove highly illuminating.

Data for Interviews with Children of Divorce (1997–2002)

1. Sex:

Males: 17 (28.3 percent)
Females: 43 (71.7 percent)

Note: It would be preferable if this number was closer to 50/50, but it must be remembered that Union's student body is roughly 65 percent female.

2. Level of conflict before divorce:

High: 19 (38.8 percent)
Low/medium: 30 (61.2 percent)
Not discernable/no information: 11

Note: The answer to this question was determined on the basis of such questions as:

a. What do you remember about your early childhood?

b. What memories do you have of your parents' relationship prior to the separation and divorce process?
c. Were you happy? Did they seem happy together?
d. Did the announcement of an impending divorce come as a surprise to you?
e. Was there any physical violence in your home prior to separation and divorce?

3. Average age of child at time of first divorce: 9.3 years
Youngest: six months

Note: Some of those interviewed experienced the divorce of their parents while in college, after the age of eighteen. Where this was the case, their data was excluded from those categories where it is not relevant.

4. Reasons for first divorce:

Major reasons:

infidelity: 34 (56.6 percent)
communication: 17 (28.3 percent)
job stress/workaholism: 15 (25 percent)
financial irresponsibility/arguments: 14 (23.3 percent)
abuse/violence: 9 (15 percent)
addictions/substance abuse: 7 (11.6 percent)

Miscellaneous reasons:

death in family: 1
mental problems/depression: 2
religious differences: 2
no sexual relationship: 1
no love: 2
midlife crisis: 1
criminal behavior: 1
general immorality/immaturity: 1
no clear reason given/known: 4

Note: Students were asked, "What would your parents say and what would you say was the reason (or reasons) for their divorce?" Any reason explicitly offered by the student was included in the above numbers, even if it differed from a reason articulated by a parent to the child. A reference to *abuse or violence* reflects either spousal abuse or child abuse. *Addictions* include alcohol, drugs, compulsive gambling, or pornography. *Infidelity* includes homosexual behavior by a husband or wife. This was rare—most infidelity was heterosexual. I counted it as infidelity for this statistic only if it occurred before the separation. *Communication* is a catch-all term for such descriptions as "they stopped talking" or "they argued/yelled all the time" or "they simply were unable to get along and fought about everything." Money-related problems were a very important reason given for divorce; I broke these down into issues related to perceived financial irresponsibility or differences over how to manage money, over against job stresses and work habits that were perceived as damaging or killing the marriage.

5. Violence:

Before divorce: 9 (15 percent)
During/after divorce or in remarriage/cohabitation relationship: 12 (20 percent)

6. Custody (original arrangement):

mother (with visiting father): 42 (79.2 percent)
split time: 7 (13.7 percent)
father (with visiting mother): 2 (3.7 percent—in one case, father became abusive; children sent to foster home)
other: 2 (3.7 percent—grandparents, children's home)
NA: 7

Note: Custody refers to the students' answer to this question: "After the divorce, what custody arrangement was in place? How closely was it followed?" My focus is on the initial legal custody decision ordered by the courts after the core parental divorce, as well as on the actual unfolding of the parent-child relationship after that.

7. Economic circumstances after divorce:

Decline: 30 (66.6 percent)
Same: 15 (33.3 percent)
No information/not discernible from interview/not applicable: 15

Note: Relevant questions here included the following:

What was the economic impact of the divorce?
Did your living arrangements change as a result of the divorce? How? Did you have to move?

8. Child had to move as result of first divorce:

27/60 (45 percent—some NA)

9. Declining quality of relationship with

Father: 41 (68.3 percent)
Mother: 18 (30 percent)

Note: This number was determined by responses to questions such as:

What custody arrangement was in place? How closely was it followed?
How much contact did you have with your father? Mother? Extended family?
What was the emotional impact of the divorce on you? Your mother? Your father?
How did your relationship with your mother, father, and siblings change as a result of the divorce?

It should also be noted that child-parent relationships develop and change over time, sometimes worsening, sometimes improving. My assessment of this category had to do with the general pattern or trajectory of the relationship since the time of the divorce.

10. Remarriages and divorces (after the end of core parental marriage):

Remarriages: 117 (1.95 per child)
Divorces: 57 (.95 per child)

Highest:

Mother: 10, 6, 5, several with 3
Father: 5, several with 3

Suggested Reading

Chapter 1

Beck, Ulrich, and Elisabeth Beck-Gernheim. *The Normal Chaos of Love*. Oxford, England: Polity, 1995. A German treatment of changing patterns in sex and family life argues that the nuclear family is indeed falling apart and that couples now must negotiate a "detraditional" family life, seeking love in a chaotic and inhospitable environment.

Bennett, William J. *The Broken Hearth: Reversing the Moral Collapse of the American Family*. New York: Doubleday, 2001. Reviews contemporary social trends and their negative consequences, argues for the superiority of the traditional family structure for both individuals and society, and proposes an agenda for action.

Coontz, Stephanie. *The Way We Never Were: American Families and the Nostalgia Trap*. New York: Basic Books, 1992. In this book and a companion volume (*The Way We Really Are,* 1997), Coontz has established herself as a leading opponent of "traditional family" arguments, marshaling historical data to argue that the family has always been in flux and that any approach to family life can succeed with the right support systems.

Gallagher, Maggie. *The Abolition of Marriage: How We Destroy Lasting Love*. Washington, D.C.: Regnery, 1996. An intense, conservative analysis of many of the trends discussed in this chapter and the social costs of our culture of divorce.

Giddens, Anthony. *The Transformation of Intimacy: Sexuality, Love, and Eroticism in Modern Societies*. Stanford: Stanford University Press, 1992. An important postmodern treatment of contemporary sexual and marriage practices.

Gill, Richard T. *Posterity Lost: Progress, Ideology, and the Decline of the American Family*. Lanham, Md.: Rowman & Littlefield, 1997. Gill offers documentation of the fading traditional family and its consequences, proposing that one key explanation for these trends is the loss of confidence in the idea of progress so central to historic American identity.

Goode, William J. *World Changes in Divorce Patterns*. New Haven: Yale University Press, 1993. An exhaustive sociological study of international divorce trends in 1950–90, finding that mass divorce is now an international phenomenon whose harsh effects have generally not been adequately addressed in either custom or law.

Hackstaff, Karla B. *Marriage in a Culture of Divorce*. Philadelphia: Temple University Press, 1992. A careful, sociological study of "marriage culture" and "divorce culture" as ways of looking at and living out married life, assessing the costs and benefits of both models through a study of two generations of married couples.

Lasch, Christopher. *Haven in a Heartless World: The Family Besieged*. New York: W. W. Norton, 1977. Written just as the divorce revolution was reaching its peak, this rather angry book, now a classic, attacks the intrusion of social science experts into the family and especially their fateful cultural impact in weakening the unique status and role of the family.

Marks, Lara V. *Sexual Chemistry: A History of the Contraceptive Pill*. New Haven: Yale University Press, 2001. A review of both the medical and social history of the birth control pill, including its triumph within both Protestant and Catholic populations.

Paul, Pamela. *The Starter Marriage and the Future of Matrimony*. New York: Villard, 2002. A striking but too sanguine study of young marriages lasting five years or less, a new and growing category contributing to the sky-high divorce rate.

Popenoe, David. *Disturbing the Nest: Family Change and Decline in Modern Societies*. New York: Aldine de Gruyter, 1988. A comparative sociological study of the changing shape of the Western family from a man who has emerged as one of the foremost academic defenders of marriage in the United States. Shows that Americans still sentimentalize marriage and are more likely than Europeans to try again rather than settle for cohabitation.

Popenoe, David, Jean Bethke Elshtain, and David Blankenhorn, eds. *Promises to Keep: Decline and Renewal of Marriage in Ameri*ca. Lanham, Md.: Rowman & Littlefield, 1996. An important collection of essays from pro–"marriage culture" intellectual leaders, tracing the decline of marriage and its consequences and proposing ways to strengthen marriage as an institution in American life.

Skolnick, Arlene. *Embattled Paradise: The American Family in an Age of Uncertainty*. New York: Basic Books, 1991. A sociological/historical analysis of changes in American family life since the 1950s, admitting that the family has changed dramatically but rejecting conservative "nostalgia" for a return to the traditional family.

Waite, Linda J., and Maggie Gallagher. *The Case for Marriage: Why Married People Are Happier, Healthier, and Better Off Financially*. New York: Doubleday, 2000. A frankly self-interest–based argument for marriage, offering empirical evidence that marriage is a better option for human well-being than its alternatives and that it should, therefore, be treated as socially preferable.

Weeks, Jeffrey. *Invented Moralities: Sexual Values in an Age of Uncertainty*. Cambridge, England: Polity Press, 1995. Offers a postmodern defense of the values of "sexual diversity" and "freedom of choice" under the rubric of "radical humanism," evidence of the scholarly ratification and articulation of the sexual revolution.

Wilson, James Q. *The Marriage Problem: How Our Culture Has Weakened Families*. New York: HarperCollins, 2002. Wilson argues that among our nation's many social divisions, the most profound is between the stably married and those who struggle in alternative arrangements. He traces the origins of our weakened institution of marriage to American individualism and, for African-Americans, slavery. A broadly learned, social scientific treatment of most key aspects of "the marriage problem" today.

Chapter 2

Basch, Norma. *Framing American Divorce: From the Revolutionary Generation to the Victorians*. Berkeley: University of California Press, 1999. Traces both the legal practice and the cultural struggle over divorce in America from 1770 to 1870, arguing that ultimately the central issue for debate concerned the legal independence of women and their autonomy relative to men.

Brooke, Christopher N. C. *The Medieval Idea of Marriage*. Oxford: Oxford University Press, 1989. A rather repetitive but still fascinating study of various ways of describing and understanding medieval marriage.

Browning, Don S., et al. *From Culture Wars to Common Ground: Religion and the American Family Debate*. Louisville: Westminster John Knox,

1997. A very helpful foray into the marriage and family debate by a group of well-informed mainline Christian scholars. Attempts to offer a "practical theology" for the contemporary setting that is informed by relevant religious, historical, and sociological awareness. One of a series of books in the Family, Religion, and Culture series offered by Westminster John Knox Press.

Cherlin, Andrew J. *Marriage, Divorce, Remarriage*. Cambridge: Harvard University Press, 1981. A careful sociological analysis of trends in American family life since the 1950s, with exploration of potential explanations and contemporary consequences.

Clapp, Rodney. *Families at the Crossroads: Beyond Traditional and Modern Options*. Downers Grove, Ill.: InterVarsity Press, 1993. A feisty Christian treatment of marriage, included here because of its unusual emphasis on the role of "advanced capitalism" in undermining lasting marriage and its overall acuteness in discussing postmodernity.

Cott, Nancy F. *Public Vows: A History of Marriage and the Nation*. Cambridge: Harvard University Press, 2000. Offers a political/legal history of American marriage laws and the massive impact of those laws on American culture.

Frum, David. *How We Got Here: The '70s: The Decade That Brought You Modern Life (for Better or Worse)*. Random House Canada, 2000. Frum's argument is revealed by the title—the 1970s (rather than the 1960s) was the decade in which the world we now live in was really created. A brief chapter on divorce as a path to self-actualization is devastating.

Graff, E. J. *What Is Marriage For? The Strange Social History of Our Most Intimate Institution*. Boston: Beacon Press, 1999. A biting, sometimes satirical rendering of the history of marriage, written by a gay marriage participant/advocate who is motivated by the desire to demonstrate that the meaning of marriage has always been contested, even as it is in our time.

Hartog, Hendrik. *Man and Wife in America: A History*. Cambridge: Harvard University Press, 2000. A thorough, scholarly treatment of American marriage and divorce, especially the legal history during the nineteenth century.

Hunter, David G., editor and translator. *Marriage in the Early Church*. Eugene, Ore.: Wipf and Stock, 2001. A nice collection of some of the most significant patristic documents, accompanied by a helpful introduction.

Mackin, Theodore, S.J. *Marriage in the Catholic Church: Divorce and Remarriage*. New York: Paulist Press, 1984. A magisterial Catholic discussion of the entire history of Catholic teaching on divorce and remarriage. A pivotal theme is that the indissolubility tradition is a deeply flawed effort to accomplish a laudable end—preventing divorce.

May, Elaine Tyler. *Great Expectations: Marriage and Divorce in Post-Victorian America*. Chicago: University of Chicago Press, 1980. A fascinating study of a neglected period of American marriage and family life—the late nineteenth and early twentieth centuries. May documents both from general trends and from specific cases show the rise in divorce during this period and the way in which the quest for happiness in personal life—through divorce—presaged the era in which we now live.

Morgan, Edmund S. *The Puritan Family*. New York: Harper & Row, 1966. A classic, sympathetic treatment of the marriage and family practices of this fascinating American subculture.

Morse, Jennifer Roback. *Love and Economics: Why the Laissez-Faire Family Doesn't Work*. Dallas: Spence, 2001. Morse offers a trenchant critique of libertarian economics/politics as a worldview applied to all areas of life, including marriage and the family where, she says, it does not work.

Phillips, Roderick. *Untying the Knot: A Short History of Divorce*. Cambridge, England: Cambridge University Press, 1991. A very helpful treatment of the history traced in this chapter.

Reynolds, Philip Lyndon. *Marriage in the Western Church: The Christianization of Marriage during the Patristic and Early Medieval Periods*. Leiden, The Netherlands: Brill Academic, 2001. A rather technical, quite thorough treatment of the subject, especially helpful in identifying ways in which the Western church "Christianized" the Roman and Germanic law codes it inherited.

Ruether, Rosemary Radford. *Christianity and the Making of the Modern Family: Ruling Ideologies, Diverse Realities*. Boston: Beacon Press, 2000. Ruether covers much of the same ground as other histories, though from a sharply feminist perspective that treats much contemporary Christian concern about the family as a veiled ideological effort to roll back changes in the role of women in society.

Tarnas, Richard. *The Passion of the Western Mind*. New York: Ballantine Books, 1991. An excellent tracing of Western intellectual history.

Whitehead, Barbara Dafoe. *The Divorce Culture*. New York: Knopf, 1997. A critically important multidisciplinary analysis of the American divorce culture, its historical roots, and contemporary impact.

Witte, John, Jr. *From Sacrament to Contract*. Louisville: Westminster John Knox, 1997. An excellent tracing of the history of marriage in Christian thought and practice, proposing five historic Western models of marriage: Catholic (sacramental), Lutheran (social estate), Calvinist (covenant), Anglican (commonwealth), and Enlightenment (contract).

Yalom, Marilyn. *A History of the Wife*. New York: HarperCollins, 2001. Covers the ground traversed in this chapter through the perspective of women's experiences as wives.

Zaretsky, Eli. *Capitalism, the Family, and Personal Life*. Revised and expanded edition. New York: Harper & Row, 1986. This groundbreaking work was the first to argue, in 1976, that the rise of capitalism caused a public/private split in capitalist societies that had an extraordinary impact on marriage and family life, including that restless search for personal identity that so characterizes the Western world.

Chapter 3

Ahrons, Constance. *The Good Divorce: Keeping Your Family Together When Your Marriage Comes Apart*. New York: HarperCollins, 1994. A leading book in the genre that attempts to "normalize" divorce and to focus on prescribing the steps needed for a successful postdivorce transition.

Amato, Paul R., and Alan Booth. *A Generation at Risk: Growing Up in an Era of Family Upheaval*. Cambridge: Harvard University Press, 1997. This volume by two sociologists offers a comprehensive overview of the contemporary experience of childhood. Perhaps the most famous finding of the book is that the impact of divorce on children is directly related to the level of marital conflict that preceded the divorce—divorces following high-conflict marriages are in children's best interest, while divorces following low-conflict marriages are detrimental to children's well-being.

Applewhite, Ashton. *Cutting Loose: Why Women Who End Their Marriages Do So Well*. New York: HarperCollins, 1997. A leading text in the school of thought that views divorce as a positive thing for women, especially if they initiate it to find liberation from an oppressive and unsatisfying marriage.

Blankenhorn, David. *Fatherless America: Confronting Our Most Urgent Social Problem*. New York: Basic Books, 1995. Perhaps the most controversial of the new wave of pro-fatherhood books, this volume is especially helpful in its argument that no substitutions for a father can take the place of the real thing.

Bunge, Marcia J., ed. *The Child in Christian Thought*. Grand Rapids: Eerdmans, 2001. An edited work offering a kind of historical theology of children, beginning with New Testament resources and extending to contemporary feminist thought. The book helps show that Christian faith does have a rich history of reflection on children, their needs, and adult moral responsibilities to children.

Dennis, Wendy. *The Divorce from Hell: How the Justice System Failed a Family*. Toronto: Macfarlane, Walter & Ross, 1998. A story from a Canadian author of the catastrophic divorce of a man named Ben Gordon and his odyssey through the Canadian legal system. One of a species of books that sides with either the man (and men) or the woman (and women) over against a legal system that the authors say is unfair to one or the other sex—and gives evidence of how our divorce culture is pitting men and women against each other in a new kind of gender war.

Emery, Robert E. *Marriage, Divorce, and Children's Adjustment*. 2d ed. Thousand Oaks, Calif.: Sage, 1999. An academic treatment of the key issues in children's adjustment to divorce, written by a clinical psychologist who specializes in divorce-related issues. Emery argues that a number of factors outside of their control affect how well children respond to divorce but that a resilient response is possible.

Gold, Lois. *Between Love and Hate: A Guide to Civilized Divorce*. New York: Penguin, 1992. A family mediation specialist walks through the entire process of divorce—from separation to the postdivorce shared parenting relationship—offering a number of helpful strategies intended to help couples avoid descending into the nastiness of postdivorce warfare that ruins so many lives.

Griswold, Robert L. *Fatherhood in America: A History*. New York: Basic Books, 1993. A thorough history of American fatherhood, focusing especially on the striking changes in the understanding of fatherhood in the twentieth century.

Hayes, Christopher L., Deborah Anderson, and Melinda Blau. *Our Turn: The Good News about Women and Divorce*. New York: Pocket Books, 1993. Another book in the "divorce-is-good" style, arguing that for many women over forty, divorce is profoundly liberating and a stimulus to reaching their full potential.

Hetherington, E. Mavis, and John Kelly. *For Better or for Worse: Divorce Reconsidered*. New York: Norton, 2002. Hetherington, a professor emeritus of psychology at the University of Virginia, offers the leading alternative to the better-known work of Judith Wallerstein on divorce and its effects. Hetherington is somewhat more positive than Wallerstein about the long-term prospects of recovery from divorce, emphasizing personal responsibility and the opportunity to make choices leading to constructive outcomes for both adults and children.

Johnston, Janet R., and Linda E. G. Campbell. *Impasses of Divorce: The Dynamics and Resolution of Family Conflict*. New York: Free Press, 1988. Two specialists on the dynamics of divorce and "family transition" dissect the causes of long-term postdivorce conflict, discuss its impact on children, and propose a model for breaking such "impasses of divorce" for the good of all concerned.

Kaganoff, Penny, and Susan Spano, eds. *Men on Divorce: The Other Side of the Story*. San Diego: Harcourt Brace and Company, 1997. A collection of narratives from men about divorce from which the editors find common themes as well as interesting connections with the stories of women after divorce.

Karbo, Karen. *Generation Ex: Tales from the Second Wives Club*. New York: Bloomsbury, 2001. Divorce has become so much of a social institution in America that it is now possible for gifted writers such as this one to offer a humorous account of the sheer complexity of the multiple divorce/remarriage way of life—the humor is most illuminating.

Larson, David B., James P. Swyers, and Susan S. Larson. *The Costly Consequences of Divorce: Assessing the Clinical, Economic, and Public Health Impact of Marital Disruption in the United States*. Rockville, Md.: National Institute for Healthcare Research, no date listed. A "seminar" rather than a book per se, this work offers a unique medical/clinical perspective on such issues as the impact of divorce and remarriage on adults and children.

Marston, Stephanie. *The Divorced Parent: Success Strategies for Raising Your Children after Separation*. New York: Pocket Books, 1994. A too upbeat how-to book for single parents (especially mothers) on parenting after divorce, written by a divorced single mother.

McLanahan, Sara, and Gary Sandefur. *Growing Up with a Single Parent: What Hurts, What Helps*. Cambridge: Harvard University Press, 1994. An influential book by two sociologists offering careful documentation and analysis of the disadvantages experienced by those growing up in a single-parent home, with a strong emphasis on its economic consequences.

Pam, Alvin, and Judith Pearson. *Splitting Up: Enmeshment and Estrangement in the Process of Divorce*. New York: Guilford Press, 1998. A deeply researched guide to the complex and difficult psychological processes associated with divorce and recovery from divorce; written at a rather technical level and aimed especially at therapists.

Popenoe, David. *Life without Father: Compelling New Evidence That Fatherhood and Marriage Are Indispensable for the Good of Children and Society*. New York: Free Press, 1996. As the title and subtitle suggest, Popenoe both offers data concerning the decline of fatherhood in America and its negative consequences and proposes concrete measures for all major sectors of society to help reverse this decline.

Royko, David. *Voices of Children of Divorce*. New York: Golden Books, 1999. A book that walks through the stages of divorce and postdivorce life from the perspective of children, based on a thousand interviews with children of divorce, who are quoted freely here. The primary goal of the book is to help divorcing/divorced parents understand their children better; a clear secondary goal is to help prevent divorce in the first place.

Wallerstein, Judith S., and Sandra Blakeslee. *Second Chances: Men, Women, and Children a Decade after Divorce*. New York: Houghton Mifflin, 1996. Judith Wallerstein, the best-known divorce researcher in America, reports on the results of her study of adults and children of divorce at the ten- to fifteen-year mark.

Wallerstein, Judith S., Julia M. Lewis, and Sandra Blakeslee. *The Unexpected Legacy of Divorce: A 25 Year Landmark Study*. New York: Hyperion, 2000. Wallerstein and associates update their study to the twenty-five-year mark; the book is different enough from *Second Chances* to merit reading both.

Winner, Karen. *Divorced from Justice: The Abuse of Women and Children by Divorce Lawyers and Judges*. New York: HarperCollins, 1996. Another attack on the legal system and its injustices, this time claiming that it is women and children (not men) who are that system's principal victims.

Wolf, Anthony E. *"Why Did You Have to Get a Divorce? And When Can I Get a Hamster?" A Guide to Parenting through Divorce*. New York: Noonday Press, 1998. A popularly written how-to guide that covers all the major divorce-related issues associated with children.

Young, Cathy. *Ceasefire! Why Women and Men Must Join Forces to Achieve True Equality*. New York: Free Press, 1999. Young nicely captures the existence of a polarizing gender war in current culture; she diagnoses the problem as largely rooted in contemporary feminism's emphasis on the victimization of women and argues for a gender-blind commitment to equality and fairness for all.

Chapter 4

Barth, Karl. *Ethics*. Translated by Geoffrey Bromiley. New York: Seabury Press, 1981. The 1928 ethics lectures of the great German theologian contain rich reflections on marriage under the rubric of calling and order in a doctrine of creation. Compare also his finished treatment of this issue in the magisterial *The Doctrine of Creation*, vol. 3 of *Church Dogmatics*. Edinburgh: T & T Clark, 1961.

Brunner, Emil. *The Divine Imperative*. Translated by Olive Wyon. Philadelphia: Westminster Press, 1957. Another brilliant neo-Orthodox treatment of marriage under the rubric of orders of creation.

Cahill, Lisa Sowle. *Sex, Gender, and Christian Ethics*. Cambridge, England: Cambridge University Press, 1996. A thorough, scholarly treatment of Christian sexual ethics from a feminist perspective anchored in historic Christian tradition.

Jewett, Paul K. *Man As Male and Female*. Grand Rapids: Eerdmans, 1975. A classic statement of a Christian theology of sexuality, rooted in very careful biblical exegesis.

Mason, Mike. *The Mystery of Marriage: Meditations on the Miracle*. Sisters, Ore.: Multnomah, 1985. A lyrical reflection on the marital estate, this book is written with a poet's sensitivity.

Molloy, Cathy. *Marriage: Theology and Reality*. Dublin: Columba; Toronto: Novalis, 1996. A brief work attempting to review the Christian theology of marriage and bring it into contact with contemporary experiences of marriage.

Oliver, Mary Anne McPherson. *Conjugal Spirituality*. Kansas City, Mo.: Sheed & Ward, 1994. A rich and innovative spirituality of marriage, well-informed by the Christian tradition, though also rather syncretistic, especially in its appropriation of Hindu themes and practices.

Post, Stephen G. *Spheres of Love: Toward a New Ethics of the Family*. Dallas: SMU Press, 1994. An overview of key issues in Christian sexual and family ethics from a careful and thorough ethicist.

Thatcher, Adrian. *Marriage after Modernity: Christian Marriage in Postmodern Times*. New York: New York University Press, 1999. An important attempt by a British Anglican theologian to offer a postmodern vision of marriage that retains contact with the Christian tradition while revising it for contemporary circumstances.

Turner, Philip, ed. *Men and Women: Sexual Ethics in Turbulent Times*. Cambridge, Mass.: Cowley, 1989. A collection of intelligent and very thoughtful essays about sexual ethics, written primarily from an Episcopalian perspective.

Wilson, Douglas. *Reforming Marriage*. Moscow, Idaho: Canon Press, 1995. A slim volume widely popular among those attracted today to a Reformed theological vision, offering a practical theology of marriage from a Reformed perspective.

Chapter 5

Allender, Dan B., and Tremper Longman III. *Intimate Allies: Rediscovering God's Design for Marriage and Becoming Soul Mates for Life*. Wheaton: Tyndale, 1995. A richly theological and practical vision of marriage, bringing together the gifts of a counselor and biblical scholar.

Brody, Steve, and Cathy Brody. *Renew Your Marriage at Midlife*. New York: Penguin Putnam, 1999. A self-help book designed especially for the midlife couple seeking renewal in their relationship.

Burkett, Larry. *Debt-Free Living: How to Get Out of Debt (and Stay Out)*. New York: Northfield, 2001. The most well-known book by the Christian financial expert who strongly recommends the goal of abolishing debt as a way to financial freedom.

Chapell, Bryan. *Each for the Other: Marriage As It's Meant to Be*. Grand Rapids: Baker, 1998. A conservative Christian articulation of a complementarian vision of marriage, oriented around the theme of mutual sacrifice.

Chapman, Gary. *The Five Love Languages: How to Express Heartfelt Commitment to Your Mate*. Chicago: Northfield, 1995. This widely used guide has become part of the standard vocabulary of marriage talk in thousands of homes and churches. Chapman argues that people use five love languages—quality time, words of affirmation, gifts, acts of service, and physical touch—but people differ in which love languages they most appreciate and need.

Christensen, Andrew, and Neil S. Jacobsen. *Reconcilable Differences*. New York: Guilford Press, 2000. The authors, both psychologist/therapists, developed a model called Integrative Couple Therapy, which they present in popular form, with a focus on conflict resolution.

Crabb, Larry. *The Marriage Builder: A Blueprint for Couples and Counselors*. Grand Rapids: Zondervan, 1992. Crabb, a founder of biblical counseling, offers a treatment of marriage marked by his characteristic rejection of self-fulfillment ideologies and call to return to biblical truth.

Doherty, William J. *Take Back Your Marriage: Sticking Together in a World That Pulls Us Apart*. New York: Guilford Press, 2001. A book directed especially at the drooping midlife marriage being crowded out by other commitments and obligations, with a strong emphasis on being intentional about marriage building and preservation.

Fein, Ellen, and Sherrie Schneider. *The Rules for Marriage: Time-Tested Secrets for Making Your Marriage Work*. New York: Warner Books, 2001. Fein and Schneider made a brief splash with *The Rules,* a feisty, neoconservative reaffirmation of traditional female approaches to dating; here they attempt something similar in relation to marriage.

Glasser, William, and Carleen Glasser. *Getting Together and Staying Together: Solving the Mystery of Marriage*. New York: HarperCollins, 2000. Based on what Glasser calls "choice theory," this book argues that we create success in marriage by the choices we make rather than being victims of incompatibility.

Gottman, John M., and Nan Silver. *The Seven Principles for Making Marriage Work*. New York: Crown, 1999. A lively, richly researched, and practical book distilling a career's worth of insights on marital success. Perhaps my favorite marriage enrichment book ever.

Gray, John. *Mars and Venus Together Forever: A Practical Guide to Lasting Intimacy.* New York: HarperCollins, 1996. Gray became famous with his *Men Are from Mars, Women Are from Venus*, a book emphasizing inherent gender differences in temperament and communication. This book seeks to apply that vision to marriage.

Harley, Willard F., Jr. *His Needs, Her Needs: Building an Affair-Proof Marriage*. Grand Rapids: Revell, 1994. A widely read book proposing that men and women have key needs in a marriage partner (men: sex, recreational companionship, attractive spouse, domestic support, admiration; women: affection, conversation, honesty, financial support, family commitment) and that failure to meet these needs opens the door to infidelity.

Moore, Thomas. *Soul Mates: Honoring the Mysteries of Love and Relationship*. New York: HarperCollins, 1994. Moore is a leading spirituality writer who here applies his mystical vision to relationships, with one chapter on marriage.

Okin, Susan Moller. *Justice, Gender, and the Family*. New York: Basic Books, 1989. A bracing discussion by a political philosopher of the neglect of an emphasis on justice in marriage and family life among even the most sophisticated (male) political philosophers, with thoughtful proposals for how to begin to do better.

Parrott, Les, III, and Leslie Parrott. *Saving Your Marriage Before It Starts: Seven Questions to Ask Before (and After) You Marry*. Grand Rapids: Zondervan, 1995. A premarriage guide designed especially for young couples, written by the marriage consulting team that was employed by the governor of Oklahoma to strengthen marriages there.

Popcak, Gregory K. *The Exceptional Seven Percent: The Nine Secrets of the World's Happiest Couples*. New York: Kensington, 2000. Popcak argues that only 7 percent of the world's couples really qualify as quite intimate and actualized in their marriages. He proposes secrets to their success including exceptional fidelity, loving, service, rapport, negotiation, gratitude, joy, and sexuality.

Ramsey, Dave. *Financial Peace: Restoring Financial Hope to You and Your Family*. New York: Viking Press, 1997. The key work by the Christian community's most well-known financial guru.

Smalley, Gary. *For Better or For Best: Understanding Your Husband*. Grand Rapids: Zondervan, 1988. A book for married women intended to help them understand men's distinctive characteristics and how to build a better marriage with their husbands.

———. *If Only He Knew: Understanding Your Wife*. Grand Rapids: Zondervan, 1988. A companion book for married men intended to help them understand women's distinctive characteristics and how to build a better marriage with their wives.

———. *Making Love Last Forever*. Dallas: Word, 1996. An upbeat summary of how to succeed at marriage from one of Christendom's most well-known marriage experts.

Stanley, Scott, Daniel Trathen, Savanna McCain, and Milt Bryan. *A Lasting Promise: A Christian Guide to Fighting for Your Marriage*. San Francisco: Jossey-Bass, 1998. A book by a Denver-based team of marital therapists/researchers, based on years of research on couples, presenting a Christian-based rendering of their approach to marital fulfillment.

Talley, Jim. *Reconcilable Differences: Healing for Troubled Marriages*. Nashville: Thomas Nelson, 1991. A book designed for those whose marriages are in serious trouble and in need of reconciliation.

Wallerstein, Judith, and Sandra Blakeslee. *The Good Marriage: How and Why Love Lasts*. New York: Houghton Mifflin, 1995. It must have been encouraging for Wallerstein and Blakeslee to turn their attention briefly away from the trauma caused by divorce to author this hopeful discussion of the keys to success in marriage.

Wangerin, Walter, Jr. *As for Me and My House: Crafting Your Marriage to Last*. Nashville: Thomas Nelson, 1990. A rich and highly personal account of marriage from one of the Christian world's most popular authors, with a strong emphasis on forgiveness.

Warren, Neil Clark. *Learning to Live with the Love of Your Life . . . And Loving It!* Wheaton: Tyndale, 1995. Previously titled *The Triumphant Marriage,* this book is based on a study of one hundred successfully married couples, offering ten "secrets" to marital bliss.

Weiner-Davis, Michele. *Divorce Busting: A Revolutionary and Rapid Program for Staying Together*. New York: Simon and Schuster, 1992. The author, a therapist, is well-known for her passionate commitment to saving marriages and resisting divorce. This book offers the essentials of her approach to "marriage-saving."

Wheat, Ed, and Gaye Wheat. *Intended for Pleasure: New Approaches to Sexual Intimacy in Christian Marriage*. Old Tappan, N.J.: Revell, 1981. Not so new anymore, this book is a classic Christian sex manual that helped prepare the way for a new frankness about sex in Christian circles.

Whiteman, Thomas A., and Thomas G. Bartlett. *The Marriage Mender: A Couples Guide to Staying Together*. Colorado Springs: Navpress, 1996. A Christian approach to marital healing, rooted in a stages-of-life approach to marriage, with a strong emphasis on communication and conflict resolution.

Wright, H. Norman. *Relationships That Work (and Those That Don't)*. Ventura, Calif.: Regal, 1998. Wright, a popular Christian marriage consultant, offers a work aimed at singles, with the hope of helping them make wise choices in a marriage partner.

Chapter 6

Brouwer, Douglas J. *Beyond "I Do": What Christians Believe about Marriage*. Grand Rapids: Eerdmans, 2001. A readable, concise pastoral theology of marriage from a Presbyterian minister, with a helpful chapter on marriage as a covenant.

Dumbrell, W. J. *Covenant and Creation: A Theology of the Old Testament Covenants.* Carlisle, England: Paternoster Press, 1984. A biblical scholar offers a theology of the Old Testament covenants, arguing for a single biblical covenant that unfolds progressively according to God's plan from Genesis to Revelation.

———. *The Search for Order: Biblical Eschatology in Focus*. Grand Rapids: Baker, 1994. The same author discussed above offers an eschatology that weaves together creation, fall, covenant, and kingdom themes.

Farley, Margaret A. *Personal Commitments: Beginning, Keeping, Changing*. New York: HarperCollins, 1990. A sensitive, popularly written but scholarly treatment of the issue of commitment (and thus covenant) by a leading Christian ethicist.

Hugenberger, Gordon P. *Marriage as a Covenant: Biblical Law and Ethics as Developed from Malachi.* Grand Rapids: Baker, 1998. An exhaustive scholarly study of Malachi 2:10–16 and the overall Old Testament understanding of marriage.

Nicholson, Ernest W. *God and His People: Covenant Theology in the Old Testament*. Oxford, England: Clarendon, 1986. A thorough review of what Old Testament scholars have written about the concept of covenant over the last century or so.

Ortlund, Raymond C., Jr. *Whoredom: God's Unfaithful Wife in Biblical Theology*. Grand Rapids: Eerdmans, 1996. The title says it all—this book explores the biblical theme of spiritual adultery, especially as articulated in the ferocious prophetic denunciations of Israel, including feminist objections to this language.

Ottati, Douglas F., and Douglas J. Schuurman, eds. "Professional Resources: Covenantal Ethics." Essays gathered in *The Annual of the Society of Christian Ethics 1996*. Washington, D.C.: Georgetown University Press, 1996. Four essays by Christian ethicists exploring covenant and its fruitfulness as a motif in Christian ethics.

Robertson, O. Palmer. *The Christ of the Covenants*. Phillipsburg, N.J.: Presbyterian and Reformed, 1980. A survey of the biblical concept of covenant from a Reformed theological perspective.

Stackhouse, Max L. *Covenant and Commitments: Faith, Family, and Economic Life*. Louisville: Westminster John Knox, 1997. A contribution to the Family, Religion, and Culture series (edited by Don Browning and Ian Evison), which explores covenantal themes in relation to family ethics.

Chapter 7

Cornes, Andrew. *Divorce and Remarriage*. Grand Rapids: Eerdmans, 1993. A thorough analysis of the biblical texts on divorce and remarriage.

Feinberg, John S., and Paul D. Feinberg. *Ethics for a Brave New World*. Wheaton: Crossway, 1993. This introductory Christian ethics text offers two thorough chapters about divorce, exploring the issue from a conservative Christian perspective and from every exegetical angle.

Grenz, Stanley. *Sexual Ethics*. Nashville: Word, 1990. One of the finest ethicist-theologians of our day offers a nice discussion of divorce in this book.

Guroian, Vigen. "An Ethic of Marriage and Family." In *From Christ to the World,* ed. Wayne G. Boulton et al. Grand Rapids: Eerdmans, 1994. Guroian, an Eastern Orthodox ethicist and theologian, articulates here a winsome and distinctively Orthodox perspective.

Harrington, Daniel, S.J. *Why Do We Suffer? A Scriptural Approach to the Human Condition*. Franklin, Wis.: Sheed & Ward, 2000. A rich biblical reflection on suffering from a Jesuit priest and New Testament scholar.

Hays, Richard. *The Moral Vision of the New Testament*. San Francisco: HarperSanFrancisco, 1996. An excellent chapter on marriage and divorce is part of this innovative approach to the New Testament's moral teachings.

Heth, William A., and Gordon J. Wenham. *Jesus and Divorce: The Problem with the Evangelical Consensus*. Nashville: Thomas Nelson, 1984. A very conservative treatment of the biblical texts related to divorce.

John Paul II. *On the Christian Meaning of Human Suffering*. Boston: Pauline Books and Media, 1984. A rich meditation on suffering from one of the twentieth century's finest Christian thinkers and leaders.

Keener, Craig. *And Marries Another*. Peabody, Mass.: Hendrickson, 1991. An exhaustive discussion of New Testament teachings about divorce and remarriage, motivated by a concern that Christians not succumb to a legalism out of keeping with Jesus' approach to divorce and remarriage.

Mayerfeld, Jamie. *Suffering and Moral Responsibility*. New York: Oxford University Press, 1999. A rich, dense philosophical analysis of suffering and its link to moral responsibility.

Soelle, Dorothee. *Suffering*. Philadelphia: Fortress Press, 1975. A searching exploration of suffering that is sensitive to the dangers of Christian masochism but equally sensitive to the dangers of contemporary nihilism; finds meaning in suffering in dialogue with biblical materials.

Thomas, Gary. *Sacred Marriage*. Grand Rapids: Zondervan, 1998. The only recent book on marriage that I have seen that devotes much attention to the spiritual challenges created by marriage and especially suffering in marriage; this book is essentially a spirituality of marriage.

Chapter 8

Chilton, Bruce, and J. I. H. McDonald. *Jesus and the Ethics of the Kingdom*. Grand Rapids: Eerdmans, 1987. A significant treatment of Jesus' kingdom teaching from leading New Testament scholars.

Horsley, Richard A., and Neil Asher Silberman. *The Message and the Kingdom: How Jesus and Paul Ignited a Revolution and Transformed the Ancient World*. Minneapolis: Fortress Press, 1997. A well-written account of the long-ago world in which Jesus and Paul lived and the transformative impact of their kingdom message.

Ladd, George Eldon. *The Gospel of the Kingdom: Scriptural Studies in the Kingdom of God*. Grand Rapids: Eerdmans, 1959. A classic popular articulation of the meaning and dimensions of the kingdom from one of the last generation's leading New Testament scholars.

McCarthy, David Matzko. *Sex and Love in the Home: A Theology of the Household*. London: SCM Press, 2001. An innovative work, badly titled, offering a richly researched theology of the household and bringing together political philosophy, economic analysis, biblical materials, and theological reflection.

Stassen, Glen H., and David P. Gushee. *Kingdom Ethics: Following Jesus in Contemporary Context*. Downers Grove, Ill.: InterVarsity Press, 2003. An introduction to Christian ethics focused on Jesus, with special attention to the Sermon on the Mount and the theme of the kingdom of God.

Witherington, Ben, III. *Jesus, Paul, and the End of the World: A Comparative Study of New Testament Eschatology*. Downers Grove, Ill.: InterVarsity Press, 1992. A thorough, scholarly study comparing the teachings of Jesus and Paul about the end of time and thus the reign of God.

Wright, N. T. *Jesus and the Victory of God*. Minneapolis: Fortress Press, 1996. Perhaps the best scholarly interpretation currently available of the life and ministry of Jesus, organized around the theme of the "victory of God."

Chapter 9

Adams, Douglas E. *Children, Divorce, and the Church*. Nashville: Abingdon, 1992. This book offers significant guidance for understanding the impact of divorce on children and suggestions for how to best organize congregational ministry to children of divorce.

Anderson, Herbert, Don S. Browning, Ian S. Evison, and Mary Stewart Van Leeuwen, eds. *The Family Handbook*. Louisville: Westminster John Knox, 1998. A kind of summary of the work of the important Family, Religion, and Culture series, this book offers significant attention to family ministry issues.

Braun, Michael A. *Second Class Christians? A New Approach to the Dilemma of Divorced People in the Church*. Downers Grove, Ill.: InterVarsity Press, 1989. A pastoral perspective on a wide variety of issues related to addressing divorce and remarriage in local church life.

Dever, Mark. *Nine Marks of a Healthy Church*. Wheaton: Crossway, 2000. An approach to church life emphasizing a vision of church identity, membership, accountability, and growth that is similar to the vision articulated in this chapter.

Doherty, William J. *Take Back Your Marriage: Sticking Together in a World That Pulls Us Apart*. New York: Guilford Press, 2001. An approach to marriage that emphasizes the need to resist cultural pressures and forces that pull couples apart. An important chapter emphasizes the significance of community support for every marriage.

Garland, Diana R. *Family Ministry: A Comprehensive Guide*. Downers Grove, Ill.: InterVarsity Press, 1999. A deeply researched and extraordinarily comprehensive survey of the landscape of Christian family ministry.

Lyon, K. Brynoll, and Archie Smith, eds. *Tending the Flock: Congregations and Family Ministry*. Louisville: Westminster John Knox, 1998. A nine-chapter book, with each chapter examining the family ministries of a particular congregation.

McManus, Michael J. *Marriage Savers: Helping Your Friends and Family Avoid Divorce*. Revised edition. Grand Rapids: Zondervan, 1995. This hugely influential book—and the ministry by the same name—focuses on the failure of the church to respond adequately to the divorce epidemic and surveys the landscape of available marriage-saving programs and ministries today.

Olson, Richard P., and Joe H. Leonard Jr. *Ministry with Families in Flux: The Church and Changing Patterns of Life*. Louisville: Westminster John Knox, 1990. A mainline treatment of changes in family life, the special needs of families taking various forms today, and constructive ministries to meet those needs.

Chapter 10

American Bar Association. *Guide to Family Law*. New York: Random House, 1996. A concise summary of the categories and key provisions of family law.

Glendon, Mary Ann. *Abortion and Divorce in Western Law*. Cambridge: Harvard University Press, 1987. The authoritative overview of Western legal treatments of these two critical issues, though by now a bit dated.

Hewlett, Sylvia Ann, and Cornel West. *The War against Parents: What We Can Do for America's Beleaguered Moms and Dads*. New York: Houghton Mifflin, 1998. A significant discussion of the structural challenges facing American parents through a combination of political, economic, and cultural forces, from two well-known cultural commentators on the left of the political spectrum.

Sitarz, Daniel. *Divorce Yourself: The National No-Fault Divorce Kit*, 3d ed. Carbondale, Ill.: Nova, 1994. A depressing representative of a genre of legal self-help books, intended to help the divorcing through the legal maze but also symbolic of our culture of divorce.

Notes

Introduction

1. Thomas S. Kuhn, *The Structure of Scientific Revolutions,* vol. 2, no. 2, 2d ed. (Chicago: University of Chicago Press, 1970), 6.

Chapter 1: *Fading Fast: The Decline of Marriage as an Institution*

1. Courtney Eldridge, "Parallels," *New York Times Magazine* (July 18, 2001): 58.

2. A leading voice for this perspective is Stephanie Coontz. See *The Way We Never Were: American Families and the Nostalgia Trap* (New York: Basic Books, 1992).

3. Susan Moller Okin, *Justice, Gender, and the Family* (New York: Basic Books, 1989), 139.

4. David Popenoe, *Disturbing the Nest: Family Change and Decline in Modern Societies* (New York: Aldine de Gruyter, 1988), 6.

5. Ibid.

6. Ibid., 9.

7. Maggie Gallagher, *The Abolition of Marriage* (Washington, D.C.: Regnery, 1996), 9.

8. The social and ethical significance of the birth control revolution is nicely assessed in Sam Torode, "Sex and Science: Does Making Love Still Lead to Making Babies?" *Books and Culture* 7, no. 6 (November/December 2001): 6–8.

9. See Charles E. Curran and Richard A. McCormick, S.J., eds., *Readings in Moral Theology*, no. 8 (New York: Paulist Press, 1993), 57–170.

10. Popenoe, *Disturbing the Nest,* 302.

11. Unless otherwise indicated, demographic statistics are from U.S. government reports, as collected and summarized in *The Statistical Abstract of the United States 2002* (Washington, D.C.: U.S. Department of Commerce, 2002) or reported on the National Center for Health Statistics web page (http://www.cdc.gov/nchs).

12. Heather MacDonald, "The Real Welfare Problem Is Illegitimacy," *City Journal* (Winter 1998): 35.

13. Willard F. Jabusch, "The Myth of Cohabitation," *America* (October 7, 2000): 15.

14. Carol DeVita, "The United States at Mid-Decade," *Population Bulletin* 50, no. 4 (March 1996): 35.

15. Quoted in Jabusch, "The Myth of Cohabitation," 14.

16. A chilling compilation of cases and research evidence can be found in John A. Barnes, "The Boyfriend Problem," *The Weekly Standard* (December 14, 1998): 21–23.

17. Quoted in Jabusch, "The Myth of Cohabitation," 15.

18. MacDonald, "The Real Welfare Problem," 36.

19. Sylvia Ann Hewlett has argued that this promise is often cruelly illusory, especially for women over thirty-five. See Hewlett's book *Creating a Life* (New York: Talk Miramax Books, 2002), chap. 5.

20. Andrew Sullivan, "Unveiled," *The New Republic* (13 August 2001): 6.

21. U.S. Department of Education, NCES, *Youth Indicators 1996*, 20–22.

22. Andrew J. Cherlin, *Marriage, Divorce, Remarriage* (Cambridge: Harvard University Press, 1981), 21–25.

23. Barbara Dafoe Whitehead, *The Divorce Culture* (New York: Knopf, 1987), 182.

24. Alex Kuczynski, "Guess Who's Coming to Dinner Now?" *New York Times*, 23 December 2001, sec. 9, p. 1.

25. Margaret Mead, quoted in Judith S. W. Wallerstein and Sandra Blakeslee, *Second Chances* (Boston: Houghton Mifflin, 1996), 297.

Chapter 2: *Structural Damage: Why Marriage Collapsed*

1. John Witte Jr., *From Sacrament to Contract* (Louisville: Westminster John Knox, 1997), 3.

2. Augustine, "The Good of Marriage," in *Marriage in the Early Church*, ed. and trans. David G. Hunter (Eugene, Ore.: Wipf and Stock, 2001), 120.

3. See Hunter's introductory essay and collection of patristic writings, *Marriage in the Early Church*.

4. Augustine, "The Good of Marriage," in Hunter, *Marriage in the Early Church*, 102.

5. It must be noted, however, that in the important 1563 Council of Trent, "companionship of husband and wife" was listed among the three reasons for marriage. See Witte, *From Sacrament to Contract*, 40.

6. Witte, *From Sacrament to Contract*, 4.

7. See Christopher N. C. Brooke, *The Medieval Idea of Marriage* (Oxford: Oxford University Press, 1989), 55–57, 274ff. Brooke argues that the sacramentalizing of marriage actually had its origins in a kind of "verbal accident"—the Latin term *sacramentum* in the Vulgate translation of Ephesians 5:32, first picked up and developed by Augustine.

8. Witte, *From Sacrament to Contract*, 28. See also Theodore Mackin, S.J., *Marriage in the Catholic Church: Divorce and Remarriage* (New York: Paulist Press, 1984), 224–365.

9. Roderick Phillips, *Untying the Knot* (Cambridge, England: Cambridge University Press, 1991), 9–10, briefly traces the varying positions affirmed by church councils through these earlier centuries.

10. Ibid., 6. The development of Catholic canon law on divorce and remarriage did open the door a crack for divorce and remarriage in cases in which the "Pauline Privilege" can be invoked; based on 1 Corinthians 7:15, this enabled divorce and approved remarriage in cases when one party to a previously nonsacramental marriage is baptized and his or her unbelieving partner "departs" from the marriage. For details, see Mackin, *Marriage in the Catholic Church*, 9–10.

11. Witte, *From Sacrament to Contract*, chap. 1.

12. Ibid., chaps. 2–3.

13. Ibid., chap. 3.

14. Phillips, *Untying the Knot*, 14–17.

15. Edmund S. Morgan, *The Puritan Family* (New York: Harper & Row, 1966), 31.

16. Richard Tarnas, *The Passion of the Western Mind* (New York: Ballantine, 1991), 367.

17. Anthony Giddens, *The Transformation of Intimacy* (Stanford: Stanford University Press, 1992), 26.

18. Ibid., 37.

19. Eli Zaretsky, *Capitalism, the Family, and Personal Life,* rev. ed. (New York: Harper & Row, 1986).

20. For a tracing of the political history of women in Western cultures, see Susan Moller Okin, *Women in Western Political Thought* (Princeton, N.J.: Princeton University Press, 1979).

21. Giddens, *The Transformation of Intimacy,* 27.

22. Nancy F. Cott, *Public Vows* (Cambridge: Harvard University Press, 2000), 6.

23. Whitehead, *The Divorce Culture,* 13–18.

24. Cherlin, *Marriage, Divorce, Remarriage,* 34–44.

25. Charles Taylor, *Sources of the Self* (Cambridge: Harvard University Press, 1989), ix.

26. Giddens, *The Transformation of Intimacy,* 27.

27. David Frum, *How We Got Here: The '70s* (New York: Random House, 2000), 76.

28. Whitehead, *The Divorce Culture*, chap. 2; Christopher Lasch, *Haven in a Heartless World* (New York: Norton, 1977).

29. Karla Hackstaff, *Marriage in a Culture of Divorce* (Philadelphia: Temple University Press, 1999), 31–35; Cherlin (*Marriage, Divorce, Remarriage*, 49–59) argues that the dramatic rise of the number of married women in the workforce is ultimately "the most important stimulus" for the increase in divorce after 1960.

30. Women do remain more economically dependent on marriage than men, and thus their exit from marriage is not always economically feasible. See Okin, *Justice, Gender, and the Family,* chap. 7.

31. Phillips, *Untying the Knot,* 230–31.

32. Cherlin, *Marriage, Divorce, Remarriage,* 49.

33. Hackstaff, *Marriage in a Culture of Divorce,* 28.

34. Giddens, *The Transformation of Intimacy,* 58.

Chapter 3: *Squandered Legacy: The Consequences of Divorce for Children*

1. Judith S. Wallerstein, Julia M. Lewis, and Sandra Blakeslee, *The Unexpected Legacy of Divorce* (New York: Hyperion, 2000), xxxiii.

2. See Paul R. Amato and Alan Booth, *A Generation at Risk: Growing Up in an Era of Family Upheaval* (Cambridge: Harvard University Press, 1997), 218–21. They found that just under a third of divorces in their study were preceded by high levels of marital conflict.

3. Ibid.

4. Here is E. Mavis Hetherington's list of key factors leading to divorce: gender-related communication and need differences, financial disagreements, sexual problems, and violence. Hetherington and John Kelly, *For Better or for Worse: Divorce Reconsidered* (New York: Norton, 2002), chap. 2.

5. Alvin Pam and Judith Pearson, *Splitting Up: Enmeshment and Estrangement in the Process of Divorce* (New York: Guilford Press, 1998), 11–12.

6. See Janet R. Johnston and Linda E. G. Campbell, *Impasses of Divorce: The Dynamics and Resolution of Family Conflict* (New York: Free Press, 1988), especially chapters 1–4, for an excellent analysis of why this bitterness develops and metastasizes. Compare the very thoughtful work by Pam and Pearson, *Splitting Up.*

7. For other children's accounts of this moment, see David Royko, *Voices of Children of Divorce* (New York: Golden Books, 1999), chap. 2.

8. It appears that no one is satisfied with how the legal process handles divorce. For narrative accounts from the United States and Canada, respectively, see Karen Winner, *Divorced from Justice: The Abuse of Women and Children by Divorce Lawyers and Judges* (New York: HarperCollins, 1996); Wendy Dennis, *The Divorce from Hell: How the Justice System Failed a Family* (Toronto: Macfarlane, Walter & Ross, 1998). On the issue of reforming marriage and divorce law, see chapter 10 of this book.

9. David Blankenhorn, *Fatherless America: Confronting Our Most Urgent Social Problem* (New York: Basic Books, 1995), 9–67; David Popenoe, *Life without Father: Compelling New Evidence That Fatherhood and Marriage Are Indispensable for the Good of Children and Society* (New York: Free Press, 1996), 19–80.

10. Blankenhorn, *Fatherless America*, chap. 8.

11. Okin, *Justice, Gender, and the Family*, chap. 7. See the careful work by Sara McLanahan and Gary Sandefur, *Growing Up with a Single Parent: What Hurts, What Helps* (Cambridge: Harvard University Press, 1994), especially chapter 2; Amato and Booth, *A Generation at Risk*, chap. 6.

12. For statistics, see Blankenhorn, *Fatherless America*, 130–31.

13. Ibid., chap. 7.

14. Okin calls this asset "professional capital"—the money-earning skill jointly invested in by both spouses but not transferable to the one who does not have it after divorce. See Okin, *Justice, Gender, and the Family*, chap. 7.

15. Wallerstein, *Unexpected Legacy*, chap. 1; Royko, *Voices of Children of Divorce*, chap. 8.

16. A similarly derisive black humor about the complexity of family forms today is found in Karen Karbo, *Generation Ex: Tales from the Second Wives Club* (New York: Bloomsbury, 2001). See especially the relationship "organization" chart, 65.

17. Wallerstein, *Unexpected Legacy*, 165.

18. Ibid., 110.

19. Pam and Pearson, *Splitting Up*, 215–22.

20. David Larson, James P. Swyers, and Susan S. Larson, "The Costly Consequences of Divorce: Assessing the Clinical, Economic, and Public Health Impact of Marital Disruption in the United States" (research study, Rockville, Md.: National Institute for Healthcare Research, n.d.), module 3.

21. Wallerstein offers a sensitive and multifaceted exploration of these issues. See *Unexpected Legacy*, 31–32, 58–63, 190–97.

22. Art Alexakis, "Father of Mine," *So Much for the Afterglow*, Everclear, 1998, Capitol Records.

23. Bob Bennett, "No Such Thing as Divorce," *Songs from Bright Avenue*, 1991, Urgent Records.

Chapter 4: *The Creation Purposes of Marriage*

1. James Q. Wilson, *The Marriage Problem* (New York: HarperCollins, 2002), 221.

2. In *Old Testament I: Genesis 1–11*, Ancient Christian Commentary on Scripture, ed. Andrew Louth (Downers Grove, Ill.: InterVarsity Press, 2001), 28.

3. Walter Brueggemann, *Genesis* (Atlanta: John Knox, 1982), 32.

4. See the discussion in Paul K. Jewett, *Man as Male and Female* (Grand Rapids: Eerdmans, 1975), 36–40. Stephen G. Post, *Spheres of Love: Toward a New Ethics of the Family* (Dallas: Southern Methodist University Press, 1994), 21, states flatly that "woman and man together constitute the image of God."

5. Brad Green, "Theological and Philosophical Foundations," in *Shaping a Christian Worldview*, ed. David S. Dockery and Gregory Alan Thornbury (Nashville: Broadman & Holman, 2002), 63.

6. Ibid.

7. Steven Ozment, *Ancestors: The Loving Family in Old Europe* (Cambridge: Harvard University Press, 2001), 111.

8. Wilson, *The Marriage Problem*, 221.

9. *Catechism of the Catholic Church* (Liguori, Mo.: Liguori Publications, 1994), #1605, 401.

10. Emil Brunner, *The Divine Imperative* (Philadelphia: Westminster Press, 1957), 344–45.

11. Jacob Neusner, "Judaism," in *The Ethics of Family Life*, ed. Jacob Neusner (Stamford, Conn.: Wadsworth, 2001), 1.

12. *Catherine of Siena: The Dialogue*, trans. Suzanne Niffke (Mahwah, N.J.: Paulist Press, 1980), 104.

13. Mary Anne McPherson, *Conjugal Spirituality* (Kansas City, Mo.: Sheed & Ward, 1994), chap. 3.

14. Karl Barth, *Ethics* (New York: Seabury Press, 1981), 232.

15. For a beautiful Christian reflection on marital sexuality, see Mike Mason, *The Mystery of Marriage* (Sisters, Ore.: Multnomah, 1985), chap. 6.

16. Theodore Mackin, "How to Understand the Sacrament of Marriage," in *Commitment to Partnership: Explorations of the Theology of Marriage*, ed. William P. Roberts (New York: Paulist Press, 1987), 51.

17. Brunner, *Divine Imperative*, 349.

18. Barth, *Ethics*, 236.

19. Brunner, *Divine Imperative*, 346.

20. *Catechism of the Catholic Church*, #1609, 402.

21. Post, *Spheres of Love*, 18.

Chapter 5: *The Skills (and Virtues) of Marriage*

1. Flyer, Barnes and Noble Bookstore, Memphis, Tennessee, August 10, 2002. Text excerpted and reproduced exactly. Author's name is pseudonymous to avoid the perception of a personal attack.

2. Thomas Moore, *Soul Mates: Honoring the Mysteries of Love and Relationship* (New York: HarperCollins, 1994), xiii.

3. Gregory K. Popcak, *The Exceptional Seven Percent: The Nine Secrets of the World's Happiest Couples* (New York: Kensington, 2000).

4. Michele Bennett, Union University student, private communication.

5. Willard F. Harley Jr., *His Needs, Her Needs: Building an Affair-Proof Marriage* (Grand Rapids: Revell, 1994).

6. On peacemaking, see Glen H. Stassen, *Just Peacemaking: Transforming Initiatives for Justice and Peace* (Louisville: Westminster John Knox, 1992), chaps. 2–4.

7. For information about PREPARE and other test instruments, see http://www.lifeinnovations.com.

8. A helpful and practical discussion of expectations is found in Scott Stanley et al., *A Lasting Promise: A Christian Guide to Fighting for Your Marriage* (San Francisco: Jossey-Bass, 1998), chap. 7. Compare Steve Brody and Cathy Brody, *Renew Your Marriage at Midlife* (New York: Penguin Putnam, 1999), 59–116.

9. An example of a work with a strong emphasis on personality types is H. Norman Wright, *Relationships That Work (and Those That Don't)* (Ventura, Calif.: Regal, 1998), especially chapters 10–14.

10. One of the most thoughtful treatments of communication (and a number of other issues) is found in John M. Gottman and Nan Silver, *The Seven Principles for Making Marriage Work* (New York: Crown, 1999).

11. Interesting treatments of the subject of male-female communication and need differences include Willard F. Harley, *His Needs, Her Needs;* the two-book set by Gary Smalley, *If Only He Knew* (Grand Rapids: Zondervan, 1997) and *For Better or For Best* (Grand Rapids: Zondervan, 1988); Douglas Wilson, *Reforming Marriage* (Moscow, Idaho: Canon, 1995); and Bryan Chapell, *Each for the Other: Marriage As It's Meant to Be* (Grand Rapids: Baker, 1998).

12. A work entirely focused on understanding the meaning of marital conflict and developing conflict resolution skills is Andrew Christensen and Neil S. Jacobsen, *Reconcilable Differences* (New York: Guilford Press, 2000).

13. A thoughtful treatment of forgiveness is found in Walter Wangerin Jr., *As for Me and My House: Crafting Your Marriage to Last* (Nashville: Thomas Nelson, 1990), 55–116.

14. See Okin, *Justice, Gender, and the Family*. Compare the similar perspective in Susan Maushart, *Wifework: What Marriage Really Means for Women* (New York: Bloomsbury, 2001).

15. Examples of works with a clear emphasis of this type are Harley, *His Needs, Her Needs;* Smalley, *If Only He Knew* and *For Better or For Best.*

16. Okin, *Justice, Gender, and the Family*, especially chapter 7. John Rawls, *A Theory of Justice* (Cambridge, Mass.: Belknap, 1999), helped pioneer recognition of justice in private and not just in public relations.

17. See an extensive discussion of these themes in Glen H. Stassen and David P. Gushee, *Kingdom Ethics: Following Jesus in Contemporary Context* (Downers Grove, Ill.: InterVarsity Press, 2003), chap. 17.

18. Okin, *Justice, Gender, and the Family,* 15, for similar depiction of justice in marriage.

19. For more on love and justice, see Stassen and Gushee, *Kingdom Ethics,* chaps. 16–17.

20. Especially significant discussions are found in Dan B. Allender and Tremper Longman III, *Intimate Allies: Rediscovering God's Design for Marriage and Becoming Soul Mates for Life* (Wheaton: Tyndale, 1995), 205–66; Mason, *The Mystery of Marriage*, chap. 6.

21. Ed Wheat and Gaye Wheat, *Intended for Pleasure: New Approaches to Sexual Intimacy in Marriage* (Old Tappan, N.J.: Revell, 1981).

22. Gallup Poll results reported at http://www.gallup.com/search/results.asp.

23. Moore, *Soul Mates,* xvii.

Chapter 6: *Covenant as the Structural Principle of Marriage*

1. See William P. Brown, "The Character of Covenant in the Old Testament," in "Professional Resources: Covenantal Ethics," ed. Douglas F. Ottati and Douglas J. Schuurman, *The Annual of the Society of Christian Ethics 1996* (Washington, D.C.: Georgetown University Press, 1996), 283–94.

2. W. J. Dumbrell, s.v. "Covenant," *New Dictionary of Christian Ethics and Pastoral Theology,* ed. David J. Atkinson et al. (Downers Grove, Ill.: InterVarsity Press, 1995), 266. For a fuller treatment, see Dumbrell, *Covenant and Creation: A Theology of the Old Testament Covenants* (Carlisle, England: Paternoster Press, 1984).

3. Margaret A. Farley, *Personal Commitments: Beginning, Keeping, Changing* (New York: HarperCollins, 1990), 124.

4. This point is made by Max L. Stackhouse, *Covenant and Commitments: Faith, Family, and Economic Life* (Louisville: Westminster John Knox, 1997), 145.

5. Gordon P. Hugenberger, *Marriage as a Covenant: Biblical Law and Ethics as Developed from Malachi* (Grand Rapids: Baker, 1998), 11–12, argues that the oath-taking dimension of covenant was central.

6. Other biblical passages in which the covenant is treated as conditional on the fidelity of God's covenant partner, normally Israel, include Exodus 19:5; Leviticus 26:15–16; Nehemiah 1:5; the whole of Deuteronomy. For more on this issue, see chapter 7.

7. Cf. Stackhouse, *Covenant and Commitments,* 140–47.

8. For more detailed discussion, see Dumbrell, *Covenant and Creation,* especially chapter 1.

9. Joseph L. Allen, "Covenant," in *The Westminster Dictionary of Christian Ethics,* ed. James F. Childress and John Macquarrie (Philadelphia: Westminster Press, 1986), 136.

10. I have been guided in this discussion by Farley, *Personal Commitments,* chap. 8.

11. Ibid., 116.

12. Hugenberger, *Marriage as a Covenant.*

13. Adrian Thatcher, *Marriage after Modernity: Christian Marriage in Postmodern Times* (New York: New York University Press, 1999), 74.

14. Hugenberger, *Marriage as a Covenant,* 83.

15. See Raymond C. Ortlund Jr., *Whoredom: God's Unfaithful Wife in Biblical Theology* (Grand Rapids: Eerdmans, 1996), chap. 2.

16. See A. Brenner and F. van Dijk-Hemmes, *On Gendering Texts: Female and Male Voices in the Hebrew Bible* (Leiden, Netherlands: Brill Academic, 1993); Renita J. Weems, *Battered Love: Marriage, Sex, and Violence in the Hebrew Prophets* (Minneapolis: Augsburg Fortress, 1995). For an alternative view, see Ortlund, *Whoredom.*

17. Thatcher, *Marriage after Modernity,* 70–71.

18. Ortlund, *Whoredom,* 163–64.

19. In ancient Israel exclusivity was qualified by the sometime practice of polygamy. Permanence was viewed as normative, but exceptions could be made as specified in Deuteronomy 24:1 and the case law that emerged from that. For more on such exceptions and the New Testament discussion of them, see chapter 7.

20. Ernest W. Nicholson, *God and His People: Covenant Theology in the Old Testament* (Oxford, England: Clarendon Press, 1986), 216.

21. Mason, *Mystery of Marriage,* 116.

22. Morgan, *The Puritan Family,* 31–47.

23. O. Palmer Robertson, *The Christ of the Covenants* (Phillipsburg, N.J.: Presbyterian and Reformed, 1980), 24.

24. Ibid., chap. 5.

25. Hugenberger, *Marriage as a Covenant,* chap. 5. Theologian Adrian Thatcher agrees that Genesis 2:24 signifies a covenant relationship. See Thatcher, *Marriage after Modernity,* 68.

26. Anna Quindlen, "In Search of a Grown-Up," *Newsweek* (August 26, 2002): 64.

Chapter 7: *Suffering in Marriage (and Divorce)*

1. Simone Weil, "The Love of God and Affliction," *Waiting for God* (New York: Putnam, 1951), 119.

2. Dorothee Soelle, *Suffering* (Philadelphia: Fortress Press, 1975), 16.

3. On the connection between suffering and desire, see Jamie Mayerfeld, *Suffering and Moral Responsibility* (New York: Oxford University Press, 1999), 19–22.

4. Mason, *The Mystery of Marriage,* 171.

5. Pope John Paul II. *On the Christian Meaning of Human Suffering* (Boston: Pauline Books and Media, 1984), 16.

6. For a strong discussion of this issue, see Daniel Harrington, S.J., *Why Do We Suffer?* (Franklin, Wis.: Sheed & Ward, 2000), chap. 2.

7. Ibid., 46–47.

8. John Paul II, *On the Christian Meaning of Human Suffering,* 17.

9. Ibid., 44.

10. Farley, *Personal Commitments,* 122.

11. Gary Thomas, *Sacred Marriage* (Grand Rapids: Zondervan, 1998).

12. Vaclav Havel, quoted in Sherwin Nuland, "The Principle of Hope," *The New Republic* (May 27, 2002): 25.

13. Among the most important of these are Andrew Cornes, *Divorce and Remarriage* (Grand Rapids: Eerdmans, 1993); John S. Feinberg and Paul D. Feinberg, *Ethics for a Brave New World* (Wheaton: Crossway, 1993); Stanley J. Grenz, *Sexual Ethics* (Nashville: Word, 1990); Richard Hays, *The Moral Vision of the New Testament* (New York: HarperSanFrancisco, 1996); William A. Heth and Gordon J. Wenham, *Jesus and Divorce* (Nashville: Thomas Nelson, 1984); and Craig Keener, *And Marries Another* (Peabody, Mass: Hendrickson, 1991).

14. Chrysostom, "Homily XIX," *Nicene and Post-Nicene Fathers*, series 1, 12: 4. Accessed at http://www.ccel.org/fathers2.

15. Philip Turner, "The Marriage Canons of the Episcopal Church: Scripture and Tradition," *Anglican Theological Review* 65: 387.

16. Farley, *Personal Commitments*, 118–20.

17. Ibid., 127.

18. Mason, *The Mystery of Marriage,* 117.

Chapter 8: *The Kingdom Possibilities of Marriage*

1. Gordon Fee, "Kingdom of God," in *Called and Empowered: Pentecostal Perspectives on Global Mission*, ed. Murray Dempster, Byron D. Klause, and Douglas Petersen (Peabody, Mass.: Hendrickson, 1992), 8.

2. Ibid., 11.

3. W. D. Davies, *The Setting of the Sermon on the Mount* (Cambridge: Cambridge University Press, 1964), 167.

4. For a much more extensive treatment of the kingdom of God, along with more copious citations, see Stassen and Gushee, *Kingdom Ethics,* especially chapter 1.

5. Mary Anne McPherson Oliver, *Conjugal Spirituality* (Kansas City, Mo.: Sheed & Ward, 1994), 29.

6. Post, *Spheres of Love*, 32.

7. See Glenn C. Loury, *One by One from the Inside Out: Essays and Reviews on Race and Responsibility in America* (New York: Free Press, 1995), 104–7.

8. For a striking emphasis on savoring and serving the neighborhood community, see David Matzko McCarthy, *Sex and Love in the Home: A Theology of the Household* (London: SCM Press, 2001).

9. Walter Rauschenbusch, *Dare We Be Christians?* (Boston: Pilgrim Press, 1914), 32.

10. A quote from an unpublished essay by Nightingale found in JoAnn G. Widerquist, "Florence Nightingale's Calling," *Second Opinion* 17, no. 3 (January 1992): 108–21.

11. Rodney Clapp, *Families at the Crossroads: Beyond Traditional and Modern Options* (Downers Grove, Ill.: InterVarsity Press, 1993), 155–57.

Chapter 9: *The Church as Marriage Counterculture*

1. Quoted in Carl E. Schneider, "The Law and the Stability of Marriage," in *Promises to Keep: Decline and Renewal of Marriage in America,* ed. David Popenoe, Jean Bethke Elshtain, and Barbara Dafoe Whitehead (Lanham, Md.: Rowman & Littlefield, 1996), 188.

2. David B. Barrett and Todd M. Johnson, *International Bulletin of Missionary Research* (January 2002). http://www.gem-werc.org/.

3. Mark Seifrid, "The Nature of Christian Community," in *Preparing for Christian Ministry: An Evangelical Approach*, ed. David P. Gushee and Walter L. Jackson (Grand Rapids: Baker, 1996), 18.

4. Ibid., 19.

5. Elizabeth Hayt, "It's Never Too Late to Be a Virgin," *New York Times,* 4 August 2002, sec. 9, p. 1.

6. For information, see http://www.divorcecare.com.

7. Michael A. Braun discusses this issue in *Second Class Christians? A New Approach to the Dilemma of Divorced People in the Church* (Downers Grove, Ill.: InterVarsity Press, 1989), 97–99.

8. Keener, *And Marries Another,* 6–11.

9. I developed this term based on my reading of Scripture without reference to any other organization or approach. After doing so, in an Internet search, I discovered one other organization using the term: a Boulder, Colorado, ministry, offering marriage enrichment cruises, founded in 1989 by Dan and Janet Hauser. For information, see http://www.marriagecruises.com.

10. One treatment of how churches can deal with addictions is found in Herbert Anderson et al., eds., *The Family Handbook* (Louisville: Westminster John Knox, 1998), chap. 17. An excellent discussion of responding to family violence is found in Diana R. Garland, *Family Ministry: A Comprehensive Guide* (Downers Grove, Ill.: InterVarsity Press, 1999), 592–601.

11. Vigen Guroian, "An Ethic of Marriage and Family," in *From Christ to the World: Introductory Readings in Christian Ethics*, ed. Wayne G. Boulton, Thomas Kennedy, and Allen Verhey (Grand Rapids: Eerdmans, 1994), 322–30.

12. Joshua Harris, *I Kissed Dating Goodbye* (Sisters, Ore.: Multnomah, 1997). For a rebuttal, try Jeramy Clark, *I Gave Dating a Chance: A Biblical Perspective to Balance the Extremes* (Colorado Springs: Waterbrook Press, 2000).

13. Michael J. McManus, *Marriage Savers: Helping Your Friends and Family Avoid Divorce* (Grand Rapids: Zondervan, 1995), chaps. 4–6.

14. Ibid., chap. 13.

15. Ibid., 319–24.

16. This theme is beginning to be recognized even outside of religious communities. See William J. Doherty, *Take Back Your Marriage: Sticking Together in a World That Pulls Us Apart* (New York: Guilford Press, 2001), chap. 11.

Chapter 10: *Marriage and the Law*

1. For a discussion of the teaching dimension of marriage and divorce law, see Milton C. Regan Jr., "Postmodern Family Law: Toward a New Model of Status," in *Promises to Keep,* ed. David Popenoe et al. (Lanham, Md.: Rowman & Littlefield, 1996), 154–86.

2. American Bar Association, *Guide to Family Law* (New York: Random House, 1996), 21.

3. Reported in http://archives.his.com/smartmarriages/0201/html.

4. *Kansas City Star*, 12 March 1998, http://archives.his.com/smartmarriages/0113/html (15 October 1998). To receive the money couples would also have to certify that they had never had a child, an abortion, or a sexually transmitted disease. These extra provisions are unhelpful.

5. Schneider, "The Law and the Stability of Marriage: The Family as a Social Institution," 196.

6. John Crouch, "Proposed language for pre-marital education provisions of divorce reform," http://www.divorcereform.org/mod.html.

7. B. J. Fowers and D. H. Olson, "Predicting Marital Success with PREPARE: A Predictive Validity Study," *Journal of Marital and Family Therapy* 12: 403–12.

8. Quoted in Pia Nordlinger, "The Anti-Divorce Revolution," *The Weekly Standard* (March 2, 1998): 27.

9. http://www.divorcereform.org.

10. Crouch, "Proposed language."

11. See Michael J. McManus, *Marriage Savers*, 2d ed. (Grand Rapids: Zondervan, 1998), chap. 7.

12. Regan, "Postmodern Family Law," 166.

13. Sylvia Ann Hewlett and Cornel West, *The War against Parents: What We Can Do for America's Beleaguered Moms and Dads* (New York: Houghton Mifflin, 1998), 242.

14. Ibid., chap. 9.

15. For a discussion of some of the starkly different approaches that go by the name of "pro-family" politics, see David P. Gushee, "Family Values?" *Prism* 3, no. 4 (May/June 1996): 15–17.

16. For the concept of marriage as a status relationship, see Regan, "Postmodern Family Law," 157–71.

17. Among the most common fault grounds that appear in state laws are adultery, physical and mental cruelty, attempted murder, desertion, habitual drunkenness, use of addictive drugs, insanity, impotence, and infection of one's spouse with a venereal disease. American Bar Association, *Guide to Family Law*, 68–69.

18. For this analysis, see Mary Ann Glendon, *Abortion and Divorce in Western Law* (Cambridge: Harvard University Press, 1987), 65.

19. Ibid., 79–80.

20. Ibid., 66.

21. Bryce J. Christensen, "Taking Stock: Assessing Twenty Years of 'No Fault' Divorce," *The Family in America* 5, no. 9 (September 1991): 3.

22. Ibid., 4.

23. See Lenore J. Weitzman, *The Divorce Revolution: The Unexpected Social and Economic Consequences for Women and Children in America* (New York: Free Press, 1985). Weitzman's dramatic findings have been modified by later research, though the negative economic impact of divorce on women and children is a settled matter in current scholarship. For an authoritative recent analysis, see the *1998 Economic Report of the President*, chaps. 3–4. Accessed at http://www.access.gpo.gov/eop (2 April 1999).

24. See Barbara Dafoe Whitehead, "The Divorce Trap," *New York Times*, 13 January 1997, A16.

25. Daniel Sitarz, *Divorce Yourself: The National No-Fault Divorce Kit*, 3rd ed. (Carbondale, Ill.: Nova, 1994), 312.

26. Amy Black, "For the Sake of the Children: Reconstructing American Divorce Policy," *Crossroads Monograph Series on Faith and Public Policy* 1, no. 2, 40.

27. See http://www.divorcereform.org/wai.html.

28. Nordlinger, "The Anti-Divorce Revolution," 26.

29. William A. Galston, "The Reinstitutionalization of Marriage: Political Theory and Public Policy," in Popenoe, *Promises to Keep*, 285–86.

30. Glendon, *Abortion and Divorce in Western Law*, 77–78.

31. Quoted in Popenoe, *Promises to Keep*, 202.

32. Glendon, *Abortion and Divorce in Western Law*, 74.

33. My proposal resembles the "Classic Marriage" model proposed by John Crouch. See http://www.divorcereform.org/cla.html.

34. Elizabeth S. Scott, "Rational Decision Making about Marriage and Divorce," *Virginia Law Review* 76 (1990): 9, in Schneider, "The Law and the Stability of Marriage," 200–201.

35. http://www.divorcereform.org/cov.html.

36. Amitai Etzioni, "How to Make Marriage Matter," *Time*, 6 September 1993, 76; for another early article, see Christopher Wolfe, "The Marriage of Your Choice," *First Things* 50 (February 1995): 37–41.

37. See Wolfe, "The Marriage of Your Choice," 37–41.

38. As reported by Religion News Service, November 11, 1997.

39. Galston, "The Reinstitutionalization of Marriage," 285–87.

40. See Wallerstein and Blakeslee, *Second Chances*. For a powerful glimpse at an all-too-typical young couple who both are children of divorce, see Tamara Jones, "The Commitment," *Washington Post Magazine* (May 10, 1998): 8ff.

41. Black, "For the Sake of the Children," 40.

42. Galston, "The Reinstitutionalization of Marriage," 286.

43. White House statement, accessed at http://www.whitehouse.gov/news/releases/2002/02/welfare-book-05.html (5 September 2002).

44. Quoted by Schneider, "The Law and the Stability of Marriage," 206–7.

45. The best available statement calling for just such a partnership is "Marriage in America: A Report to the Nation," authored annually by the Council on Families in America. See Popenoe, *Promises to Keep*, 293–318.

Epilogue: *Why Christians Divorce "Just like Everyone Else"*

1. Information from Barna Research Group web page, http://www.barna.org/cgi-bin/PageCategory.asp#Divorce.

2. Information from Barna web page, http://www.barna.org/cgi-bin/PageCategory.asp#Definition.

3. Information from Barna web page, http://www.barna.org/cgi-bin/PagePressRelease.asp?PressReleaseID=106&Reference=C.